The History of
North American
STEAM

Christopher Chant

The History of
North American
STEAM

Christopher Chant

**CHARTWELL
BOOKS, INC.**

This edition published in 2012 by
CHARTWELL BOOKS, INC.
A division of BOOK SALES, INC.
276 Fifth Avenue Suite 206
New York, New York 10001
USA

Reprinted 2013

The Manor House
High Street
Buntingford
Hertfordshire
SG9 9AB
United Kingdom

www.regencyhousepublishing.com

ISBN-13: 978-0-7858-2933-1

Printed in China

CONTENTS

CHAPTER ONE
THE ORIGINS OF STEAM LOCOMOTION IN THE U.S.A.

The start of the 19th century marked the emergence of still more momentous times for the United States of America. In the last quarter of a century the country had secured a national identity by winning independence from the United Kingdom, and in much the same period had achieved a measure of internal security by removing the threat of risings by the indigenous Native North American population. The achievement of political and social stability had in itself opened the way to the growth of the new country's economy, and this too was a spur to an increase in population, which soon after the start of the 19th century rose to about 8.35 million persons. While this rise in population helped to spur the economy of the original part of the U.S.A. along the Atlantic seaboard by creating a larger workforce and also a bigger customer base, it also created the demand for additional land by a people who have always evinced a dislike of being hemmed in, and in the short term wanted more acreage to be brought under the plough. The inevitable consequence was the start of the succession of westward migratory movements that were to witness the U.S.A's eventual arrival on the western seaboard of the North American continent, namely the shore of the Pacific Ocean in the regions that were to become the states of California, Oregon and Washington.

The driving force in this first stage of the U.S.A.'s westward expansion was a combination of factors; the most important of these were the three represented by an increased level of taxation, the escalating cost of land (especially for farming), and the steadily more rigid nature of the social order in the most heavily populated regions of the 13 'original colonies' that had rebelled against

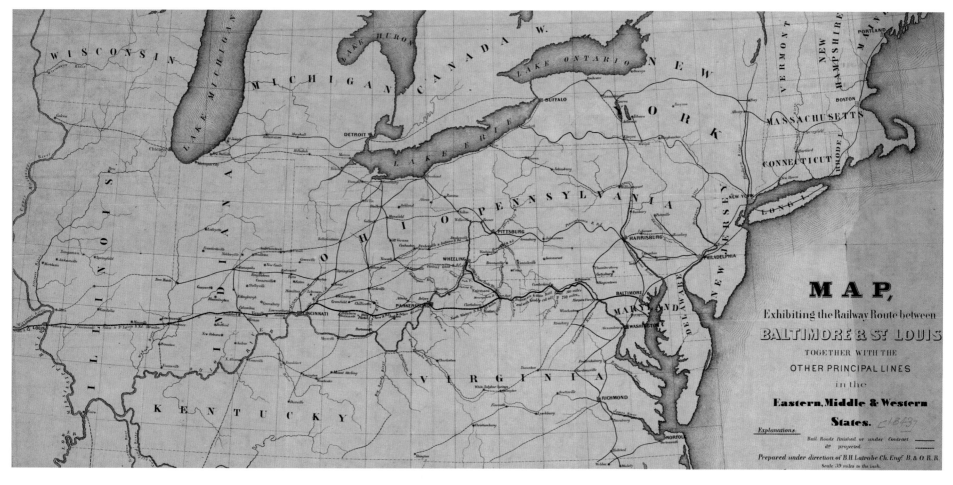

British rule. To these three primary factors should be added, in the case of the inhabitants of the more southerly states, a steady diminution of the fertility of the land and the rise of the plantation culture, which made it increasingly difficult for small farmers to make a secure living from the land.

Inevitably, therefore, large numbers of Americans looked to the virgin lands west of the limit of American habitation at that time,

and started to plan new lives for themselves, their families and, in more limited circumstance, their communities. At this stage in the evolution of the U.S.A., about 80 per cent of the population lived in the regions along the Atlantic seaboard, and of the other 20 per cent the majority inhabited the valley of the Ohio river with the minority (albeit a steadily growing one) moving toward and then down the valley of the Mississippi river.

The first stage of movement of Americans toward the regions west of the originally settled areas was based inevitably on the use of land transport, mostly along a growing network of new roads (initially nothing more than tracks) driven through these heavily wooded and forested regions. The three primary axes of the westward expansion were the northerly route from New England in general (and Boston in particular), along the

This 1843 map by Benjamin H. Latrobe reveals the route of the Baltimore & St. Louis Railroad connecting Baltimore at the head of Chesapeake Bay and St. Louis on the confluence of the Missouri and Mississippi rivers, and thus one of the primary lines opening the interior of the U.S.A. Also evident are the other principal railroad lines of the time in the eastern, central and western parts of the eastern U.S.A. at this time.

9

RIGHT
The map by L. Jacobi lays out the routes and profiles of the Baltimore & Ohio Railroad during 1858, together with its branches and immediate tributaries. At this time the Baltimore & Ohio Railroad was the single most important artery in the U.S.A.'s national route between its eastern and western halves.

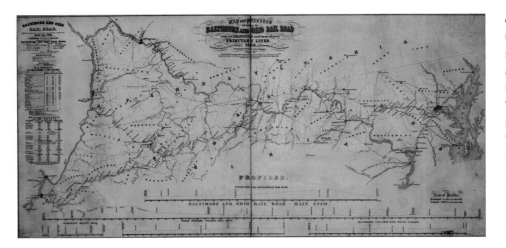

cases over the Appalachian Mountains toward the upper reaches of the valley of the Ohio river, and the southern route from the cities and plantations of Virginia and North Carolina toward the lower reaches of the valleys of the Tennessee and Ohio rivers in the regions around Nashville and Louisville respectively. This was about the westward limit of the regions which the migrants could reach by land transport. For destinations still farther to the west, which soon became more popular as the regions of the first wave of movement began to be filled, water transport by river,

valley of the Mohawk river toward Lake Erie, the central route from Maryland and southern Pennsylvania in general (and Philadelphia and Baltimore in particular) through and in many

RIGHT
The important place they occupied, and knew that they occupied, in the development of the U.S.A. is clearly evident in this painting of the directors of the Baltimore & Ohio Railroad.

FAR RIGHT
A naïf illustration shows the engine and coaches of the first railroad service to be run from Baltimore to York in the course of 1838.

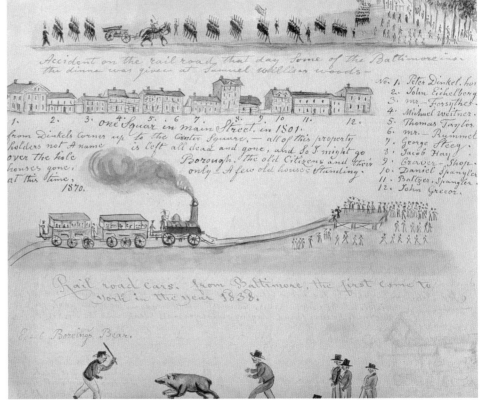

An early goal of the U.S.A. was a physical linkage between its eastern and western coasts offering faster and more reliable services than could be managed by wagons and/or riverboats, or alternatively sea-going ships that had to negotiate Cape Horn in the far south of the Americas. This connection came into existence only after the end of the Civil War, and was instrumental in opening vast tracts of the western hinterland to settlers and commerce. The creation and operation of the transcontinental railroad was beset by enormous physical problems, as can be gauged by this illustration of a Standard- type locomotive hauling a service along the side of the Truckee river in the Sierra Nevada in 1871.

canal and lake became necessary. Thus, during the first quarter of the 19th century, a number of new routes came into being to satisfy the steadily growing demand for movement into the more open lands to the west, and also to maintain links between the newly settled regions and the rest of the U.S.A.

The nature of the growing significance of

the westward movement is attested by the completion in 1818 of the paved National Road to Wheeling on the banks of the Ohio river, the opening in 1825 of the Erie Canal linking the upper reaches of the Hudson river with Lake Erie across the northern part of New York state, and the introduction during this period of paddle-wheeled steamers able to

progress up the rivers from the south to reach the fertile farmlands of Ohio, Indiana and Illinois.

This process of creating and maintaining land and water links between the newer and older populated regions of the U.S.A. had not only a large element of the social dynamic about it, but also a growing element of the

A photograph of the 1920s shows the paired road and rail bridges, the latter of the Baltimore & Ohio Railroad, over the junction of the Potomac and Shenandoah rivers at Harpers Ferry, West Virginia. The scene can have changed only in details over the previous three-quarters of a century.

goods, as their industries grew, by the stimulation of a larger domestic market. Obvious outlets for manufactured goods were the new centres of population that were springing up to the west of the established Atlantic seaboard communities. But while the new communities could be brought into being through the use largely of primitive transport links, the fostering of the economic conditions that would make them customers for the new and growing plethora of American manufactured goods demanded the establishment of better transport links for the westward movement and sale of manufactured goods that would be bought with the money derived from the eastward movement and sale of agricultural products.

In general, the pioneers of the movement to the west were farming families and those who in other ways depended on farming for their own way of life. The first demand of any movement to the west was the rapid development, once the migrants had reached the area they wanted to settle, of self-sufficiency in terms of food and other vital commodities. But once the means to sustain life had been provided and larger areas of land had been brought under cultivation, there developed a demand for 'consumer goods', leading to the development of towns that could provide otherwise isolated farming families and villages with such amenities as a general store, a blacksmith and other artisan services. The steady enlargement of the area of fertile land now under cultivation produced quantities of grain and other agricultural produce increasingly too great for merely local consumption.

The development of railroad stations went hand-in-hand with the growth in the fortunes of the railroad companies that built them. This is the station at Camden in 1869, clearly reflecting the solid nature and great prosperity of the Baltimore & Ohio Railroad at this time, when the end of the Civil War was followed by a period of rapid economic and population growth.

economic dynamic in its make-up. During this period, between 1800 and 1825, the U.S.A. had started on what was, for the time, a major economic boom. The primary causes for this rapid growth, most visible in the U.S.A.'s manufacturing industries, were the Napoleonic Wars, the War of 1812 with the U.K., and the import tariff introduced in 1816. These and other circumstances pushed the U.S.A. increasingly toward the concept of meeting its own requirement for manufactured goods and then further developing the market for these

Seen late in the 19th century, this is the station of the Baltimore & Ohio Railroad in Washington, D.C. It was situated on the corner of New Jersey Avenue.

History often seems to be populated by happy coincidences, and this period was no exception for the people of the U.S.A. So while the westward expansion was progressing and beginning to pay dividends in terms of much enlarged potential availability of agricultural produce, there was a major surge in the industrialization of the north-eastern states of the U.S.A. and in the large-scale succession of conventional food-producing agriculture with the planting of cotton in the southern states. This meant that three different areas were producing three different types of saleable commodities. The solution was obvious to the merchants of the east coast states: handsome profits could be made by bringing agricultural produce from the west for sale in the cities of the eastern seaboard, and buying cotton and moving it north for processing into cloth and finished garments. This process would also provide the money

PETER COOPER'S "TOM THUMB" 1829-30 BALTIMORE & OHIO R. R.

with which the western and southern communities could buy the goods and equipments manufactured in the east. Thus every part of the American population would benefit (but the middlemen in particular) if only one problem could be overcome. This problem was that of transportation, or rather the lack of transportation: only after the establishment of effective transport links would it be feasible to undertake the process of moving raw materials and finished goods in a system that offered the type of reliability and speed that would yield cost-efficiency and therefore profit.

As the benefits of the USA's belated but now speedy industrialization began to be felt, its existing system of transport was obviously incapable of satisfying the needs of the American economy that was beginning to emerge from a larger and more productive population enjoying the benefits of a greater area of cultivation and an increasing capacity for the manufacture of finished goods. The roads across the mountains between the original states and the new lands to the west were too limited for the large-scale transportation of grain and the speedy delivery of more perishable agricultural products, while

the alternative route down the rivers to New Orleans before the produce was embarked on ships for the passage through the Gulf of Mexico and round Florida to the ports of the eastern seaboard was both slow and climatically damaging to perishable foodstuffs.

The first attempt to create a more useful northern link between east and west was the Erie Canal, and marked a considerable success in trimming the temporal and financial cost of moving people and all manner of goods. The primary beneficiary of the advantages accruing from the opening of the Erie Canal was New York city, the eastern seaboard which lies at the mouth of the Hudson river and marked the south-eastern end of the navigable freshwater transport network of

ABOVE
The *Stourbridge Lion*, brought to America from the U.K. in 1829 to work the Delaware & Hudson Railroad.

ABOVE LEFT
Built by Peter Cooper, the *Tom Thumb* was a one-horsepower experimental engine mounted on a car frame and geared to one of the two axles. The boiler tubes were apparently made from musket barrels and the engine's one cylinder had a diameter of just 5in (127mm). Nonetheless, it was able to transport the directors of the Baltimore & Ohio Railroad in a boat-shaped car from Baltimore to Ellicott's Mill and back on 28 August 1830, becoming the first locomotive in the U.S.A. to haul a passenger load.

which the canal was a part. New York soon became the most important trading centre of the region, and the city's growing importance (and related affluence) rapidly became a cause for concern for other port cities of the north-east. These rivals to New York could easily see the nature of the processes that were responsible for the advance of the city, and rapidly urged the creation of comparable links with more western regions. Because of the success of the Erie Canal, the thoughts of New York's rivals were directed at first to the establishment of their own canal networks. It soon became clear, though, that a number of major geographical obstacles, of the type New York had avoided, militated against the successful creation of canal networks that would have to be built, or rather driven, through the mountains lying between the other eastern port cities and the agricultural regions to the west. A number of canals were nonetheless schemed and constructed, but the basic cost-inefficiency of fighting against rather than co-operating with nature can be see in the unhappy experience of Philadelphia, which cajoled the government of Pennsylvania to undertake the construction of a canal system that linked Philadelphia on the south-eastern side of the state with Pittsburgh in the state's north-western region: the system had been completed by 1834 but had to cross a mountain range in a process that necessitated the haulage of goods 10 miles (16km) up a series of inclined planes before coasting down on the other side to complete its journey. The Chesapeake and Ohio Canal, started in 1827 as a joint project by Baltimore in Maryland and Washington, D.C., was another

attempt to create a rival to the Erie Canal.

In the same year, however, an entirely new concept, which was rapidly to render the canal obsolete, was launched and quickly began to revolutionize the concept of high-capacity and what was, for the time, high-speed transport in the U.S.A. This was, of course, the railroad. (It is worth noting at this stage, however, that although it was 1827 that marked the practical beginning of U.S. railroads, the concept of the railroad in the U.S.A. was already 12 years old, for as early as 1815 John Stevens had received the first state charter to undertake the construction of a railroad.) The conceptual impetus for the first U.S. railroads was the pattern now beginning to characterize the first British railways, pioneered at a slightly earlier time and currently starting to reveal technical and commercial success. The primary

attractions of the railroad were, naturally enough, firstly that it was relatively cheaper to construct than a canal, and secondly that a loaded train could travel at up to 15mph (24km/h), which was something in the order of four times the speed attainable by the fastest canal boat.

The task of launching a railroad industry was greatly facilitated by the fact that from virtually the first flush of westward migration from the eastern seaboard there had begun the process of surveying routes and mapping the country into which the migrants were moving, in the process allowing the creation of geographical knowledge rolling steadily to the west. Thus came the time for railroads to supplement the current system in which the first privately owned toll or turnpike roads had already been followed by steam ships on

navigable rivers and lakes, and then most recently by boats on a small but growing network of canals.

The first railways had been pioneered in England during the 17th century as a way to reduce friction in moving heavily loaded wheeled vehicles. The first North American arrangement of this 'gravity road' type was built during 1764 for military purposes at the Niagara portage in Lewiston, New York, under the impetus of Captain John Montressor, a British engineer and cartographer. The earliest American map showing the course of a commercial 'tramroad' was drawn in Pennsylvania in October 1809 by John Thomson, and revealed the railroad that Thomas Leiper was contemplating as a means

OPPOSITE
The Roundhouse Museum of the Baltimore & Ohio Railroad, housing a 'must-see' collection of historical locomotives.

ABOVE LEFT
Built in 1927, this is the Baltimore & Ohio's working replica of the first Lafayette-class locomotive No. 13, originally introduced in 1837 as a 4-2-0 of the Norris type.

ABOVE
A 1941 replica of the Camden & Amboy Railroad's *John Bull*, originally built in 1831 by George and Robert Stephenson in England as a 0-4-0 unit (seen here) but later revised to the 4-2-0 configuration. It is the world's oldest working locomotive.

BELOW
A replica of the *Best Friend of Charleston*. The original was built in 1830 as a 0-4-0 tank engine for the South Carolina Rail Road, which operated the Americas's first commercial railroad service in January 1831. In June of that year the locomotive had the dubious distinction of being the first to kill its fireman after this unfortunate had become so annoyed by the sound of steam escaping from the safety valves that he had tied down their operating lever, resulting in a boiler explosion. Tamper-proof valves then became the norm.

OPPOSITE
A map by Rand McNally & Company of the Baltimore & Ohio Railroad's route network in 1876, together with this operator's major connections.

of moving dressed stone from his quarry at Crum Creek to a point on Ridley Creek at which the stones could be embarked on boats. An affluent Philadelphia tobacconist, Leiper was the owner of quarries near Chester and, using this map, Thomson helped Reading Howell, another celebrated mapmaker and now the engineer for the project, to lay the first practical wooden trackway for a tramroad.

During 1826 another commercial tramroad was surveyed and built at Quincy, Massachusetts, by Gridley Bryant. The relevant machinery was created by Solomon Willard, and was based on the use of horses to haul granite (being used in the construction of the

Bunker Hill Monument) from Quincy quarries over a distance of some 4 miles (6.4km) to a jetty on the Neponset river for further movement to Boston.

These initial uses of tramroads for the guidance of heavily-laden wagons were moderately effective for short-distance movement, but were limited in overall terms by their restriction to gravity and horsepower as their motive force. The creation of real railroads demanded the introduction of an alternative means of generating motive power, and this arrived in the form of the steam engine, which created a genuine revolution in transportation. The improvements to the steam

engine of the British engineer James Watt were adopted and modified by John Fitch in the U.S.A. during 1787, as a means of propelling a vessel on the Delaware river, and in the same year by James Rumsey to move a vessel on the Potomac river. However, it was with Robert Fulton's *Clermont* and a vessel built by John Stevens that steam power became fully accepted as the primary means of moving vessels. It is worth noting, however, that the concepts of the railroad and steam motive power developed independently of one another, and it was not until the first took on board the key technology of the second that the railroad could begin to emerge as an effective commercial undertaking.

The 'father of the American railroad' is generally considered to be Colonel John Stevens, who in 1826 first demonstrated the feasibility of steam locomotion on an experimental circular track he built on his estate in Hoboken, New Jersey. (It is interesting to note that this was three years before George Stephenson perfected a practical steam locomotive in England.) As noted above, although the first North American railroad charter had been granted to Stevens in 1815, there followed other grants to a number of persons, and this paved the way for the start of work on the first American railroads intended for commercial service rather than experimental use.

Before progressing to the development of the first railroads, and the locomotives that hauled the services over their tracks, it is worth considering the way in which the railroads were aided in becoming commercially successful, and therefore worthy of investment and further

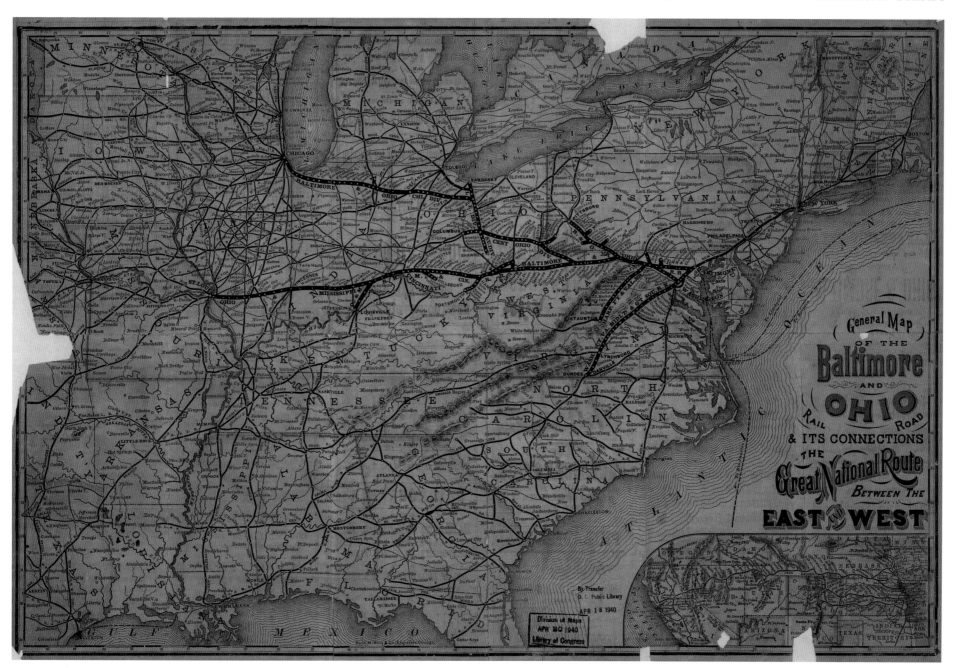

TOP
A replica of the *De Witt Clinton*, a 0-4-0 locomotive originally built by the West Point Foundry for the Mohawk & Hudson Railroad in 1831. The engine hauled the first train in New York state, from Albany to Schenectady, on 25 June 1831.

ABOVE
The *South Carolina*, placed in service during 1832 by the South Carolina Canal & Rail Road Company, was an unusual 2-4-2 freight-hauling locomotive that was in effect two 2-2-0 units attached back-to-back and controlled from a position above the junction of the two units.

development. Oddly enough, given the U.S.A.'s later commitment to private enterprise as the core of its financial system, the establishment of transport links between the longer-established cities of the Atlantic seaboard states, and the steadily increasing number of communities developing in the U.S.A.'s hinterland, were reliant to a marked degree on the support of the federal and state governments. In the first stages of the development of such links there was strong competition between communities who wanted these links to reach them as quickly as possible. Such communities appreciated that the early creation of such transport links would provide them with a commercial

advantage over their neighbours. Thus there came into being a system whereby companies prepared to create such links (turnpikes, followed next by canals and finally by railroads) and received from the federal government, state authorities or other interested bodies large tracts of publicly owned land over which to establish the links. However, it is easy to overstate the amount of such land that the railroads received, which led to the erroneous belief that virtually all of the American railroad system was created over such grant-in-aid land. In fact only some 8 per cent of the railroad system came into being in this way.

Moreover, it should be remembered that

only a comparatively small proportion of these grant-in-aid lands were outright gifts to the railroad companies. The majority of the land grants thus came with strings attached, and were therefore akin to standard commercial transactions. In return for the receipt of federal land grants, for instance, the railroad companies often had to agree to the movement of government traffic at reduced rates: the system was finally ended by an act of Congress in 1946, by which time the money saved by the federal government has been assessed as nine times the value of the land grants originally involved. Among the other types of transaction by which the railroad companies received federal and state aid were loans, which the companies had to repay over a set period complete with interest: some of the companies defaulted by going out of business, but the majority of those that did receive such loans did repay them along purely commercial lines. Another form of federal and state aid took the form of investment in the railroad companies, a process which saw a not inconsiderable quantity of railroad company stock pass into the control of the federal and state governments. As late as 1950, four of these bodies (the states of Georgia, North Carolina and Virginia, and the city of Cincinnati in Ohio) retained such ownership.

The first U.S. railroad to begin services was the Baltimore & Ohio. Work on this system began on 4 July 1828 when Charles Carroll, the only surviving signatory of the Declaration of Independence, turned the first sod of earth to mark the start of the project. Within 10 days the company had asked for

Truly one of the most remarkable photographs ever to have emerged from the annals of American steam locomotion, this reveals the Baltimore & Ohio Railroad's locomotive No. 7, named *Andrew Jackson*, disguised as the operator's original *Atlantic*, a 0–4–0 Grasshopper-type locomotive. The flavour of the 1830s is completed by the period-dressed 'passengers' embarked on the two replica carriages whose design clearly reveals the origins of the first passenger carriages as stagecoach bodies, with highly-exposed 'upper decks', adapted for installation on two-axle cars.

Baldwin built the *Old Ironsides* for the Philadelphia, Germantown & Norristown Railroad in 1832.

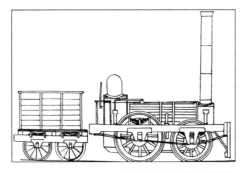

John Jervis made this experimental 4-2-0 locomotive, *Experiment*, at the West Point Foundry in 1832.

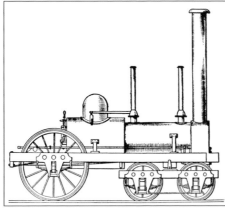

One of the first successful 4-2-0 locomotives was this unit manufactured by Baldwin in 1837 for the Utica & Schenectady Railroad.

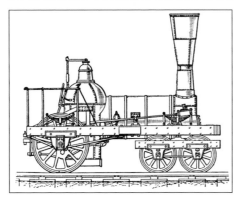

tenders for the construction of the first 12 miles (19.3km) of track, linking Baltimore with Ellicott's Mill (now Ellicott City). This section opened for business on 24 May 1830, and the line was pushed forward to reach Harpers Ferry in Virginia during 1834, Cumberland in Maryland during 1852 and Wheeling in Virginia in 1853. An extension was added during 1835 in the form a branch line from Relay in Maryland to Bladensburg near Washington, D.C., and the main line was extended by a combination of purchase and new construction to push through to the Ohio river, the Great Lakes, Chicago in Illinois and St. Louis in Missouri.

The railroad's first services were undertaken with horse-drawn wagons. The first practical steam locomotives had not reached the U.S.A. until 1829, when the distinction of being the first to run on an American railroad, in this instance the Delaware & Hudson Railroad, was secured by the *Stourbridge Lion,* which was one of four locomotives bought in England and shipped across the Atlantic. The advent of steam locomotion was not without incident, however, for the first services revealed that the locomotive was too heavy for the trackway, which was of iron-plated wooden construction, and the Delaware & Hudson was thus compelled to return to horsepower for several more years.

From a time early in its existence, the Baltimore & Ohio Railroad had great ambitions and planned to develop a route that extended from the port city of Baltimore, at the head of Chesapeake Bay, right the way through to the Ohio river. Here the railroad could link up with the river network that carried most of the trade in this region of the U.S.A.'s rapidly growing interior. The link between Baltimore and the Ohio river represented a distance of 380 miles (612km); among the physical problems that the railroad's surveyors and builders had to overcome, were the crossing of a significant range of mountains and the completion of a route that was more than 10 times longer than any hitherto built.

The construction of the railroad's infrastructure and track was particularly difficult for men who, quite naturally, lacked any real experience in the difficulties of building and running a railroad. Yet the Baltimore & Ohio Railroad's team of planners and builders pressed ahead with the tenacity and ingenuity that were already becoming a trademark features of American engineering. The task of surveying the planned route was entrusted to a team of men supplied by the U.S. Army's engineer service, and the surveyed route extended up the Patapsco river before striking off across country to reach the Potomac river, which was then followed upstream through the Caboctin mountains.

Within three years, profits from the initial horse-drawn traffic over the first few miles of track were sufficient to persuade the railroad's board of directors to take a bold new step toward the aim of improving the service their operation offered, and in the process boosting ticket and freight income. Thus the board offered first and second prizes of $4,000 and $3,500 respectively for the best steam locomotives delivered by 1 June 1831. The requirement was that the contenders should weigh less than $3\frac{1}{2}$ tons and in trials confirm their ability to pull a train weighing 15 tons at a speed of 15mph (24km/h).

The U.S.A., as noted above, had already

The first Grasshopper 0-4-0 locomotive was made by Davis & Gartner for the Baltimore & Ohio Railroad in 1836. This pioneering engine is seen here in 1864, by then relegated to service as a switching locomotive at the operator's celebrated Mount Clare workshops.

seen trials with a number of primitive steam locomotives. The first of these was the small engine made by John Stevens and tested on a small track built specially for the purpose on his estate. The first commercial locomotives were imported from the U.K., and resulted from an order placed by Horatio Allen on behalf of the Delaware & Hudson Canal Company. As indicated by its name, this was

concerned primarily with the construction and operation of canal systems, most specifically that linking Rondout in the state of New York with the Carbondale mines in the north-western part of the state of Pennsylvania. The final stretch of the planned route, which comprised the 16-mile (26-km) section from Honesdale, was geographically so difficult for canal-building purposes that John B. Jervis,

the company's chief engineer, came to the conclusion that it would be technically and commercially sensible to replace a canal with a railroad over this stretch. Thus Allen was dispatched to England with the task of purchasing iron rails and any locomotive engines that he considered suitable. The first of these, manufactured by Robert Stephenson and named *America*, reached New York City in January 1829. The other three locomotives ordered by Allen were manufactured in Stourbridge by the Foster, Rastrick company: the *Hudson* and the *Delaware* were destroyed when a fire gutted the shed in which they were being accommodated after their delivery to Rondout, while the *Stourbridge Lion* (page 15), after its arrival in the U.S.A. in May 1829, was evaluated at the West Point Foundry and then transferred to Honesdale.

On 8 August 1829 the locomotive was prepared for its first trip, which Allen decided to operate on his own because of the difficult and wholly experimental nature of the route along a twisting course over wooden rails liable to distortion as a result of natural warping. The *Stourbridge Lion* grumbled into movement along the 500-ft (152-m) straight track leading into a sharp curve and then a trestle bridge, and although many thought that the locomotive would fail to negotiate its way round the first curve, the *Stourbridge Lion* encountered no difficulty, progressed over the bridge, and then steamed another 3 miles (4.8km) along the track before Allen halted and then returned to his starting point. This constituted the first real journey by a steam locomotive in the U.S.A., and Allen may be regarded as fortunate, for in the following journeys the *Stourbridge Lion* began to suffer problems: the locomotive was derailed on a number of occasions and was then retired to static service as a boiler in the company's Carbondale foundry.

Of great historical importance, the locomotive was later restored to its original condition for exhibition at the Chicago Railway Exposition of 1884, and is now preserved by the Smithsonian Institution.

While these first efforts toward the hauling of freight loads by steam locomotives were being essayed, the Baltimore & Ohio Railroad had begun its first passenger operations. During 1830 Peter Cooper, one of the railroad's shareholders, manufactured the first wholly American-built steam locomotive. Intended as a type to demonstrate the steam locomotive's capabilities, the *Tom Thumb* (page 15 et seq.) weighed a mere 1 ton and its internal features included gun barrels used as boiler tubes and an axle-driven fan to create the draught needed for effective burning of the fire. Experimental though it may have been, the *Tom Thumb* was no slouch in terms of its performance: on 28 August 1830 the locomotive drew one coach, with 36 passengers on board, along the 15-mile (24-km) line from Baltimore to Ellicott's Mill, reaching a speed of 18mph (29km/h) in the course of its run. On the return journey, the *Tom Thumb* was challenged to a race by a horse-drawn rail car on a parallel track: the steam locomotive gained the first advantage, but the horse-drawn car eventually prevailed after the *Tom Thumb*'s fire died following the failure of the draught arrangement as a result of drive-belt slippage.

Despite the result of the 'race', the overall advantage enjoyed by the steam locomotive over the horse-drawn car was fully evident. The Baltimore & Ohio Railroad pressed forward with the competition mentioned above, but the only locomotive that met its complete requirement and which thereby became the winner was the locomotive named *York*. This had been designed by a Philadelphia watchmaker named Phineas Davis, and the railroad then ordered 20 examples of an improved version. These upgraded locomotives were known as Grasshoppers, as a result of their actions, which were based on the combination of a vertical boiler and rocking beams to drive the wheels. Ungainly though they may have appeared, each of these could haul a 50-ton train along the railroad's winding track. So successful and reliable were they that many of the Grasshoppers remained in service for about half a century, and the last of them was not retired until 1893.

The potential of the steam locomotive was already attracting the interest of a number of engineering companies, and there began to appear a number of other. Thus 1830 saw the appearance of the West Point Foundry's *Best Friend of Charleston* (page 20), designed for the Charleston & Hamburg Railroad, whose track was being laid by the South Carolina Canal & Rail Road, which employed Allen to supervise the task. In the course of its first run, the *Best Friend of Charleston* suffered a broken wheel, but on its second attempt attained a speed of 20mph (32km/h) while hauling a car carrying a load of 40 men. The *Best Friend of Charleston* was destroyed just a few months later by a boiler explosion, but before this there had appeared another West Point Foundry locomotive, in this instance named the *West Point* and notable for having a horizontal boiler rather than the *Best Friend of Charleston*'s vertical one. A third West Point Foundry locomotive completed in 1830 was the *South Carolina* (page 22). This was characterized by yet another variation in the powerplant arrangement, in this instance two boilers, each driving one centreline cylinder on separate four-wheel bogies.

It was the *Best Friend of Charleston* that on 25 December 1830 undertook the first steam-hauled regular schedule in the U.S.A., the service taking place on the Charleston & Hamburg's 6 miles (9.65km) of track.

By this time the West Point Foundry was starting to gain a good reputation for its locomotives, a fact that was attested by a swelling number of orders from several railroads. In 1831 the company delivered the *De Witt Clinton* (page 22), named for the governor of New York state and designed by John B. Jervis, to the Mohawk & Hudson Railroad. This had been established by financial interests in Albany and Schenectady to provide an effective land link between Albany and the eastern end of the Erie Canal. In the following year the *Experiment* (page 24), another Jervis design for the Mohawk & Hudson, confirmed the progress of the West Point Foundry along effective technical lines, for while earlier locomotives from this manufacturer had been troubled by a measure of instability, the new locomotive proved very steady. The instability was largely a result of the indifferent, and indeed often poor, tracks on which the locomotives ran. The earlier locomotives were four-wheel units with rigid frames, and the uneven and twisting nature of the tracks was readily transmitted directly through to the locomotive. The problem was solved by the West Point Foundry's introduction of three-point suspension: the axle for the main driving wheels was carried by two bearings, one at each end, and the front of the locomotive was

now supported by a four-wheel bogie attached to the underside of the locomotive by a single centreline pivot. The new arrangement proved efficient as it allowed the forward four-wheel bogie to conform to variations in the track; this type of 4-2-0 layout soon became standard for the locomotives, not only of the West Point Foundry but also of the increasing number of companies which were becoming involved in this growing market.

One of these other companies was the Philadelphia-based company headed by Matthias Baldwin. Baldwin entered into the arena of steam locomotive design with a comprehensive assessment of the *John Bull* (page 19), a Planet-type locomotive from the Stephenson company. This was imported into the U.S.A. during 1831 by Robert L. Stevens for the Camden & Amboy Railroad in the state of New Jersey. After assessing the *John Bull*, Baldwin built a basically similar locomotive of this 0-4-0 type as the *Old Ironsides* (page 24) to a contract from the Philadelphia, Germantown & Norristown Railroad. Baldwin learned quickly, however, so his next locomotive, the *E.L. Miller* for the Charleston & Hamburg, was of the far superior 4-2-0 layout with a 'haystack' firebox. A similar arrangement was used by William Norris, another Philadelphia manufacturer, in the *George Washington* of 1836; the stream of configurational development embodied in these locomotives was taken one step further by Henry Campbell in a 4-4-0 unit he created for the Philadelphia, Germantown & Norristown during 1836.

It was in 1838 that the major breakthrough in locomotive design arrived, the decisive factor being Joseph Harrison's

patented system of equalizing beams to support the coupled driving wheels. In combination with the pivoted leading bogie, this type of suspension made it possible for all the wheels to remain in contact with the track, despite the latter's variations.

It would have been impossible for these locomotive improvements to have been created and introduced if the American railroad system had not grown as it did during the period in question, for it was the growth of the overall system and the success of its services in attracting and keeping passengers and, to a lesser extent, freight, that created the growing operating profits that allowed the railroad companies to invest in newer and more advanced locomotives. This, in turn, allowed far-sighted companies to offer services better than those of less prudent rivals, which in turn allowed the generation of healthier profits and the expansion of the railroads with greater track lengths and still more capable locomotives.

In general, the growth of the railroad industry had been received with great commercial and social enthusiasm, though proximate causes of this enthusiasm were different in various parts of the country. Thus, while the success of the Erie Canal had inspired the Baltimore & Ohio, as well as other north-eastern railroads, to enter the railroad market, the motivation of ports such as Richmond, Charleston and Savannah in the south-eastern states was the intention to link trading areas coming into existence farther to the west, as the practice of cotton-planting extended in that direction. The establishment of the South Carolina Rail Road to Hamburg on the Savannah river represented an attempt

to divert river trade to Hamburg and thus away
from Savannah; after the completion of the
South Carolina Rail Road financial interests in
Charleston put their money into the Georgia
Railroad so that its route could be extended to
Athens and Atlanta.

Savannah responded to these attempts to
erode its pre-eminent trading position by
furthering the establishment of the Central
Railroad of Georgia, backed by the state
administration, reaching toward Macon, and the
Monroe Railroad providing a link between
Macon and Atlanta. Richmond, the capital of
Virginia and the other most significant
commercial centre of the region, planned to use
its canal to Lynchburg as the base on which the
Lynchburg & New River Railroad would be
launched in the direction of the increasingly
important region along the Ohio river.

In the west, the new states were at first
happy to allow eastern interests to undertake
the commercial risks of constructing the
railroads that would boost the prosperity of
both areas, but were then faced increasingly by
the difficulties of handling the constantly
enlarging volumes of grain and other produce
resulting from the arrival of more farming
families and introduction of more intensive
cultivation. The time was now ripe, it was
appreciated by all concerned, for the
improvements of communications between the
eastern and western states.

That most important icon of the opening of
the Ohio river valley and other parts of the
American hinterland's northern regions to
westward migration, the Erie Canal was the

This Baldwin-made 4-4-0 unit is typical of the American or Standard type of locomotive that was so important in the development of the U.S. railroad system. The locomotive was manufactured in Philadelphia for the Wilmington & Weldon Railroad in the course of 1859, and was later sold to the Atlantic Coast Line Railroad.

stimulus for most of the western states's initial involvement in the establishment of canals and then, and considerably more importantly in the longer run, railroads. The states of the region (Ohio, Indiana, Illinois and Michigan) all undertook major programmes of canal construction. The new systems were designed to connect existing canal and river routes with the Great Lakes, so removing the need for the farmers of the region to rely on the transport of their produce by ship down the Mississippi and other rivers to New Orleans in Louisiana. All concerned with the programme knew that the capital cost of the effort would be very considerable, but firmly believed that the higher profit margins resulting from this

simpler method of getting their produce to the markets and consumers of the eastern states would soon make it possible for the required loans to be paid off. In the 1830s the advent of the railroad as a burgeoning economic force then dictated a major modification of the canal-building programme. Canals were all very well for the cheap movement of bulk products such as wheat, whose delivery was in no significant way time-critical, but were less well suited to the movement of more perishable agricultural produce. Here there seemed to be the possibility of a mutually beneficial symbiosis between the canal and the railroad. As the western states soon discovered, however, the rate of canal building

was considerably slower than that of agricultural demand for the services that should have been provided by the canals. Moreover, the slow development of the canals, and therefore the limited income derived from their use, meant that state governments found it increasingly difficult, if not impossible, to service the interest now growing on the vast sums they had borrowed to finance the programme. In 1837 the result was a financial crisis and then an economic downturn, which saddled the states with vast and still-growing debts but with little to show for them.

In Ohio two systems, those of the Little Miami and the Mad River & Lake Erie, were conceived as the means of connecting

Springfield with Cincinnati and the Ohio river in the southern part of the region, and with Sandusky on Lake Erie in the northern part. Ordaining that state would buy one-third of the stock of any railroad which had raised the other two-thirds of the capital it needed, a law enacted in 1837 then saw $3,000,000 disappear into the hands of 40 not-existent 'builders', and was thus repealed in 1840. Farther to the west, vast sums expended by the state of Indiana resulted, before the railroads were sold, in only a few miles of preparatory work for routes designed to connect Madison with Lafayette and New Albany with Crawfordsville.

Another state government that encountered major problems was that of Illinois farther to the north: in 1837 the authorities here agreed to fund the construction of the Illinois Central Railroad from Cairo in the south to Galena in the north-west, and also the Northern Cross and Southern Cross railroads to provide the associated east/west lateral links. But by 1842 only half the Northern Cross Railroad, from Quincy to Springfield, had been completed. Farther still to the north, the Erie & Kalamazoo Railroad, the first to be established in the western hinterlands, launched the construction of its line from Toledo and reached Adrian by 1836. Becoming a state in 1837, and thereby gaining a freer hand in the control of its own affairs, Michigan planned a network of northern, central and southern railroads, but as was so often the case in other states, the authorities raised and allocated vast sums of hard-earned cash only to have the guarantor banks collapse; work was accordingly halted in 1842.

This is just some of the evidence of what had become in effect 'railroad mania' in the U.S.A. And though it is worth recording that the failure of some of the schemes was certainly the result of fraud, others came to nought as a result of the increasingly difficult economic situation of the period, or as a result of wild over-ambition or muddled thinking. This last was frequently overlooked by potential and actual investors desperate to place their money in what was seen as little more than a sure-fire way to vast profit.

It must also be admitted that the railroad mania was just as prevalent in the more southerly states. Here, again, city fathers and the leaders of local businesses were sure that the establishment of railroad links to other cities inside and then, with a modicum of luck, outside their own commercial bailiwick would liberate their cities and regions from financial thraldom to the operators of the riverine and maritime transport lines on which they were currently dependent. A typical example can be

ABOVE LEFT
This 4-4-0 American-type locomotive was built by Baldwin of Philadelphia in 1875 for the Virginia & Truckee Railroad.

ABOVE
Baldwin was truly one of the greatest names in American steam locomotive engineering and manufacture over a protracted period. This Mogul-type 2-6-0 locomotive, manufactured in 1875 for the Virginia & Truckee Railroad, shows that the company was looking to the future, here recognizing that while the Standard type of locomotive was still important and one of its mainstays, there was a steadily growing market for larger and more powerful locomotives to haul the passenger and freight services which the success of the Standard-type had helped to create.

Caught by the camera in 1858 on the line along the Potomac river near Cumberland, Maryland, this 4-4-0 American- or Standard-type locomotive of the Baltimore & Ohio Railroad had been manufactured by the William Mason Company at Taunton, Massachusetts in the previous year. The American or Standard type of locomotive was made in vast numbers to basically the same pattern by companies in many parts of the industrialized U.S.A.

found in the Louisville, Cincinnati & Charleston Railroad, an undertaking launched jointly by the states of Kentucky, South Carolina and Tennessee: the idea may have been sound, but the planning and execution were not, and by 1839 continued construction of the railroad's track and other infrastructure had been terminated through a shortage of capital and, it must be added, intractable

argument by the three states about the precise alignment of route, which each believed to favour the other two.

In another part of the southern U.S.A., ambitious plans were laid for the creation of a series of short but interconnected railroads that would, in their entirety, constitute a rail link between Memphis in Tennessee and the port city of Charleston in South Carolina: by 1837,

when the whole programme fell into abeyance as a result of a financial panic, a mere 8 miles (12.9km) of track had been completed. Lying on the Mississippi river and up to this time wholly reliant on river transport to the port city of New Orleans, so that the goods of the area could be taken by sea to the cities of the eastern seaboard, Vicksburg at this stage planned a railroad route to Charleston in the east. However, by the time the concept was abandoned in 1840, only the link between Vicksburg and Jackson, farther to the east in Mississippi, had been built. These and other railroads with what was basically an east/west alignment were complemented by a number of lines with a north/south alignment essentially parallel to the Mississippi river. The railroads included links between Mobile and Chattanooga and between New Orleans and Nashville, but like the east/west routes these saw the completion of only short stretches of their ambitiously planned routes before they too fell into abeyance.

In summary, therefore, it is easy to see that while some early technical and commercial successes were achieved by the railroad pioneers, the development of the first and essentially limited plans had created a railroad mania that then, after only a very short time, became a source of disapproval among members of a public alarmed that altogether too large a proportion of the railroad schemes were now facing increasingly severe financial problems; there was now conclusive evidence that very large sums of money, raised by taxation to pay for loans, had been squandered and, in a number of instances, been lost to fraud.

The year 1837 was therefore a turning point, although only of limited duration, in the development of American railroads. There were still considerable quantities of private money, most of it from larger investors, available for railroad schemes, but the state authorities, mindful as they were of the need for periodic re-election by a public already sceptical of the way in which large amounts

of their taxes had been allocated, became ever more circumspect in dealing with the railroad companies' requests for further investment. Inevitably, therefore, large numbers of schemes either failed to get themselves up and running, or failed for lack of further injections of capital.

What cannot be denied, however, is that many of the schemes were right in their basic thinking. Thus these and the other state-backed railroads of the 1830s soon re-emerged as the foundations on which the edifice of American railroads began to rise. However, while these primary building blocks had been initially funded with public money, the later implementation of the programmes came to rely almost exclusively on private investment. The result, of course, was that the later profits went into the bank accounts of private individuals rather than into the public purse.

The process also had ramifications outside the purely financial field, however, in the political and social as well as economic development of the eastern part of the U.S.A.: there were few individuals in the southern states with the wealth and the temperament to favour investment in the railroads, so the financing of the railroad revival, when it came, was left to the men who had created their wealth in the industrialization of the northern states. Naturally enough, the additional wealth that the investors gained from railroad investments gravitated to the northern states, and in the process aggravated the already clear-cut divide between the northern and southern states in their respectively financial strengths and stabilities.

Thus the revival of the fortunes of the railroad companies in effect speeded the relative impoverishment of the south by comparison with the north.

As these events in the western states were unfolding, progress was being made among some of the railroads extending through and from the eastern states. The Baltimore & Ohio Railroad had reached Cumberland, a little over half way to its originally planned terminus, during the course of 1842, but the railroad managed to maintain its existence through the depression and in 1848 began further construction work so that the line had reached Wheeling on the Ohio river by 1853. The Baltimore & Ohio Railroad also planned to construct a lateral spur to Pittsburgh in Pennsylvania, and this so concerned financial interests in Philadelphia, which was at that time Pittsburgh's primary trading partner, that in 1847 these interests began the Pennsylvania Railroad, which linked the two cities by 1853.

Meanwhile the Mohawk & Hudson Railroad in the state of New York had been joined from 1836 by the Utica & Schenectady Railroad: the Mohawk & Hudson Railroad had received a charter from the state of New York in April 1826 to establish a railroad connecting the Hudson and Mohawk rivers. The start of work on the railroad's infrastructure was delayed by legal problems but finally began in July 1830, and it was on 9 August of the following year that the operator initiated its first passenger service between Albany and Schenectady. The 1836 combination of the Mohawk & Hudson and the Utica & Schenectady railroads opened the

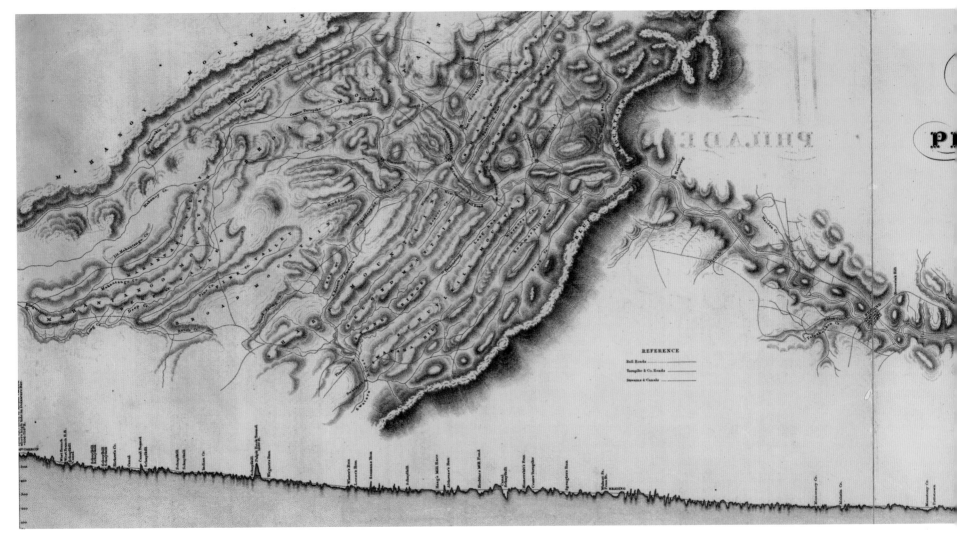

way to the establishment in the 1840s of railroad links between the towns along the Erie Canal, so creating a system of rail transport connecting Albany with Buffalo on the southern shore of Lake Erie. Then in 1851 and 1852 the completions of the Hudson River Railroad (operating between New York City and Troy, near Albany) and the New York & Harlem Railroad established a link between Albany and New York along the valley of the Hudson river.

Other operators notable in the early stages of the development of American railroads were to be found in several different parts of the country. The South Carolina Canal and Rail Road Company, which later became part of the Southern Railway System, began during February 1829 in Charleston, in the state of South Carolina. When this 136-mile (219-km) system was completed to Hamburg, also in the state of South Carolina across the Savannah

Topographical Plan & Profile

OF

THE

...ADELPHIA AND READING RAIL ROAD

SCALE OF MILES

This topographical plan and profile of 1838, drawn by R. B. Osborne, reveals the line for which the Philadelphia & Reading Railway received a charter from the Pennsylvania state legislature on 4 April 1833. The line extended for 58 miles (93km) and work began in 1835. Sections of the line were in service by 1838, and the whole line had been completed by 1842.

river from Augusta in the state of Georgia, during the course of 1833, it was the longest railroad in the world.

The first railroad in New England was the Boston & Lowell, which later became an element of the Boston & Maine Railroad. This received its charter in 1830 and launched its first services in June 1835. Another opening in the same month was that of the Boston & Providence Railway, which was the earliest ancestor of the later New York New Haven & Hartford Railroad: this operator's service connected Boston in the state of Maine with Providence in Rhode Island. The completion during the following month of the Boston & Worcester Railroad, which later became an element of the Boston & Albany Railroad and, as such, a component of the New York Central System, established railroad communication between the two name cities in the state of Massachusetts.

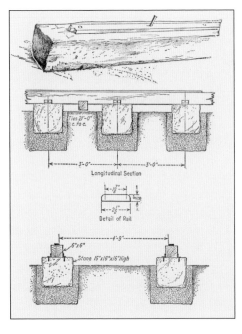

Right down in the south of the U.S.A., the Pontchartrain Railroad (later absorbed by the Louisville & Nashville Railroad Company) received its charter in January 1830 to establish a short railroad line in Louisiana to link New Orleans and Lake Pontchartrain, an extension of the Gulf of Mexico penetrating through the state's coastline. The Pontchartrain Railroad opened for business during April 1831.

The Richmond & Petersburg Railroad, which came into being during 1836, was the start of the later Atlantic Coast Line Railroad, while the later Seaboard Air Line Railway could trace its origins back to the charter received in March 1832 to create a short line between Roanoke and Portsmouth, two cities in the state of Virginia. The City Point Railroad was chartered in 1836 and started

commercial operations during April 1837, and became the parent of the Norfolk & Western Railroad. The Louisville & Nashville Railroad received its charter from the states of Kentucky and Tennessee early in 1850, and operated its first through service between these cities at the end of October 1859. The Chesapeake & Ohio Railroad originated with the charter received from the state of Virginia in February 1836 by the Louisa Railroad, and by 1873 extended between Chesapeake Bay and the Ohio river.

The Pennsylvania Railroad had its origins in popular demand for a railroad to provide through services between Philadelphia and Pittsburgh, so eliminating reliance on the system of canals and inclined planes then existing between the Susquehanna river and

Pittsburgh. The Pennsylvania Railroad was incorporated in April 1846, and began construction of its infrastructure in 1847 from both Harrisburg and Pittsburgh. A through service linking Philadelphia and Pittsburgh came into operation on 10 December 1852, and on 15 February 1854 the use of inclined planes to cross the Alleghenies was finally discontinued. Even before the completion of its own railroad line, the Pennsylvania Railroad had started to offer financial aid to the railroads prepared to provide its connections to destinations farther to the west. Through the buying of securities, the institution of traffic arrangements and, eventually, the effecting of long-term leases and corporate consolidations, the definitive system was created to comprise a system of

railroad lines extending from the Atlantic seaboard as far to the west as the Great Lakes, as well as to economically vital cities such as Chicago, Cincinnati, Louisville and St. Louis.

As noted above, the 1851 completion of the Erie Railway (later Railroad) between two cities in New York state (Piermont on the Hudson river just above New York city and Dunkirk on the southern shore of Lake Erie) created the first single-railroad link between the Atlantic Ocean and the Great Lakes.

Up to the later part of the 1840s, American railroads had extended westward only to the region of Chicago at the southern end of Lake Michigan in the state of Illinois. Yet by now the steady westward movement of the U.S.A.'s migratory expansion toward the Pacific Ocean was paving the way for further expansion of the American railroad system. The railroads began to extend west from Chicago in 1848 when the Galena & Chicago Union Railroad, which later became part of the Chicago & North Western Railroad system, reached the Des Plaines river, some 10 miles (16km) from the city. The first operator to link Chicago with the Mississippi river, however, was the Chicago & Rock Island Railroad, which later became part of the Chicago, Rock Island & Pacific Railroad organization. After just two years in existence, this operator had extended its line to the Mississippi river by 1854, and it also became the first to complete a bridge across the Mississippi river. However, only a short time after the bridge's completion, a river boat collided with it and caught fire, and in the ensuing conflagration both the bridge and the steamboat were burned. A subsequent lawsuit,

Despite the odd nature of the passenger carriage, this is believed to be an accurate representation of a service on the Erie & Kalamazoo Railroad on the 33-mile (53-km) stretch between Toledo and Adrian in 1837. Started in 1831, the 4-2-0 locomotive was the 80th to be completed by Baldwin of Philadelphia, the railroad later becoming one of the core elements of the Lake Shore & Michigan Southern Railroad system.

launched in an effort to prevent the bridge from being rebuilt, was successfully fought for the railroad by Abraham Lincoln.

Lines that later became components of the Chicago, Burlington & Quincy Railroad organization reached the Mississippi at a point opposite Burlington in the state of Iowa during 1855 and at Quincy in Illinois during 1856. An extension of the Galena & Chicago Union Railroad reached the Mississippi river at Fulton, Illinois, during 1855. Thus, in a period of a little more than five years, the railroad advances to the bank of the Mississippi river allowed the railroad companies to draw off much of the relevant regions's trade that had previously travelled by river boat to and from New Orleans. Yet this was still only an early stage of the process of railroad building and

later of railroad consolidation attendant on the westward expansion of the U.S.A. in the north-central part of the country. During 1856 the Illinois Central Railroad was completed between Chicago and the junction of the Mississippi and Ohio rivers at Cairo in the state of Illinois, which meant that by 1860 there was a railroad network able to offer through services along all of the route between Chicago and New Orleans, except for an 18-mile (29-km) ferry link between Cairo and Columbus in the state of Kentucky.

The establishment of railroads to the west of the Mississippi river began in July 1851, when the Pacific Railway of Missouri began the construction of the infrastructure it needed for a line that by July 1853 had progressed some 37 miles (59.5km) to the west; it was on

Crews pose with their three switch engines in front of the former station at Pacific Junction, Iowa, during 1905. Pacific Junction marked the point at which the line linking Kansas City and Council Bluffs crossed the main line to Lincoln. Here, trains for Council Bluffs and Omaha turned north to steam up the valley of the Missouri river. The engine on the left is an E-class, with engine 1390 in the centre and a G-class locomotive on the right.

this line that the first locomotive to operate west of the Mississippi river ran its first 5-mile (8-km) service from St. Louis during December 1852. The railroad later became a component of the Missouri Pacific System, whose route network extended to New Orleans in Louisiana and Denver in Colorado, and also to destinations in the south-western states of the U.S.A.

The next major obstacle after the Mississippi river was the Missouri, and the rails reached this mighty river in 1859 with the completion of the Hannibal & Saint Joseph Railroad, which later became part of the Chicago, Burlington & Quincy Railroad. The Chicago & North Western Railroad also reached the Missouri at Council Bluffs in the state of Iowa early in 1867.

All of these early operators were comparatively small and therefore lacked strategic and financial weight, however, so in 1853 the advantages of a consolidation of the local railroad operators were so abundantly clear that all of these small railroads merged into the New York Central Railroad. This was a far more effective operator, whose railroad lines covered the area between New York City and the southern shore of Lake Erie. The New York Central Railroad was able to rationalize many of its smaller constituent elements's equipment and operating practices to create a more cost-effective network, but the feature that most appealed to passengers of the consolidated operator was the fact that on longer journeys they no longer had to change trains in the fashion that had been inevitable when the route network was the responsibility of a larger number of operators. Farther to the south in the lower part of New York state, but at much the same time, the New York & Erie Railroad re-emerged after it had become bankrupt during the depression of the 1830s. Thus an operator that had gone out of business in 1832 was re-established so successfully that by 1851 is had created a network that extended from Piermont on the bank of the Hudson river to Dunkirk on the shores of Lake Erie. This was the first rail connection by a single operator between the Atlantic seaboard and the Great Lakes.

At this stage it is necessary to backtrack a little and flesh out the details of the expansion in the region westward from the valley of the Ohio river to Chicago. By the middle period of the 19th century, the major railroad companies fully appreciated that they had to create viable links to the railroads springing up in the west if the steamboat operators of the Mississippi and other rivers were not to gain a stranglehold of trade into and out of these states. The key area in this thinking was that to the west of the Ohio river, and it was the influx of financial resources from the east that now allowed a resumption of railroad building after the problems of the late 1830s and the 1840s. First off the mark was the Mad River & Lake Erie Railroad, revived in 1846 and reaching Sandusky on the Ohio shore of Lake Erie in just two years. At the same time the completion of a line between Sandusky and the Ohio Canal paved the way for new railroads, completed in 1852, connecting Cleveland, another port city on the southern shore of Lake Erie and a commercial rival to Sandusky, with the inland cities of Cincinnati and Columbus. In 1853 there opened the westward extensions to Cleveland and Toledo

of the New York Central and Erie systems, and over this short period the Pennsylvania Railroad was extended westward from Pittsburgh in the direction of Chicago.

Lying on the southern tip of Lake Michigan, Chicago was a city of rapidly growing commercial significance, a fact signalled by the establishment of the Chicago & Galena, the Chicago, Burlington & Quincy and the Chicago & Rock Island railroads, all of which fanned out to the west of Chicago. Most important of all these developments was the start of renewed work on the Illinois Central, which was now schemed as the railroad link connecting Cairo, lying on the

junction of the Ohio and Mississippi rivers in the south of Illinois, with Chicago and Galena in the north. The links with Galena and Chicago were finished in 1855 and 1856 respectively. What was notably interesting about this renewed effort was the way in which it was financed: the state gave the Illinois Central land grant sections, alternating on each side of the line, for sale to realize the money needed for construction: the concept of land grants was destined to become a major factor in the financing of future railroads. The completion of these new links was just as important within the context of the shaping of the U.S.A.'s patterns of trade and passenger

With its rapidly-growing population and commercial importance, the Chicago of the mid-19th century was a natural nexus for the development of railroads, such as the Illinois Central Railroad, to link the city with outlying communities and the rest of the U.S.A., including destinations west that soon began to ship vast numbers of cattle to the slaughterhouses of the city for processing and onward shipment to the east.

movement. The western states were now connected by rail to the ports of the north-western states, rather than by water to the ports of the south.

The ending of the depression and the resumption of interest in railroad construction also meant that work was restarted on a number of the southern railroads, albeit at a comparatively slow rate. The number of railroad links connecting the Mississippi, Gulf of Mexico and ports of the eastern seaboard with the leading cities of the U.S.A.'s inland regions began to grow, but oddly enough no real attempt was made to create any significant links with the railroad systems of the north. The situation was also made more inconvenient by the fact that the majority of the southern railroads were built to the 60-in (1.52-m) gauge first adopted by the Charleston

& Hamburg rather than the 56-in (1.42-m) gauge that was common but certainly not universal among the northern railroads.

These latter continued to forge ahead to the west during the 1850s. A notable event, taking place in 1854, was the arrival of the Rock Island Railroad on the eastern border of Illinois at the bank of the Mississippi river. This was next to be spanned by a bridge based on Rock Island, which had given the railroad it name; however, against the vehement opposition of steamboat operators fearing the loss of their livelihoods, the bridge was completed to take the railroad over the river to Davenport in Iowa. Only a short time after this, the wooden bridge itself was burned to destruction after a steamboat had struck one of the bridge's supports. The result was a series of legal actions whose upshot in the U.S.

Supreme Court was a decision that the railroads had as much right to bridge rivers as the steamboats had to ply them.

Henry Farman, president of the Rock Island Railroad, was already looking farther to the west. He established the Mississippi & Missouri Railroad to take railroad transport across Iowa. Other operators followed suit: the Missouri Pacific Railroad departed from St. Louis in Missouri toward Kansas City on the border between Missouri and Kansas, and the Chicago & North Western drove forward over the Mississippi at Clinton in Iowa toward Council Bluffs on the Missouri river. In the event, these two operators lost out to a Missouri-based company, the Hannibal & St. Joseph Railroad, which secured federal land grants and began work in 1851: early in 1859 sections of the railroad, being built simultaneously from the east and west finally met.

The acceleration in the rate of railroad construction is attested by the figures: in 1840 the U.S.A. had 2,799 miles (4504km) of railroad, by 1850 this figure had increased to 8,683 miles (13974km), but only 10 years later still in 1860 the figure had been enlarged dramatically to 30,283 miles (48734km). In terms of changes to the patterns of trade in the U.S.A. the alterations had an equally significant effect: whereas New Orleans had been the leading American port for the export trade, by 1850 its position had been usurped by New York, which benefited from the opening of a host of railroad connections to it, and also from the U.K.'s 1846 repeal of the Corn Laws, which now permitted the import of wheat.

The Pacific type of locomotive was arguably the single most important type of fast passenger locomotive ever created, the type having its origins in a locomotive designed for New Zealand service in 1901 by Baldwin. The capabilities of the Pacific-type locomotive, with a large, wide firebox over a two-wheel pony truck and designed to burn low-grade coal, soon became so clear that Pacifics were built in very large numbers for the U.S. as well as export markets. This is a Pacific of the Illinois Central Railroad.

CHAPTER TWO
STEAM SPANS
THE NATION

The United States of America was transformed in 1846 when the nation gained California from Mexico and secured a definitive border between Oregon and Canada with the U.K. In two strokes the U.S.A. now had a well populated and prosperous Pacific coastline that was linked to the eastern part of the country by ship or, under very limited and dangerous conditions, by horse. The crux of the matter lay in the fact that the Atlantic and Pacific seaboards, together with their increasingly important hinterland regions, were separated from each other by the Great Plains and the Rocky Mountains, which had been explored only to a limited extent and were the homes of many Native American tribes.

By the time the U.S.A. gained its Pacific seaboard presence, there were already in existence a number of proposals for a transcontinental railroad link from 'sea to shining sea'. Some of these proposals were fanciful, to say the least, but there were also a number of suggestions that were more feasible, at least at the technical and financial levels, if one ignored the political and military aspects of the presence of a large 'population

hole' in the middle of the U.S.A. Among the more practical suggestions for a transcontinental railroad was the 1845 concept put forward by Asa Whitney, a New England trader who saw in the transcontinental railroad

link the best way of opening trade with the Far East. Whitney's concept was based on the notion of a federal grant-in-aid transfer to him of a strip of land no less than 60 miles (97km) wide between the Great Lakes and Oregon:

Men of the U.S. Army's Railroad Construction Corps work along the tracks of the Orange & Alexandria Railroad at Devereaux Station near Bull Run, Virginia, probably in 1863. Fought between 1861 and 1865, the American Civil War was the first major conflict anywhere in the world to have made considerable use of railroads for logistics and military, both tactical and strategic. The Federal armies made considerably better use of the railroads than their Confederate opponents, largely negating the latter's advantage of interior lines of communication.

The *General Haupt* was a 4-4-0 Standard- or American-type locomotive, manufactured in 1863 for the U.S. Military Railroad. This was the railroad run for and by the Federal forces in the American Civil War.

Whitney proposed to introduce settlers and extend American civilization along this strip, thereby generating the financial and physical resources to make it feasible for him to construct a railroad extending from the current western limit of construction right through to the shores of the Pacific Ocean. There was strong opposition to Whitney's proposal, most notably from railroad entrepreneurs in other

Though it made extensive use of the railroad system in the American Civil War, the Federal army's railway corps built little new track mileage, but concentrated instead on the exploitation of existing track, which had constantly to be repaired and improved. This 1864 photograph shows Federal troops working on a four-tiered wooden trestle bridge, 780-ft (238-m) long, at Whiteside, Tennessee.

regions which saw themselves as the natural starting point for a transcontinental railroad endeavour. The opposition to Whitney was as fragmented as the schemes proposed by several other protagonists of a transcontinental railroad, but in concert the opposition was significant and when Whitney's proposal came before the Congress in 1848, the bill to authorize it was defeated, albeit by only a narrow margin.

By this time there was considerable public as well as entrepreneurial clamour for the establishment of a transcontinental railroad link, which was clearly of vital importance in drawing the two halves of the country together, and also in paving the way for the wholly undeveloped region between the eastern and western halves of the country to be opened up to settlement and commercial development. In 1853, therefore, the Congress ordained that the U.S. Army send out teams of surveyors and engineers to complete a thorough examination of routes that could be used for a transcontinental railroad.

The U.S. Army proposed any of four possible routes, two of them located in the north and the other two in the south. The northern routes were those between Lake Superior and Portland on the Oregon coast on the one hand, and through South Pass to San Francisco in California on the other. The southern routes were those to southern California along the line of the Red river or through southern Texas. At this juncture there was an intervention by Stephen A. Douglas, an Illinois senator who had been a major force in the issue of grant-in-aid lands to the Illinois Central Railroad. Douglas now urged the

development not only of one but rather of three transcontinental routes: one in the north to the Oregon coast, one in the centre to San Francisco, and one in the south from Texas to southern California. So pregnant with commercial possibilities was the whole concept of the transcontinental railroad, moreover, that there were several other proposals. The third and fourth proposals to gain a significant level of geographical and financial credibility were those promulgated by the backers of the Leavenworth, Pawnee & Western Railroad, a company which currently operated no track but had rights to large areas of Native American land in Kansas on its route schemed as a line west from the border of Missouri and Kansas, and by the backers of the Hannibal & St. Joseph Railroad, who wished to extend their line to the west along the route pioneered by the Pony Express mail service, which had been started from St. Joseph during 1860.

This was only part of the story, however. These and others were concerned to ensure that the transcontinental railroad or railroads were launched from the east to drive through to the Pacific coast, providing easy and therefore earlier recouping of current investment as migrants moved in behind the railheads on their progess west toward the Pacific coast. There was also, however, a growing number of entrepreneurs and visionaries based on the west coast of the U.S.A., and these were avid proponents of the concept that the railroad or railroads should be driven eastward from the Pacific coast to link up with the railroad networks of the U.S.A.'s eastern half somewhere as close to the line of

the Missouri and Mississippi rivers as possible: in this way, of course, the Pacific coast entrepreneurs saw themselves as opening up the west and securing the returns that would otherwise have ended up in the pockets of eastern entrepreneurs.

A major force in the technical aspects of the proposal that the transcontinental railroad should be constructed from the west coast was Theodore Judah, an engineer who had been born and raised in Connecticut but who had moved to California when he was appointed to oversee the construction of a short railway linking Sacramento and the mining area near Placerville. Judah's thinking caught the attention of businessmen such as Charles Crocker, Mark Hopkins, Collis P. Huntington and Leland Stanford. In 1860 Judah failed to win federal approval for his concept, so the four California businessmen formed a high-powered consortium to promote Judah's idea. The first practical stage in the consortium's effort was a survey to find a route superior to that which had been recommended by the U.S. Army's teams of surveyors. The consortium assessed the Sierra Nevada region in the summer of 1860 before fixing the route of the railroad it planned: this route extended through the Donner Pass, so lopping more than 100 miles (160km) from the route planned by the U.S. Army's survey teams, and opened the way for the provision of potentially very lucrative services into the valley of the Carson river, where new mines were coming into production.

The consortium's next move was the acquisition of federal approval, which would bring in its train all-important federal subsidies or money and/or land. In 1861 the consortium created the Central Pacific Railroad of California with $200,000 of capital, and Huntington left the west coast to collaborate with Judah in the pressing of the consortium's case in Washington, D.C. Washington was now the capital of a nation at war, or more realistically the capital of one of the two sides involved in the American Civil War, which started in 1861.

Though the expansion of the railroads was not one of the factors responsible for the situation that led directly to the start of the Civil War, it was responsible in part for the manner in which the warring parties divided into their two camps, and also the manner in which this first of what can be regarded as modern wars would be fought. The expansion of the U.S.A.'s railroad system, which was weighted more strongly to the north than to the south, had already laid the foundation for what was increasingly an interrelated economic entity of the northern states, and at the same time helped to foster the strong individualistic feelings of the southern states. Here there were considerably fewer great railroad networks to bolster the suggestion of some type of national unity, and as a result there was a strong feeling of the rights of the southern states, individually and collectively, to decide their own futures. In 1860 the American railroad network covered 30,283 miles (48734km), as noted above, but only 8,838 miles (14223km) were in the southern states (south of the Ohio and Potomac rivers and east of the Mississippi river but including Louisiana). This meant that 21,445 miles (34511km) or 70.82 per cent of the American

railroad network lay outside the southern states. Of this total, 3,660 miles (5890km) were in the New England states (Maine, New Hampshire, Vermont, Massachusetts, Rhode Island and Connecticut), 6,353 miles (10224km) in the mid-Atlantic states (New York, Pennsylvania, New Jersey, West Virginia, Maryland, Delaware and the District of Columbia), 9,592 miles (15436km) in the north-central states (Michigan, Indiana, Illinois, Ohio and Wisconsin), and 1,840 miles (2961km) in the states west of the Mississippi river (including Minnesota). The ratio of railroad mileage lying on the 'northern' and 'southern' states was to prove as crucial to the conduct of military operations in the Civil War as it had already been in fostering the development of the higher level of industrial capacity and wealth in the northern states.

Although it was the matter of state rights that was the root cause of the Civil War, the factor that brought this to the fore was slavery. Slavery had been permitted when Arkansas became a state in 1836, largely as a result of the Missouri Compromise of 1820, which allowed slavery in the region on the condition that it would not be allowed in the remaining lands west and north of the Arkansas border. During the 1850s the frontier moved steadily westward, more and more people then pouring into the region in their search for land, and this made it essential that a new wave of organization should be implemented. This had major implications for the routes that the transcontinental railroads would use.

One of the first to appreciate this fact was Stephen Douglas, who foresaw that a single territory to the west of the Mississippi river

would have as its first settlers migrants from Arkansas and Missouri. These would doubtless create their main city in the south of the area, leading to a shift to the south of the proposed railroad's course. Douglas wanted Chicago as the eastern end of the transcontinental railroad, so he planned a division of the area into two, with the question of slavery to be left to the people who reached the area: in this way Douglas hoped to make the area attractive to migrants from the north and the south. The result of this process was a 1854 Congressional act repealing the Missouri Compromise and establishing the territories of Kansas and Nebraska. The act did not have the effect anticipated by Douglas, however. The northern opponents and southern proponents of slavery were respectively angered and pleased by the repeal of the Missouri Compromise, and in Kansas there developed an increasingly bitter and bloody 'war' between the two sides. This bitterness was reflected in the 1860 presidential elections, in which the success of Abraham Lincoln and the Republican party led to the secession of the southern states, led by South Carolina, from the Union and then the outbreak of the civil war between the Union and the Confederacy in the spring of 1861.

In simple terms, the dividing line between the two sides extended along the northern borders of Virginia, Tennessee and Arkansas. As noted above, in the northern states of the Union lay more than 70 per cent of the USA's railroad mileage total, which also constituted a more useful concentration and connectivity of transport capacity than the more fragmented railroad network that was now left to the

A wood-burning Standard-type locomotive seen on the City Point Line during the American Civil War. Behind the freight cars is a 13-in (330-mm) mortar nicknamed *The Dictator*. It was used in the final stages of the war during the Federal siege of Petersburg, and used a 20-lb (9.1-kg) black powder charge to project its explosive-filled 200-lb bomb into the Confederate defences.

The locomotive *Firefly* passes over a trestle bridge, on the Orange & Alexandria Railroad, supported by masonry buttresses at each end.

As one of the most important cities of the Confederacy and a major rail junction, Atlanta, Georgia was a prime target for the Federal armies in 1864 during the later stages of the American Civil War. This photograph reveals the locomotives *Telegraph* and *O.A. Bull* by the ruins of the Confederate machine-house at Atlanta after the Federal forces had taken the city.

southern states of the Confederacy, as a result of the region's history of more disjointed railroad development. Both sides were equally dependent on the portion of the complete railroad system that lay in the areas they controlled, the nature and extent of the system being, to a very large degree, responsible for the way in which the war between the states developed and was fought. Only the

availability of railroad transport permitted the war to be fought in the way that it was waged, for the increasingly large armies mustered by each side were reliant mainly on the railroads, not only for strategic transport but also for the very considerable quantities of food, clothing, equipment and munitions that had to be delivered over considerable distances.

That this would be the case had been clear

right from the beginning of the Civil War, and as a result railroads became targets for raids from the start of hostilities. For example, the Baltimore & Ohio Railroad's bridge at Harpers Ferry had been destroyed by John Brown's raid on the town in 1859 and had then been reconstructed, only to be attacked by Confederate forces under 'Stonewall' Jackson in 1861 and destroyed once more. Jackson also commanded a raid on Martinsburg, where the Confederate attack destroyed some 44 of the Baltimore & Ohio Railroad's locomotives. The same company's lines was also frequently sabotaged by the Confederates. Farther to the south, the Norfolk & Petersburg and the South Side railroads suffered major damage as battles were fought along their length. In many other parts of the railroad network, raiding parties from each side attacked the other side's rolling stock and installations, burned bridges, cut telegraph lines and destroyed tracks.

As the Civil War progressed, railroad transport became increasingly important at the strategic, and to a more limited extent, tactical levels for the movement of each side's war-making capability (troops and all their equipment and munitions). This was the case from an early time, for in the war's first major battle, fought in July 1861 and known as the 1st Battle of Manassas to the Confederacy, and as the 1st Battle of Bull Run to the Union, victory went to the Confederate forces as a result of the timely arrival by railroad of reinforcements. But as the war continued, it was the Union that was inevitably better placed to exploit its advantages in railroad transport, not only in capacity but also in

A typical scene in what is now Seven Valleys but was then, in 1864 in the midst of the American Civil War, Hanover Junction. It is believed that the tall figure in the centre of the image wearing a stovepipe hat, is President Abraham Lincoln, the architect of the Federal victory and thus responsible for maintaining the U.S.A. as a single nation.

One of the greatest raiders of the war was a Confederate officer, General J.E.B. 'Jeb' Stuart, who commanded a large body of fast-moving and aggressive cavalry. Seen here is some of Stuart's handiwork after his attack on the railroad supplying the Federal forces of General John Pope after the 2nd Battle of Bull Run in August 1862.

connectivity. The lack of this latter was a decided disadvantage for the Confederacy: in July 1862, for example, General Braxton Bragg was able to move his army of 35,000 men from Tupelo in Mississippi to Chattanooga in Tennessee, but only via Mobile on Alabama's Gulf of Mexico coast along a route nearly three times longer than any straighter railroad linkage would have been.

The limitations of the railroad system with which the Confederacy started the war were exacerbated by lack of industrial resources. The production of all the hardware associated with railroad operations was concentrated almost exclusively in the states of the Union, and the Confederacy was further hampered by continued commercial rivalry between several of the railroad operators, which frequently caused the Confederate armies intractable logistic difficulties. Railroad problems were not limited entirely to the Confederacy, though, for while the Union's railroad system was more extensive, better integrated, and supplied with superior equipment, it also suffered from a number of problems, including tracks of several different gauges. One of the keys to the Union's eventual victory in 1865 was not so much the possession of a superior railroad network, but rather the maximization of the capabilities provided by this network. It was only in 1865, when it was teetering on the edge of defeat, that the Confederacy brought its railroad network wholly under military control, but it was in 1862 that President Lincoln had gained Congressional authorization to take over any railroad he considered necessary to the war effort.

Another and perhaps still more important key to the Union's eventual victory was the establishment of the U.S. Military Railroad organization, which was controlled directly by the Department of War. Led by Daniel C. McCallum, the U.S. Military Railroad built almost 650 miles (1046km) of new track and large numbers of bridges, and finally had under its control more than 2,000 miles (3220km) of track as well as more than 400 locomotives and 600 cars.

From a time in the middle of the war, the Union was sufficiently skilled in effective exploitation of the railroad system to ensure the timely movement of large numbers of

MAP OF ROUTES
FOR A
PACIFIC RAILROAD

Compiled to accompany the Report of the

HON. JEFFERSON DAVIS, SEC. OF WAR

In Office of P. R. R. Surveys
1855.

Statute Miles

The several schemes for the transcontinental railroad scheduled for construction in the 1860s are detailed on this map drawn to accompany the overall report to the U.S. Congress of the Honourable Jefferson Davis, soon to become the president of the breakaway Confederate States of America.

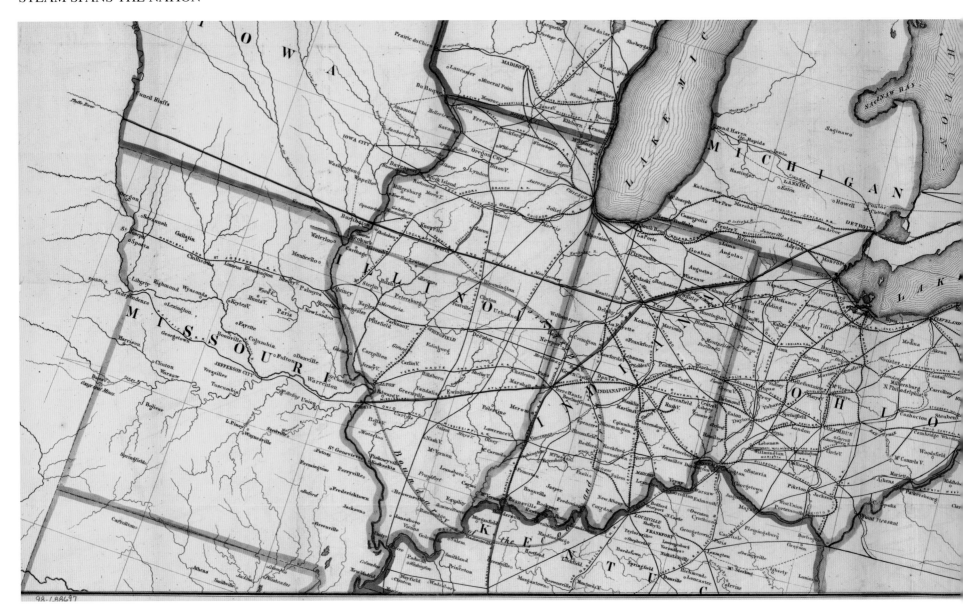

RAIL ROAD MAP
accompanying the Report and Exhibit
of the CHIEF ENGINEER *of the*
LOGANSPORT & NORTHERN INDIANA RAILROAD
Showing its connections and the
Through Route from St. Louis to New York
of which this road forms a part.
Logansport. Indiana May 1st 1854.
L. S. Nash
Chief Engineer.

Map accompanying the report and exhibit of the Logansport & Northern Indiana Railroad, showing its connections and the through route from St. Louis to New York, of which this road forms a part. May 1854.

men. In September 1863, for example, the Confederate victory in the Battle of Chickamauga resulted in the siege of Chattanooga, where more than 20,000 Union soldiers and large quantities of weapons and equipment were trapped. In 12 days, however, the Union command was able to move two corps of the Army of the Potomac some 1,190 miles (1915km) from defensive positions near Washington, D.C., to Bridgeport, one of the two points from which the relief of Chattanooga could be undertaken.

The appreciation of the significance of the effective use of railroad transport for military operations was one side of the coin whose other was the appreciation that the denial of this facility to the other side was just as important. Throughout the Civil War, therefore, each side made efforts to deny or, failing this, to hamper the other side's use of the railroad system. These efforts usually involved raids and sabotage, and the threat of such efforts meant that a modest yet important part of each combatant's overall strength had to be used for the railroad's protection, the need to protect the railroads being in itself a testament to their importance.

Among the first officers to grasp the implications of this factor was General William Sherman in the course of his 1864 campaign against the Confederate forces. Sherman first built up his supplies at Nashville and Chattanooga in Tennessee, and then drove the Confederate forces along the line of the railroad toward Atlanta in Georgia, in the process severing the Confederacy's railroad links from Atlanta to Macon and Montgomery. This compelled the Confederacy to retire its

Army of Tennessee south-east in the direction of Atlanta. Fully appreciating the importance of possessing what it was worth denying to the opposition, Sherman ensured that the railroad, crippled by the retreating Confederates, was repaired as he moved forward to allow the timely delivery of reinforcements, equipment and food. Reaching a point north-west of Atlanta and taking this key Confederate city under siege, however, Sherman found that he had to use about half of his available strength to protect the railroad. This was one of the reasons for a classic change of tactics. Toward the end of the year, Sherman decided to abandon the railroad and its promise of resupply, instead striking off to the south-east in the great 'March to the Sea', in which his forces lived off the land. Lasting from 15 November to 21 December, this took Sherman's forces in a wide swathe to Savannah in Georgia, and in the process divided the Confederacy into two portions that could then be defeated in detail.

The railroad network of the southern states was a shattered wreck over much of its more important sections by the time the Civil War ended in April 1865. Even when they had not been deliberately destroyed, many sections were in very poor condition after years of neglect and the absence of operational equipment. On the other side of what had been the front line, the situation was altogether different, for the years of the Civil War had seen extensive development of the northern states's railroad system. There had been considerable standardization of gauges, the tracks were in generally superior condition following the introduction of steel as a

replacement of iron, and the replacement of wood by coal as locomotive fuel was offering great advantages.

At the same time, a new way of thinking had entered into all matters relevant to the building and operation of railroads. Nowhere was this more striking than in the question of the transcontinental railroad. Even during the war, agitation for the creation of this link had continued, and the significance of establishing this link, initially seen mainly in financial terms, had acquired elements of national reconstruction: improved communications inside the U.S.A. would become a means of deterring other secessionist ambitions, perhaps by the states of the south-west and west. The task of planning the transcontinental railroad had been simplified by the outbreak of Civil War, however, for the implementation of any southern route was now clearly out of the question, certainly in the shorter term, as the proposed southern routes had their eastern termini in great cities of the Confederacy, while a starting point in Missouri was also impossible as there was still fighting in the region. Lincoln had signed the act authorizing the transcontinental railroad on 1 July 1862, establishing the legal framework for the construction of a railroad and parallel telegraph line from the Missouri river to the Pacific Ocean, and specifying an eastern starting point on the western side of Iowa's border. The new link was to be built simultaneously from the west and the east by the Central Pacific Railroad and the newly created Union Pacific Railroad respectively.

The Congress imposed a mass of conditions on the construction of the transcontinental railroad. The companies were required to lay a single-track railroad and a telegraph line; the California/Nevada border marked the dividing line between the two companies's operations, with the Central Pacific Railroad and the Union Pacific Railroad working respectively to the west and east of the dividing line; only American-produced iron and steel were to be used. The companies were each allocated a right of way 400-ft (122-m) wide, together with five alternating sections of land on each side for every mile of track completed, a loan of S16,000 for each mile of track, rising to $32,000 and $48,000 per mile in the foothill and mountain sections respectively. Both companies made notable use of the relevant departments's imaginations to boost the miles of 'foothill' and 'mountain' their lines had to cross, with the result that the Union Pacific Railroad received $27 million and the Central Pacific $24 million, granted as first mortgages on the railroads. The railroad companies were also permitted to offer 100,000 $100 shares to the public, although no person was allowed to purchase more than 200; it was also ordained that the start of work would not be authorized until one-fifth of the shares had been sold, giving each company another $2 million of working capital. In order to benefit from these terms the Union Pacific Railroad was required to complete 100 miles (160km) of track within two years and 100 miles per year thereafter, while the equivalent figures for the Central Pacific Railroad, which had to lay its track over more difficult terrain, were half of those demanded of the Union Pacific Railroad.

To broaden the benefits offered by the new railroad connection to areas to each side of the transcontinental railroad's eastern reaches, authority was also granted for the construction of lines east of 100° W to provide connections with cities such as Kansas City, Leavenworth, Omaha, Sioux City and St. Joseph.

At the other end of the transcontinental railroad, equally momentous events were taking place in California. Even as Huntington was receiving the charter to build the Central Pacific Railroad, Leland Stanford was elected governor of California and the Central Pacific Railroad received a state loan of $1.659 million. More money was found by selling bonds to the communities along the route, yielding large sums which included no less than $1 million from San Francisco alone. Bond buying was stimulated by the fears of inland cities that their failure to subscribe would cause the railroad's planners to bypass their communities, which would then suffer the financial consequences. Among the first of such subscribers were Sacramento and Placer County, which subscribed $848,000.

With the Civil War still raging in the east, Stanford broke the ground of the Central Pacific Railroad's starting point on the eastern bank of the Sacramento river during 8 January 1863. While Huntington and Stanford were leading the Central Pacific Railroad's political and financial approaches to the mighty task of building the western end of the transcontinental railroad, another man had been playing a less obvious but just as important role. This was Charles Crocker, whose task it had been to create at Sacramento the stockpile of equipment and supplies that

would be needed. Once work had started, Crocker became the operation's general superintendent and, as such, the head of the construction effort. By July, Crocker's teams had graded 18 miles (29km) of track in preparation for rail laying, and built a 400-ft (122-m) trestle bridge over the American river, the first of a huge number of obstacles to the railroad's continued eastward progress. The first 20 miles (32km) of track from Sacramento, only a modest height above sea level, to Roseville, were characterized by modest gradients, but eastward from Roseville the gradients became steeper and, as the year advanced, the weather deteriorated.

One of the most important requirements faced by the construction effort was large numbers of men to hack out and remove rock, level the roadbed, and lay the ties and rails. Bridges up to 500-ft (152-m) long and 100-ft (30.5-m) high had to be constructed across many deep ravines interrupting the route, and tunnels 500-yards (457-m) long or more had to be smashed through stone ridges. Yet the railroad offered a maximum of only $3 per day for such work, always hard and occasionally dangerous, when the Californian labour market was being drained by the lure of the gold and silver mines able to offer considerably higher wages. Crocker found a solution in the Chinese enclave of San Francisco. Although an initial force of only 50 Chinese was employed, these 50 proved so effective that a major programme of Chinese recruitment was launched. Once all the available Chinese labour in California had been recruited, the railroad was forced to look for additional workers in China and then ship

This is a train derailed during the retreat of General John Pope's Federal forces after their defeat in the 2nd Battle of Bull Run in August 1862. Destroyed track was comparatively easy to repair, both sides discovered, but the loss of locomotives and rolling stock was a task more difficult, and therefore more time-consuming and costly, to rectify.

The Federal army made extensive use of the railroad system, wherever it could, to effect the movement of large numbers of men and all their equipment to attack the Confederate forces where they least expected it. These are Federal troops waiting at City Point, Virginia, for the train that will move them up to the front sometime in 1864.

them across the Pacific. By the summer of 1865 some 3,500 of the Central Pacific Railroad's force of 4,000 labourers were Chinese, and the railroad planned to double the number.

It is worth noting that about this time the senior officers of the Central Pacific Railroad launched an imaginative scheme to support their financial planning and boost income. For this purpose they created the Contract and Finance Corporation, and subcontracted the construction work to this. The Central Pacific Railroad eventually paid the Contract and Finance Corporation almost $80 million, perhaps twice what the work actually cost, and very substantial amounts of federal and shareholder money passed from the Central Pacific Railroad to the Corporation. In 1866 the Congress authorized the Central Pacific Railroad to continue construction work beyond the state line that it had originally fixed as its eastern limit. The increase in the labour force, and the imaginative use of its financial resources, allowed the Central

Pacific Railroad to speed its construction programme. During June 1864 the railroad issued its first timetable, a schedule for the 31-mile (50-km) route linking Sacramento and Newcastle: each day, one train carrying passengers and mail and the other two passengers and freight were interleaved with the trains carrying labourers and materials to the railhead. The next 12 miles (19km), climbing 800ft (244m) to Clipper Gap, took 12 months, but in the following two months 11-miles (18-km) more were added. Grading of the trackway continued through the winter, and by the end of 1866 the track had reached Cisco, only 92 miles (148km) from

OPPOSITE

This is the 4-4-0 locomotive *Fred Leach* of the U.S. Military Railroad after its escape from a Confederate raiding party near Union Mills on 1 August 1863 while operating on the tracks of the Orange & Alexandria Railroad. The smokestack reveals clear evidence that the locomotive was struck by Confederate fire.

LEFT

A major 'weapon' in the rapid construction of railroad track was the construction train. This is such a train from General Casement's outfit near Bear River City. The trains included flat cars for tools, a fully- equipped blacksmith's forge, accommodation coaches for the work crew, and other cars for cooking, eating and the storage of equipment and food.

Built in the yards at Chattanooga, Tennessee, this is locomotive No. 137 of the U.S. Military Railroad. It is seen in 1864 with troops mustered in the background ready to embark.

Sacramento but at an altitude of almost 6,000ft (1830m).

The following winter was dire: during February and March the snow was more than 10-ft (3-m) deep on average, apparently interminable blizzards battered the work camps, and the cold was intense. Even so, work on the track continued as the railroad could not afford to pay men who were not working, or to lose a workforce which was now very skilled. As a great snowplough was used to keep open the track back to Sacramento and snowsheds were erected to protect the track behind and the newly graded roadbed ahead, the labourers began work on the 1,660-ft (506-m) Summit Tunnel at an altitude of 7,017ft (2139m), a force of some 8,000 men blasting and hacking their way from each end and also in both directions from a central shaft. The snow behind the tunnel entrance from the west was so heavy and

Built by Danforth, Cooke & Company, locomotive No. 133 of the U.S. Military Railroad is a 4-4-0 seen at City Point, Virginia, in 1864.

compacted that the snow plough could not be shifted, even by a team of 12 locomotives, so oxen had to be used to keep the labour gangs supplied with the timber, explosives and other items they needed.

Progress continued, the next major feature the railhead crews reached being the Donner Pass: in 1867 the last snow did not disappear from the pass until June, when the disappearance of the last patches permitted the laying of ties and rails. By the middle of 1867 the Central Pacific Railroad had pushed its railhead forward some 130 miles (209km), but it was the end of the year before the rails could be laid though the Summit Tunnel. This made it possible for three locomotives to haul cars to the summit, and then followed all the requirements for another 50 miles (80km) of

RIGHT
The 'Heathen Chinee', a coloured engraving of the period, belittles the Chinese who were imported in large numbers during the building of the first transcontinental railroad. However, without the perseverance and endurance of its many thousands of Chinese labourers, the Central Pacific Railroad would have been hard-pressed to complete its portion of the railroad.

OPPOSITE
This still from Cecil B. de Mille's epic film, *Union Pacific*, highlights the decisive moment when the final golden spike was driven at Promontory Point, Utah, to mark the meeting of the western and eastern parts of the first transcontinental railroad on 10 May 1869. It was now possible to cross the U.S.A. by rail.

THE "HEATHEN CHINEE."

"But the hands that were played, by that heathen Chinee
And the points that he made were quite frightful to see
Till at last he put down a right bower
Which the same Nye had dealt unto me."

track. Even so, ox teams had to be employed to move supplies past a gap in the rails. Adverse weather was still a major factor in the railroad's infuriatingly slow progress at this stage throughout 1867, when the railroad completed the laying of only another 40 miles (64km) of track to reach the California/Nevada border during December, the point originally established as it eastern end, despite the fact that there was a gap of 7 miles (11.25km) near Donner Lake, where work had been halted by snow.

The track reached the new city of Reno in Nevada during the spring of 1868, the gap in the rails near Donner Lake was filled and,

with equipment and supplies now brought up more easily, the railhead drove east across Nevada toward Utah. The Central Pacific Railroad now began to derive income from the track that had been completed, with traffic to and from the mining areas of Nevada boosting revenues quite dramatically. It was now the intention of the railroad's board of directors to reach Ogden before the westward progress of the Union Pacific Railroad claimed it.

The Union Pacific Railroad did not start work on its route to the west until after the Central Pacific Railroad's effort had been under way for some time. The company received its charter by an 1862 Congressional

act that named 158 commissioners. Some of these conducted a preliminary meeting in Chicago during September 1862, when William B. Ogden was elected as president. Thomas Durant, the man behind the Rock Island Railroad and its subsidiary, the Mississippi & Missouri Railroad, wanted another man, however, and set about overturning this initial decision. In March 1863, with only 150 shares on the Union Pacific Railroad sold, Durant used the names of friends to evade the restrictions on share ownership, and by disposing of his holding the Mississippi & Missouri Railroad gained control of the 20,000 shares that had to be sold before work could begin. In October 1863, therefore, Durant was able to use the major shareholding he now controlled to replace Ogden with John A. Dix, previously the figurehead president of the Mississippi & Missouri Railroad.

On 2 December of the same year, ground was broken at the start of the Union Pacific Railroad's eastern end at Omaha in Nebraska. But by the spring of 1864 the Union Pacific Railroad had completed only a few of the initial gradings and work had halted for lack of adequate funding. Durant's solution was to create the Credit Mobilier of America as a holding company, and to persuade the Congress to double land grant-in-aid made to the Union Pacific Railroad and to include with it any mineral deposits under the land, to convert the company's federal loans into a second mortgage, and to increase the permitted number of shares from 100,000 to one million. A final touch in Durant's plan for the completion of the railroad, and in the

process the considerable enrichment of himself, was the replacement of Peter Dey, the chief engineer who had estimated costs at between $20,000 and $30,000 per mile, by Colonel Silas Seymour, who had prepared a more circuitous line of advance, and the arrangement with the Credit Mobilier for work to be completed on the basis of $50,000 per mile.

Most of these moves were dubious, to say the least, but did succeed in securing enlarged financial resources, which allowed the resumption of work on the railroad on a more effective basis. This was just as well for the Union Pacific Railroad, for the Leavenworth, Pawnee & Western Railroad was, in its new form as the Union Pacific, Eastern Division, and with its own federal land grant agreed, already advancing its track west from the Missouri river; the Atchison & Topeka Railway, under Cyrus K. Holliday, had also received federal land grants encouraging it to revise its original thinking, based on the laying of a railroad from Atchison on the Missouri river to Topeka, the capital of Kansas, to ambitious plans for a westward extension along the line of the Santa Fe Trail to the Pacific.

Events soon revealed that Seymour had been a poor choice by Durant to supervise the construction of the Union Pacific Railroad's line, as only 15 miles (24km) of track had been laid by October 1865. Seymour was therefore replaced by General Grenville Dodge, who had assisted Peter Dey on the Rock Island Railroad, been involved in the Mississippi & Missouri Railroad surveys, and had made a considerable name for himself

during the Civil War. At much the same time, in the spring of 1866, the company took on General John S. Casement and his brother Daniel to supervise construction. The changes had the desired effect, and progress accelerated. The ferry landing at Omaha on the western bank of the Missouri river was rapidly transformed into a major industrial site as workshops were built, boats delivered increasing quantities of equipment and supplies, and a construction force of 10,000 men and vast numbers of draft animals were assembled.

As the Union Pacific Railroad's track moved west, use was made of an accommodation train incorporating triple-deck bunks so that the work crews did not need to be ferried back and forth between more permanent accommodation and the railhead, and trains were used to carry ties and rails as close as possible to the railhead, which was finally reached by horse-drawn wagons. Ahead of the railhead proper, the grading teams preparing the way for the laying of the track were supplied by trains of ox-drawn wagons, and still farther forward the precise alignment of the route was surveyed and marked by special parties. The reorganization of the whole process along these lines was characterized by a sevenfold increase in the speed of the railroad's advance, and by October 1866 the Union Pacific Railroad had crossed 100° W, slightly less than 250 miles (400km) to the west of Omaha. Just a few weeks later, temporary winter quarters were built at North Platte.

In the spring of 1867 the Chicago & North Western Railroad reached Council

Bluffs, which greatly eased its supply problems, while at the same time the Union Pacific Railroad resumed work with the improvement in the weather. By the beginning of the winter of 1867–68, progress had been sufficient for a new temporary winter camp to be established at Cheyenne. In the spring of 1868 the Union Pacific Railroad pushed forward through the Black Hills at about the time that the Central Pacific Railroad was advancing into Nevada after passing over and through the mountain barrier that had given it so many problems.

Advancing from the west and east, both railroads were now aiming to be first into Utah, Dodge announcing his intention that his railroad should double the 500 miles (805km) already laid and reach Ogden by the end of 1868. In pursuit of their objectives, the Union Pacific and Central Pacific railroads each contracted with the Mormon religious community in Utah to start grading routes far ahead of their rails but, unfortunately for both companies, many miles of parallel routing were graded before the federal authorities fixed on Ogden as the meeting place.

The laying of track had by now become a highly standardized operation that progressed with an extraordinary rapidity. Before work began in 1868, 3,000 men were employed to fell trees and position their stripped trunks along the Union Pacific Railroad's line of advance; the work train was further increased in size to allow it to carry butchers, bakers and their equipment, and even visitors such as newspaper publishers. In the wake of the railhead, the less salubrious aspect of the progress was the appearance of all the

OPPOSITE
Featuring prominently in the 'golden spike' ceremony at Promontory Point was the Central Pacific Railroad's 4-4-0 locomotive Jupiter.

OPPOSITE
The Union Pacific Railroad's counterpart to the *Jupiter* at the golden spike ceremony was another 4-4-0 locomotive, the more prosaically named No. 119.

dissolute elements wishing to separate the men of the workforce from their hard-earned pay. This body of camp followers, with their portable saloons and brothels, became known as 'Hell on Wheels', and pursued the railhead as it advanced through Laramie, Benton, Red Desert, Black Butte, Green River, Salt Wells, and Bitter Creek in southern Wyoming.

Before the winter of 1868–69 slowed the construction season once more, the Union Pacific's railhead had progressed 995 miles (1601km) to the west of Omaha and was now at Wasatch in the mountains of the border between Wyoming and Utah, just 67 miles (108km) from Ogden, while coming up from the west, the Central Pacific Railroad had driven 446 miles (718km) east from Sacramento to reach Carlin in the north-eastern part of Nevada. With Ogden so close, neither railroad seriously entertained a winter break, despite the desperately bad conditions in the mountains. The pay of the workforce was doubled, work continued, and by the spring both railroads were racing across the plains of Utah. First to reach Odgen on 8 March, was the Union Pacific Railroad, and the railhead of the Central Pacific Railroad was only some 50 miles (80 km) distant. Even so, it was only pressure exerted by President Ulysses S. Grant that finally compelled the two railroads to agree a meeting place, namely Promontory, some 53 miles (85km) west of Ogden.

As the railheads advanced, the copper wires for the parallel telegraph system had been strung on poles alongside the tracks, and with this system completed shortly before the two railroads met at Promontory Point, the daily newspaper reports of the rival organizations's

progress had caught the imagination of the country. Reflecting this fever, Crocker and the Casements responded by speeding the progress of their lines still further, each railhead finally advancing between 6 and 8 miles (10 and 13km) each day. There was also an intense rivalry, or even antipathy, between the Central Pacific Railroad's predominantly Chinese and the Union Pacific Railroad's generally Irish workforces, and there were even instances of the work gangs of one operator deliberately setting off explosive charges round the location of the other's.

It was on 28 April 1869 that the transcontinental railroad effort finally reached its peak when, with only 20 miles (32km) of track still to be laid, Crocker decided a $10,000 bet he had made with Durant by putting together a special team to lay 10 miles (16km) of rail in only 12 hours. It was all over in just a few more days. On 10 May officers and workers of the two railroads gathered at Promontory Point for the placing of a silver-wreathed laurel tie and the driving of a golden spike to mark the junction of the rails from the east and west. The Union Pacific Railroad's locomotive *Jupiter* (opposite) and the Central Pacific Railroad's No. 119 crept forward to touch each other, while a telegraph message signalled the completion of the first transcontinental railroad, which extended over a distance 1,776 miles (2858km).

Celebrations of this great achievement swept like a blizzard though the U.SA., especially in the north. But the jubilation was soon followed by a period of reflection as details of the transcontinental railroad's real cost began to emerge. The Union Pacific

Railroad had received land grants-in-aid amounting to 24 million acres (9.713 million hectares), and the Central Pacific Railroad 9 million acres (3.64 million hectares) for a combined total of more than 50,000 square miles (129500 km²). Financial grants to the two companies from the federal government amounted to $27 million and $24 million respectively, and further huge sums had been raised by the sale of stock. Even in 1869, few felt that this was money that had been well spent. It began to emerge that the rail lines, especially those of the Union Pacific Railroad, were of poor quality, but even this was initially overlooked as people were dazzled by the enormity of the overall achievement. Other factors that could be overlooked in the excitement of the moment or explained by the speed with which the two railroads had pushed forward their work were the random spacing of ties placed directly on the ground without intervening ballast; the use of soft, wholly unseasoned pine for ties that started to rot even as they were laid; bridges of poor design and construction; embankments without any shoring to support them against lateral movement and collapse; and poor joining of the sections of rail. Quite apart from these technical matters, there was also the fact that route alignments had deliberately been made to meander so as to increase their lengths and maximize the federal land grants-in-aid that extended to each side of the tracks's length.

The general feeling was that the most important aspect of the whole effort was that rail communications across the country were now possible, and that time would see the

RIGHT & OPPOSITE
Though the speed with which the two railroad operations that met at Promontory Point meant that considerable improvement of the infrastructure soon had to be undertaken, the golden spike ceremony on 10 May 1869 was of great significance in American history as it marked the completion of the first genuinely effective transcontinental route.

RIGHT
The *Jupiter* forms a fitting backdrop in this photograph of the Promontory Point celebrations featuring bandsmen of the 21st Infantry Regiment, currently stationed at Fort Douglas, Utah. (See also page 67.)

OPPOSITE
Rand McNally and Company's map of the Union Pacific system of railroad and steam ship lines, 1900.

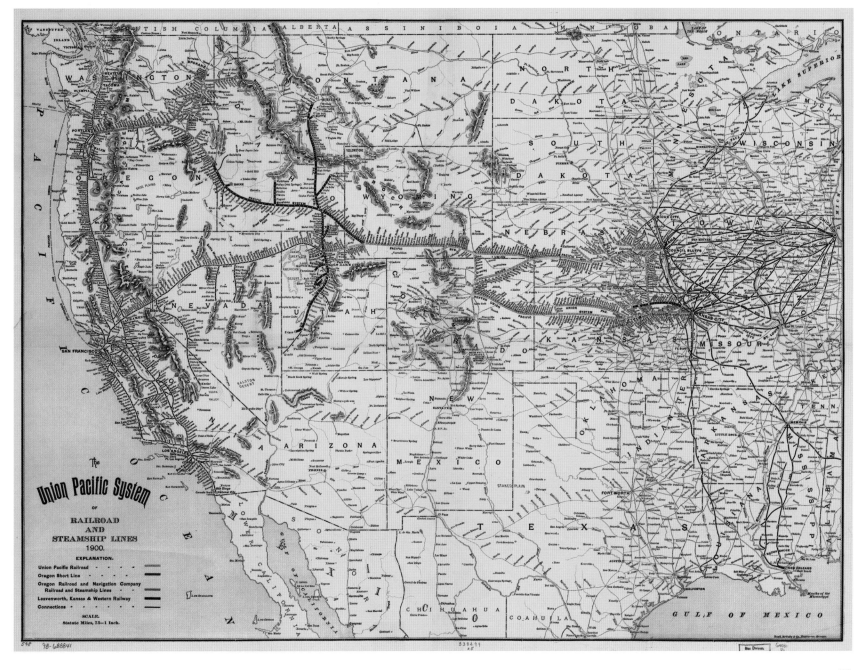

The
Union Pacific System
OF
RAILROAD
AND
STEAMSHIP LINES
1900.

EXPLANATION.

Union Pacific Railroad
Oregon Short Line
Oregon Railroad and Navigation Company
Railroad and Steamship Lines
Leavenworth, Kansas & Western Railway
Connections

SCALE.
Statute Miles, 75=1 Inch.

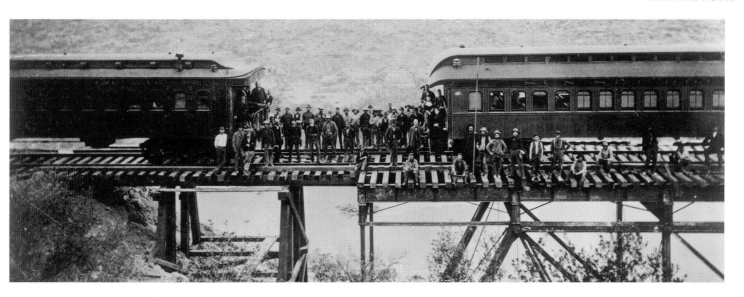

improvement of the track and the straightening of the route. It was in 1873 that the real shock arrived, for it now emerged that many members of the Congress had received stock in the Credit Mobilier, which had been able to pay huge dividends on the basis of its fraudulent dealings with the Union Pacific Railroad. The revelations of the Credit Mobilier rcaused a national scandal that quickly eroded the public's faith in the railroads, an immediate result being a steep and disastrous decline in the Union Pacific Railroad's share value: by the end of 1873 each share had dropped from $100 to $14, a fact that caught the attention of Jay Gould, who had established himself as a hard-headed businessman in his battles with Cornelius Vanderbilt over the New York railroads.

THE GREAT RACE FOR THE WESTERN STAKES 1870

CHAPTER THREE
THE CONSOLIDATION OF THE
STEAM RAILROADS

OPPOSITE
Edwin F. Johnson's map of the proposed
Northern Route to the Pacific, published in
1853.

BELOW
U.S. railroad stations embodied the value
that the Victorian age placed on monumental
and well-constructed buildings. This is the
depot of the Erie Railroad at Elmira in New
York state.

The railroads had been popular with financial speculators since the 1830s, when they emerged as what were in essence the only large industrial organizations to appear in the U.S.A. before the outbreak of the Civil War. Then, in the course of the Civil War, several men, including Cornelius Vanderbilt, had made fortunes from speculation in railroad shares. By the end of the war Vanderbilt had used his holdings in the Harlem Railroad to force the directors of the New York Central Railroad, which was reliant on the Harlem Railroad for its connection to New York, to surrender control of their operation to him. At the same time two younger financial adventurers, Jay Gould and Jim Fisk, had managed to gain control of the Erie system from one of the first railroad speculators, Daniel Drew, who had taken over the Erie in the 1850s, not through any real interest in the construction or operation of railroads but merely to facilitate his speculations in its shares. And while Vanderbilt's New York Central system was soundly organized and well run, the Erie system was notable for the neglect of its operating conditions and consequently a high accident rate, as nothing but the most meagre resources had been expended on track and rolling stock.

Gould and Fisk built still further on the Drew pattern of manipulation of the Erie, and in the late 1860s their battles with Vanderbilt reached an extraordinary level. Early in 1868, for example, they were forced to flee New York to avoid arrest, and then based themselves in Jersey City. Following a series of legal and political conflicts in which judges and state legislators were bribed liberally, often by each side, Fisk and Gould were later able to return to New York, basing the headquarters of their operation in a vaudeville theatre whose basement accommodated the printing press from which there streamed Erie stock certificates.

The Erie battle ended in compromise, and Gould started to look for railroad targets further removed from the north-eastern part of the Atlantic seaboard. Beginning with speculation in the Wabash and Lake Shore lines, operating along the southern shores of the Great Lakes, he developed his operation into an effort to corner the U.S.A.'s entire gold supply: this he saw as a means toward the reduction in the export price of grain to stimulate traffic on the grain-carrying Wabash. The scheme was stymied by federal intervention but, just in time, Gould managed to sell his interest in the Wabash and Lake Shore operation, and after the Credit Mobilier scandal began to buy the low-cost stock of the Union Pacific Railroad. As had been the case with his Erie operation, Gould saw this as an exercise in pure speculation, and controlled

RIGHT
The problem of hauling heavy loads up steep gradients has long been solved by the process of 'double-heading', that is the addition of another locomotive at the head of the train to increase by a large percentage the quantity of tractive power available. This is a double-header of the Norfolk & Western Railroad at Blue Ridge, Virginia.

OPPOSITE
Since the effective demise of steam locomotion as a prime mover on North American railroads in the late 1950s and early 1960s, the survival of steam locomotives as working engines has depended largely on the existence and motivation of a swelling base of avid steam locomotion fans, who will pay for the privilege of making a special trip on a train hauled by steam. Seen here is such a service, hauled by the Chesapeake & Ohio Railroad's locomotive No. 614 over the tracks of the old Erie Railroad at Point Jervis in New York state.

the Union Pacific Railroad only as long as it took to make enormous sums for himself by declaring unjustifiably high dividends before he sold his holdings at the inflated prices this produced. In 1878 Gould switched his attention to the Kansas Pacific Railroad, which had recently become bankrupt, and after settling with the bondholders announced his plan to construct a line from Denver to the west coast. This forced the new board of the Union Pacific Railroad to take over the Kansas Pacific as a means of protecting its route monopoly, the price of Kansas Pacific Railroad stock climbed rapidly, and Gould was in the position once again to sell at an enormous profit.

Whereas Gould was a speculator pure and simple, the Huntington interests were controlled in a financial manner that was both sound and conventional. Huntington was a man with an eye on the future of the American railroad industry, thinking which went somewhat beyond Durant's concept of exploiting just one railroad. Though he was akin to Gould in having a strong desire to increase his wealth, Huntington was sure that his objective could be achieved in a businesslike manner that would ensure the longer-term survivability of the interests he intended to hold rather than sell. Huntington therefore expanded his interest to west coast shipping and other related industries and, even before the 1869 junction of the two parts of the transcontinental railroad at Promontory Point, also started to plan a second transcontinental railroad independent of the first. Thus in 1868 Huntington and his associated group of investors bought the

OPPOSITE
The last use of steam locomotion for commercial purposes on the U.S.A.'s main railroads was for the haulage of heavy freight trains over long routes. This is the Union Pacific Railroad's locomotive No. 3985, a Challenger-class 4-6-6-4 unit, at Union Junction, Oregon.

LEFT
The same locomotive is caught in close-up at Portola, California.

charter for the Southern Pacific Railroad as a first step in consolidating their Californian interests, and replaced the Contract and Finance Corporation, which had received $79 million for its part in the construction of the Central Pacific Railroad, by the Western Development Company, to boost the group's ability to exploit the development of California, which was recognized as being very fertile but also decidedly underpopulated.

The Western Development Company's initial step was the building of a railroad through the San Joaquin valley from San Francisco to Los Angeles with the aid of generous land grants from Los Angeles, the new line being completed by 1876. Next came a determined effort to prevent the implementation of other railroads's efforts to create a second transcontinental railroad to the west coast along a path more to the south than the first route. The most important of these was the Texas & Pacific, which had been chartered with federal grant-in-aid lands totalling 18 million acres (7.28 million hectares) along the Mexican border, and was headed by Thomas A. Scott, the president of the leading eastern railroad operator, the Pennsylvania Railroad. Scott had previously tried to run the Union Pacific Railroad but had soon abandoned the idea and now employed Grenville Dodge to plan and build the new railroad. In 1873 the Texas & Pacific Railway ran into problems as the revelation of Dodge's implication in the Credit Mobilier scandal checked receipt of funds. Though it reached Dallas in 1873, the Texas & Pacific finally ran short of financial resources in 1876 after reaching Fort Worth, less than 200 miles

(322km) from its starting point at Marshall. In 1877 an agreement was reached between Scott, Huntington and the federal authorities whereby the Southern Pacific Railroad would keep control of the Californian end of the new transcontinental route, and Scott would extend the Texas & Pacific Railway to Yuma on the Arizona/California border and thus provide a southerly connection to the east.

After extending the Southern Pacific Railroad as far as Yuma, however, Huntington was determined that there was still scope for further expansion of his interests in the western part of the U.S.A., and thus arranged for the territorial governments of Arizona and New Mexico to provide him with the charters that enabled him to start the process of getting round his lack of federal authorization and backing. A first step in this process was to build a railroad bridge over the Colorado river when, in the face of this *fait accompli*, presidential approval was given to Huntington for a continuation of railroad construction to the east. The competing railroads eventually decided on a junction at El Paso on the New Mexico/Texas border, and the two lines met here in 1882 to complete the construction of the second transcontinental railroad.

In 1883 the Southern Pacific Railroad acquired its own route across Texas by taking over the Galveston, Harrisburg & San Antonio Railroad and, after taking control of a number of other small operators, the Southern Pacific Railroad had a route to New Orleans. In 1895 the Central Pacific Railroad was finally absorbed into the new system.

During this same period the concept of the transcontinental railroad had attracted other

railroad operators in the south-west of the U.S.A. The Denver & Rio Grande Railroad was established by citizens of Denver as a means of bolstering efforts to develop new mines in the Rocky Mountains in Colorado. The Kansas Pacific Railroad had created a railroad link between Denver and Kansas City, and was also linked into the Union Pacific Railroad at Cheyenne by a branch line to the north. The new line also extended south toward Santa Fe, also the immediate objective of the Atchison, Topeka & Santa Fe Railway. Since receiving its Kansas land grant-in-aid during 1863, the Atchison, Topeka & Santa Fe had managed only limited progress until 1870, when it began building across Kansas to gain a foothold in the burgeoning cattle trade centred on Dodge City. The Atchison, Topeka & Santa Fe Railway reached Dodge in 1872, which opened the way for the lucrative transport of beef cattle, which had arrived at Dodge after long trail drives toward the ever-growing population centres of the U.S.A.'s more eastern regions. In 1873 the Atchison, Topeka & Santa Fe's line reached La Junta in south-east Colorado, and at much the same time the Denver & Rio Grande Railroad reached Pueblo, 70 miles (113km) farther to the west. The further extension of both lines was then delayed by lack of funding in the aftermath of the Credit Mobilier scandal, but by 1876 the Atchison, Topeka & Santa Fe Railway had also reached Pueblo.

At this juncture, what had been financial and political battles began to acquire physical dimensions as armed clashes began to erupt between the men of the various companies. The immediate cause was the availability of only two routes south to Santa Fe, through the Raton Pass on the New Mexico border, and to the mining area around Leadville to the west of Pueblo through the Royal Gorge of the Arkansas river. Having negotiated with the operator of the toll road through the Raton Pass, the Atchison, Topeka & Santa Fe sent its construction teams into the area during February 1872 for the start of route-grading work. Here they met armed employees of the Denver & Rio Grande Railroad, but aided by a strengthening of local feeling against the Denver & Rio Grande as a result of its dubious real estate operations, the men of the Atchison, Topeka & Santa Fe prevailed and won the route to the south. Similar events followed on the Royal Gorge route, but court cases finally settled the matter in favour of the Denver & Rio Grande Railroad.

Then the Atchison, Topeka & Santa Fe took the decision to concentrate its efforts on the areas farther to the west. In 1880, therefore, it purchased the old charter for the Atlantic & Pacific Railroad. This had been planned as a means to link St. Louis and southern California, but at the time reached no farther than the western border of Missouri. In the east a line was built from the Atchison, Topeka & Santa Fe Railway's tracks at Wichita to a junction with the Atlantic & Pacific Railroad at Pierce City, near Springfield in Missouri, giving the Atchison, Topeka & Santa Fe a link to the east at St. Louis. In the west, the charter of the Atlantic & Pacific Railroad included large grant-in-aid lands in Arizona and New Mexico, and this allowed the Atchison, Topeka & Santa Fe to build a new line to Albuquerque in New

Mexico. This meant that the city of Santa Fe was now served only by a branch, while the main line carried on to the California border at Needles, one of the few places on the Colorado river where current technology allowed a bridge to be built. The Southern Pacific Railroad had already completed its own line to Needles, so a sensible agreement allowed the Atchison, Topeka & Santa Fe to operate its trains to Los Angeles and San Francisco over the tracks of the Southern Pacific Railroad, thereby creating the third transcontinental line.

None of these three served the needs of the states and territories of the U.S.A.'s north-western region. During the same basic period, however, another railroad to the Pacific coast was being created to satisfy this demand. This was an offshoot of the Northern Pacific Railroad, and its alignment was basically that between Lake Superior and Portland in Oregon, that had been suggested by Asa Whitney as early as 1845. During the Civil War, when the Pacific railroad charters were being allocated, the Northern Pacific Railroad had received grant-in-aid lands totalling 47 million acres (19.02 million hectares) in the north-western region of the U.S.A. between Minnesota and Washington states. There were no financial arrangements associated with the grant-in-aid lands, however, which checked the start of work by five years. The key figure in the eventual launch of the construction programme in 1869 was Jay Cooke. Cooke was a Philadelphia financier who had vastly increased his wealth through the sale of the government bonds that financed the Union's efforts in the Civil War and then reinvested

much of this wealth in major land purchases in Minnesota. After organizing, at his own expense, a survey of the Northern Pacific Railroad's allocated route, Cooke became the railroad's financial agent. He hired newspaper editors and public figures to extol the advantages of the north-western part of the U.S.A. as little short of a second Garden of Eden: so attractive did the advertising make the region seem that the curved belt of land in the associated maps became generally known as 'Jay Cooke's Banana Belt'. This publicity campaign aimed to sell $100 million of bonds in order to finance the building of the railroad.

Work on the construction of the new transcontinental railroad started in 1870, and it was not long before branches from Duluth and Minneapolis met at Brainerd before being driven westward across Minnesota and Dakota to the banks of the Missouri river, where in 1873 the new town of Bismarck was established. The naming of this city after the 'iron chancellor' of the newly unified German empire represented an effort to draw both immigrants and investment from Germany. Cooke saw large-scale immigration as the optimum means of filling the vast tracts of land he owned in the region; moreover, the investment was sorely needed as work on the new railroad was costing somewhat more than Cooke could raise money for in the short term through the sale of bonds: this meant that Cooke's bank was subsidizing the railroad to the extent of some $5.5 million. Cooke attempted the sale of a new issue of bonds, but there was little market for these in the aftermath of the Credit Mobilier scandal and the spread of an increasing number of rumours

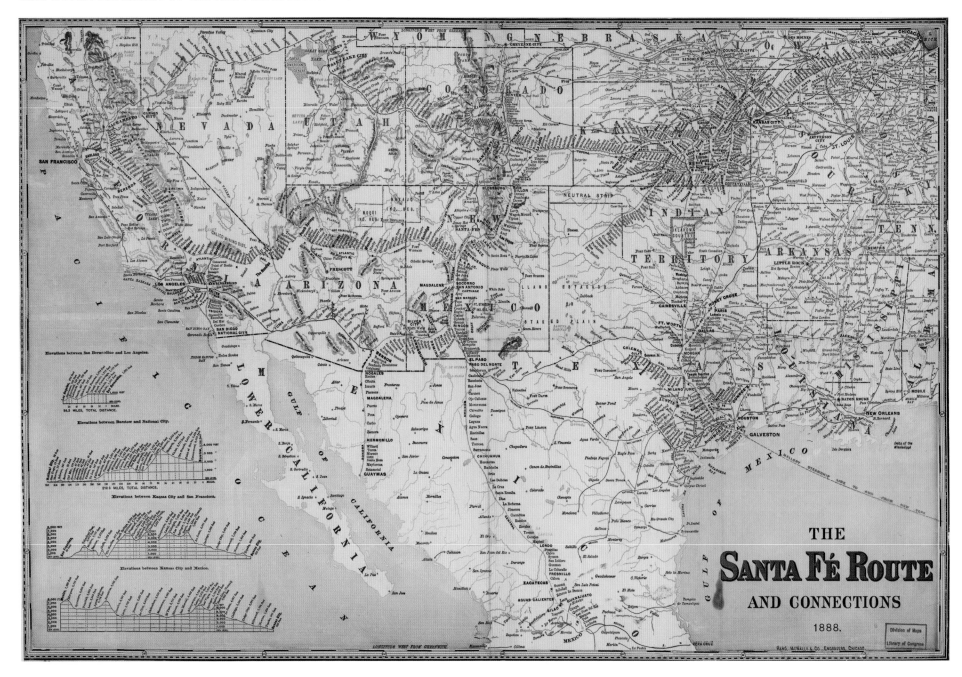

THE
Santa Fé Route
AND CONNECTIONS
1888.

Published by Rand McNally and Company, this map shows the routes and, just as importantly, the connections of the Santa Fe system in 1888.

LEFT
Locomotive No. 497, a Baldwin-built K37-class 2-8-2 engine, is caught by the camera at Windy Point on the line of the Rio Grande Railroad over the Cumbres Pass, Colorado.

RIGHT
A freight service of the Missouri Pacific
Railroad awaits the order to move off.

OPPOSITE
This S. W. Eccles map highlights the lines,
connections and extensions of the Denver &
Rio Grande Railroad in 1881, and also
reveals the relative position of the Denver
& Pueblo Railroad as well as the main
towns and mining regions of Colorado and
New Mexico.

concerning the Northern Pacific Railroad's difficulties. Now these rumours were exacerbated by adverse reports about the real and decidedly less attractive geographical and climatic conditions along the 'Banana Belt', and made it very difficult to move new railroad bonds. The problems of the Northern Pacific Railroad were further adversely complicated by the fact that the Franco-Prussian War of 1870–71 had slowed to a trickle the flow of European capital to North America, with the result that 18 September 1873 saw the closure of the New York offices of Cooke's bank and marked the beginning of a major 'crash'.

It is worth noting that by this time the railroads had received some $3 billion from the authorities and the public, and between 1865 and 1870 the total route mileage of the American railroads had increased from 35,000 to almost 54,000 miles (56325 to almost 86900km). The increase was decidedly impressive, but so too, on the debit rather than the credit side of the railroad businesses' ledger, was the poor state of the investment market supporting the railroads: in 1860 each mile of railroad had been backed by an average of 1,026 investors, but by 1873 that figure had declined to just 590. Inevitably, the result was a collapse of the financial system and with it the failure of many American railroads, though the Northern Pacific Railroad actually managed to evade bankruptcy until 1875.

Lack of adequate capital investment was one of several problems now checking the continued development of U.S. railroads. Another of the problems, for instance, was the

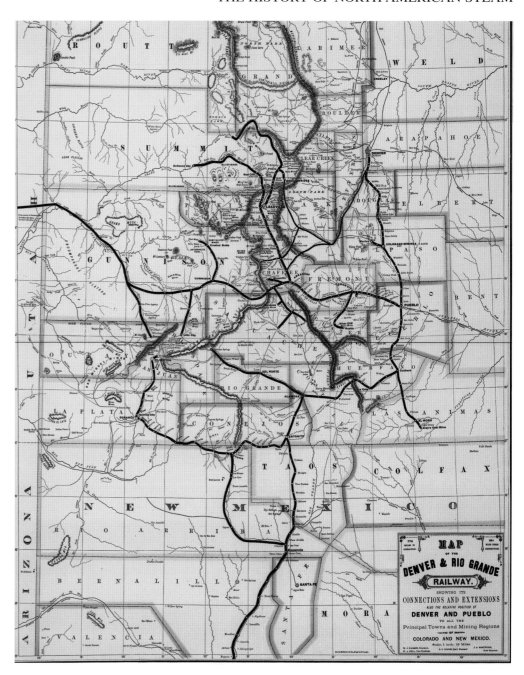

fact that in the north-west part of the U.S.A. the Native Americans, who had been steadily driven north by the westward encroachment of the railroads into their hunting grounds, now refused to move further or to allow more railroad construction. The military expedition to crush this resistance culminated in the defeat of Colonel George A. Custer's U.S. 7th Cavalry Regiment in the Battle of the Little Big Horn in 1876. After this success, however, Chief Sitting Bull led the tribes north into Canada and this allowed the re-establishment of peace in the north-west. At much the same time the railroad industry's financial situation improved in line with that of the rest of the country, which opened the way to revived interest in the transcontinental railroad link over the northern route.

Originally a German journalist, Henry Villard had gained a considerable reputation and following for his representation of German bondholders seeking repayment in the bankruptcy of the Kansas Pacific Railroad, and was now commissioned to look after the interests of a comparable group of investors in the Oregon & California Railroad, which had also gone into bankruptcy. Villard began by incorporating the Oregon Railway & Navigation Company, which soon became the single most important transport organization in the area. The Oregon Railway & Navigation Company built railroads along the valleys of the Columbia and Willamette rivers, and this interested Villard in the concept of constructing a transcontinental railroad. The Northern Pacific Railroad still controlled the vital grant-in-aid lands, however, and from 1875 this railroad was transformed for the

better by the arrival on the scene of Frederick Billing, under whose dynamic leadership it began to push its track forward not to Portland in Oregon, 100 miles (160km) inland, but toward Tacoma in Washington state on the natural harbours of the Puget Sound.

Villard offered the use of his Columbia river valley tracks to the Northern Pacific Railroad but was rejected, and created a 'blind pool' (money raised from a number of investors without disclosure of the purpose), thus managing to secure control of the Northern Pacific Railroad. Villard was now getting out of his financial depth, however, and the cost of construction, especially over the immensely difficult sections of the Rocky Mountains, far exceeded the railroad's financial backing, as a result of which the Northern Pacific Railroad had become bankrupt. Villard resigned and the railroad was then reorganized financially and completed to Tacoma.

Even though vast grant-in-aid lands seemed to have given the Northern Pacific Railroad an unchallengeable hold over the northern transcontinental route, James J. Hill, who had made a fortune in the grain trade of St. Paul in Minnesota, now set his ambitions on the region. Hill's opportunity was provided by the 1873 bankruptcy of the St. Paul & Pacific Railroad. In 1862 this company had been chartered and had received grant-in-aid lands totalling 5 million acres (2.0235 million hectares) of Minnesota. Then the St. Paul & Pacific Railroad had pushed its construction forward only as far as a connection with the Northern Pacific Railroad's route at Brainerd and the creation of a branch line toward the

Canadian border. In 1878 Hill was able to gain control of the St. Paul & Pacific Railroad, buying its stock for a fraction of the face value and then making a very considerable profit by selling its grant-in-aid land. Hill changed the name of the company to the St. Paul Minneapolis & Manitoba Railroad, which now possessed the financial resources to extend its line in the direction of the Canadian border and a junction with the new Canadian Pacific Railway at Pembina.

Large-scale immigration to northern Minnesota combined with several excellent grain harvests to increase the wealth of Hill, who used the opportunity to extend the railroad. It is worthy of note that Hill represented a railroad builder of a somewhat different type to many of the other great names of this and earlier periods, for rather than being an entrepreneur looking for a quick return on his investment, it was his intention to proceed slowly and carefully in the creation of efficient operations that also charged lower rates than its main competitor, the Northern Pacific Railroad. Hill's aim in this practice, which seemed senseless to his competitors and rivals, was the creation of a contented customer base that would in all probability stay with Hill's railroad and therefore increase its chances of securing a regular flow of income. During the 1880s the railhead of Hill's operation was extended slowly but steadily to the west through the timber and the copper-mining areas of Montana.

It was in January 1893 that the Great Northern Railway's route to Puget Sound at Seattle in Washington state was completed, but before the end of the year the Northern

The Union Pacific Railroad's locomotive No. 934 heads a block fruit train (before the development of refrigerated cars) somewhere in Wyoming or Nebraska in about 1890. Agricultural produce was one of the staples of the railroad freight business, and the cost and timeliness of the service provided by the railroads was often a bitter bone of contention between the farming community and the railroads.

Pacific Railroad, of which Villard had managed to regain control in 1889, was bankrupt once more, and by 1896 Hill had gained control of the route parallel to the one that he himself had built. Hill had further railroad ambitions, however, and now refocused his ambitions south-eastward toward Chicago and the Midwest. There were two possible means of achieving his new objectives. One was the Chicago, Burlington

& Quincy Railroad, that had been created in 1856 through the amalgamation of small operators in the Chicago area, and over the years had developed through line construction and purchases into a system of over 6,000 miles (9656km) extending from Chicago to destinations such as Denver, Kansas City, Minneapolis, St. Louis and cities in Montana. The other was the Chicago Milwaukee & St. Paul Railway, but this had the backing of

William Rockefeller, the creator of Standard Oil, and was not for sale. In the circumstances, therefore, Hill took the course of lesser resistance and purchased the Chicago, Burlington & Quincy Railroad.

Though the period is known to later generations as that of the transcontinental railroads, it should not be imagined that the word 'transcontinental' still retained the same hold on the imaginations of the public and the

railroads that it had in the 1860s. The reason for this is partially the dire financial climate of the 1870s and the revelations of the chicanery that had accompanied the construction of the first transcontinental route, but also a more blasé feeling about what was now a well-established element of the American commercial and social scene. Moreover, there was no single route that operated directly between the U.S.A.'s Atlantic and Pacific seaboards. The only man who came within striking distance of this objective, albeit some 10 years into the future, was George Gould, who numbered the Denver & Rio Grande Western, the Wabash and the Western Maryland railroads among his extensive railroad interests up to 1907, and the onset of another railroad panic; with the completion of his Western Pacific Railroad in 1909, linking Ogden and San Francisco, Gould came close to achieving a system that actually spanned the continent.

The establishment of transcontinental links was the dream of men with very big ideas, but there were others with more modest ambitions. Operating mainly in the western part of the U.S.A., these latter were happy to construct railroads wherever they perceived a niche requirement. For example, in the Rocky Mountains area of Colorado the Denver & Rio Grande Railroad was one (though the largest) of several railroads serving the region's mining towns. Much of the Denver & Rio Grande's track was originally built to the 36-in (0.914-m) gauge that was popular among western railroads from 1870, despite the fact that this narrow gauge made it impossible for any such railroad to exchange traffic with the

operators of standard-gauge lines. This was a limiting factor with adverse financial consequences and, seeing the error of its ways, the Denver & Rio Grande Railroad soon started the process of converting most of its track to standard gauge.

There was still one more transcontinental line to be built. The completion of this route was typical of the profligate waste that was so typical of much railroad construction in the 19th century, for it competed directly with two existing systems, yet it nonetheless became one of the most advanced railroad operations. The line was the result of Hill's determination: prevented from securing control of the Chicago Milwaukee & St. Paul Railway as a complement to his transcontinental Great Northern and Northern Pacific routes, Hill was able to gain control of the Chicago, Burlington & Quincy Railroad, which in 1905 persuaded the Chicago Milwaukee & St. Paul to establish its own north-western route to the Pacific. Even though it had no grant-in-aid lands, in a mere three years the Chicago Milwaukee & St. Paul Railway completed its line linking Chicago and Seattle by a route shorter than those used by either of its competitors. Though in many respects a technical triumph, the new route was completed only at great cost and by adopting an alignment including several very severe grades over mountain ranges. As a result of the operational difficulties and challenges resulting from these facts, the railroad (with the word Pacific added to its full title but soon universally known as the Milwaukee Road) started an ambitious programme of electrification in the Rocky and

Bitter Root Mountains. Two sections were equipped with an overhead electrical supply. That between Harlowtown and Avery was opened in 1917, and that between Othello and Seattle in 1920: together they represented 656 miles (1056km) of electrified main line, the longest in the world at the time and using the most advanced system available.

Toward the end of the 19th century there were very large numbers of U.S. passenger and mixed freight/passenger railroads varying in size from the huge to the tiny, and between these any number of specialized freight railroads concentrating on the movement of just a single product such as coal, ore and lumber; there were also suburban railroads providing short-distance commuter transport services into and out of the U.S.A.'s apparently ever-swelling cities. The railroad industry has emerged from the American ideal of private enterprise even in the completion of great enterprises, but aided by financial incentives from federal, state and other administrations. What was also becoming abundantly clear, though, was that the country's system of railroads was not an intrinsic part of the American economy, and was therefore approaching the point at which it was too important at the strategic, economical and social levels to be left virtually exclusively to the financial and personal whims of entrepreneurs.

The U.S. railroad system that had begun to stabilize in the last quarter of the 19th century was very much the child, in its deeper origins, of the way that the whole industry had begun in the second quarter of the same century. Before the outbreak of the Civil War

OPPOSITE
The Milwaukee Road's locomotive No. 261, an Alco-built 4-8-4 unit, hauls a service at Vernon, Wisconsin.

LEFT
This is the same locomotive, the Milwaukee Road's No. 261, painted as locomotive No. 1661 of the Lackawanna & Western Railroad.

in 1861 the railroads had started with charters issued by individual states, and this exercised a very major influence on their core routes. A typical example can be found in the Erie Railway, which in the southern part of New York state followed a route that was selected more for its relationship to the state border than for any practical consideration. Then, applied first to the transcontinental railroads and then to railroads in the territories that later became the western states, the system of grant-in-aid lands furthered the emergence and growth of systems more concerned with long-

OPPOSITE & BELOW
The Northern Pacific Railroad's locomotive No. 328 was an Alco-built 4-6-0.

LEFT
The same locomotive is seen as its hauls a service over the steel trestle bridge over the St. Croix river in Wisconsin.

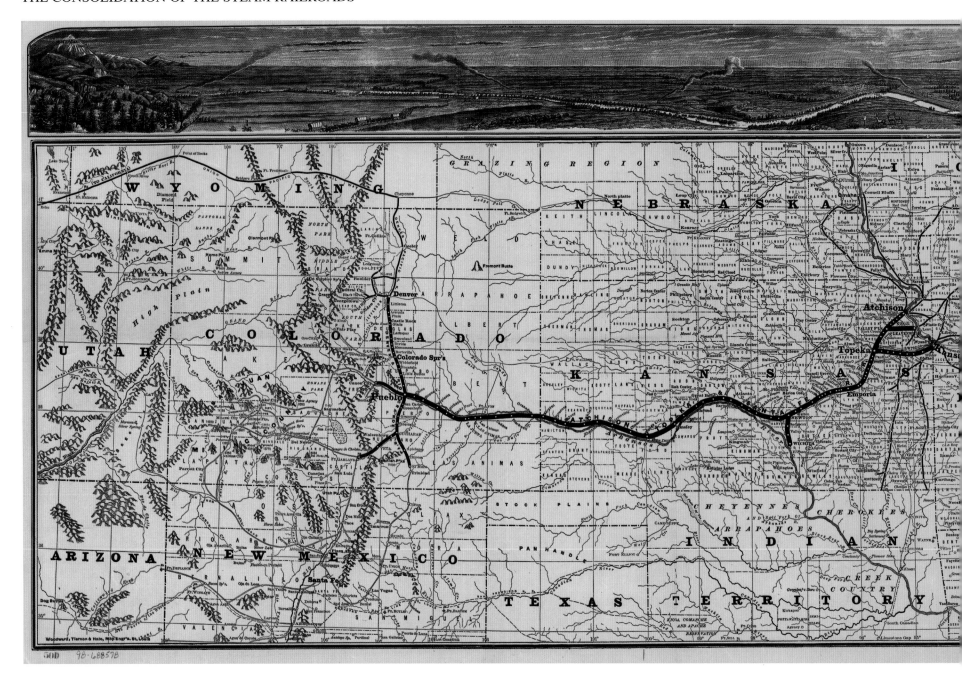

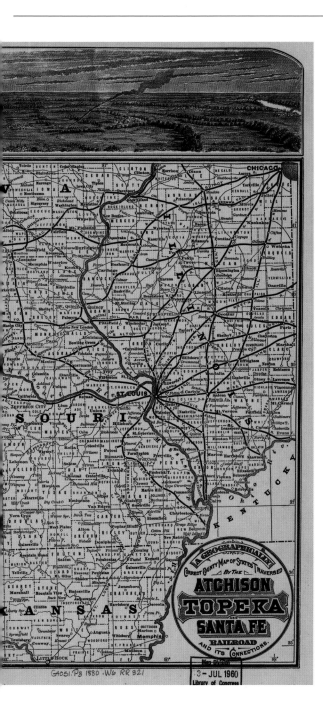

distance travel than local needs, and the need to cater for both shorter- and longer-distance travellers and freight transport opened the way for the mergers of individual railroads, smaller as well as larger, to create interstate carriers able to satisfy regional demands. The trend toward this type of amalgamation was left at first to the initiative of individual managements, which saw the possibility of greater profit, and this led to the type of railroad operations that reflected the nature of their leading lights. Under the leadership of J. Edgar Thompson and later of Thomas A. Scott, the Pennsylvania Railroad was typical of this process, in which it became probably the most efficient railroad system anywhere in the world: its track was the best, its rolling stock (and especially its locomotives) was excellent, and the overall level of its services was first class. There were many operations that compared most unfavourably with the Pennsylvania Railroad, however; in many of these other railroads the nature of the competition between the railroads stemming from the emergence of interlocking systems created the potential for good management capabilities but also for companies often lacking in any type of scruples.

Lack of probity on the part of railroad managements sometimes exerted an adverse effect on the return yielded to investors, but more frequently worsened the lot of the railroads's users, who thus became the victims of very poor safety standards, which were most evident in the continued use of unsafe track, which therefore caused frequent accidents.

The transport of freight was one of the

LEFT
A geographically correct county map by Woodward, Tiernan and Hale of the states traversed by the Atchison, Topeka & Santa Fe Railway (1880).

could attempt to extract the maximum possible financial reward from the market was the charging of different freight rates for different commodities or for the transport of freight over different journeys. This meant that major customers, which were mainly those moving large quantities of freight, were in the position to demand lower rates and, with the proviso that these rates would cover the railroad's operating costs, it was tempting for the railroads to accede to these demands, even if it was for no purpose other than to deprive a rival operator of the trade. The requirement for fixed costs to be met from other sources in this concept of railroad operations had the effect of subsidizing the larger customer at the expense of the smaller. When faced with no competing company, the railroad could charge whatever rate it thought it could manage to extract from its customers, who had no alternative but to pay up with whatever grace they could muster. Moreover, there were so-called rate pools, which rival railroads created as a cartel that charged rates of a uniformly high level to avoid the costs of competition.

The freight-reliant railroad clients who suffered most from these and other financial abuses were those in the agricultural industry, who had to have not only freight transport, but that which was also rapid and reliable to get their produce to market before it began to spoil. Consequently, it is hardly surprising that it was the agricultural industry which was the leading light in the growing resistance to these practices by the railroad companies. In 1867 the agricultural industry had established a trade organization that was formally known as the Patrons of Husbandry, but more popularly

Although it was the larger units that hauled freight and passenger services on the main lines that have always attracted the lion's share of interest in steam locomotives, these magnificent creatures would have been lost without the ancillary services of the smaller and altogether less glamorous locomotives, such as this 0-4-0 unit, of switching and other humdrum tasks.

aspects of railroad operations that possessed ramifications beyond those that might be immediately apparent. Competition with regard to the rates that the railroads levied for the movement of freight was based on the two types of costs incurred by the railroads: these were firstly the fixed costs of maintaining the railroad system, and secondly the running costs of moving a load of a specific weight and size over a specified distance. On a route where a railroad operator faced competition, it

was faced with the temptation of undercutting the opposition by calculating the freight rate on the basis of running costs alone, with the fixed costs then left for covering by other sources. These latter were generally any other of the operator's routes in which the company enjoyed the commercial benefits of a monopoly and could therefore charge (and get away with charging) a somewhat higher rate than would otherwise have been possible. Another way in which the railroad operator

Taken in 1873, this photograph reveals the first railroad passenger station built in Minneapolis. The passenger station is at the left, with the freight depot at the centre, the latter on the site of what was later the Great Northern Railway's freight depot on 4th Avenue. The St. Paul & Pacific Railroad was the first such operation on the north-west portion of the U.S.A., and operated services between St. Paul and Minneapolis, which was then known as St. Anthony. The St. Paul & Pacific Railroad was later acquired by James J. Hill and his associates, who developed it into the Great Northern Railway.

Union Station in Worcester, Massachusetts.

North Station in Boston, Massachusetts.

called the National Grange. Though at first a social and educational body of limited size and ambition, by the 1870s it was beginning to appreciate that it could extend its influence beyond these limited aims. During the 1870s almost 1 million farmers, most of them in the Midwest region of the U.S.A., became members of the organization, and the National Grange swiftly and perhaps inevitably developed into a political force that could effectively co-ordinate the votes of its members and so virtually ensure the election of a state government sympathetic to its cause. Thus it was predisposed to the enactment of legislation to remove the most common commercial abuses against the agricultural community.

The railroad operators were also a force experienced in the ways in which political and judicial processes could be manipulated for their own purposes, so the members of the National Grange were highly encouraged when appeals against the new measures by the railroad operators were dismissed by the Supreme Court. But during 1886 the Supreme Court reversed its earlier decision, handing down a judgement that the individual states lacked the authority to regulate rates on traffic that was transported beyond their own borders. This cut the ground from under the foundation on which the National Grange had erected its resistance to the pressures exerted by the railroad operators, and at the same time brought to the fore the realization that the effective solution to the problem, which extended far beyond the agricultural industry and the railroad operators, could be imposed only by the federal authorities, who could look at the problem at a national level rather than on a state-by-state basis.

The process creating the competition that paved the way to the railroad freight tariff 'wars' was the consolidation of the smaller operators into increasingly large railroad systems, in a process that was speeded rather than slowed by the anti-railroad sentiments that were becoming increasingly vocal and numerous. In the later stages of the 19th century the railroads saw that consolidation rather than confrontation between themselves would be the decisive factor, and the leading light in this process was J. Pierpont Morgan, who was the most important American banker and financier of the period. Morgan had first become involved in railroad operations during one of what might be described as the skirmishes typical of the 'Erie wars' in the late 1860s. After reaching a compromise solution in their dispute with Vanderbilt, Gould and Fisk had seen the very distinct possibility of enhancing their capabilities by buying one of the railroad companies involved in the rapidly growing market for the transport of coal from the mines of northern Pennsylvania. In 1869 the Albany & Susquehanna Railroad was on the verge of starting operations as a new link between Binghamton and Albany. Using the Delaware & Hudson Canal Company as their front organization, Gould and Fisk sought to purchase a controlling interest in the Albany & Susquehanna Railroad. There was considerable opposition from Morgan and the Lackawanna & Western Railroad, however, and the struggle for control of the Albany & Susquehanna finally terminated in a trackside battle, in which the victory of Morgan's men

persuaded Gould and Fisk to halt their combined legal and political effort to seize control of the Albany & Susquehanna Railroad.

The fact that his banking empire was growing in size and importance at the same time that the American railroads were burgeoning into a system that was poorly co-ordinated but of increasing national importance, created the conditions in which Morgan inevitably became embroiled in railroad matters. By 1879 Morgan had become a director of the New York Central Railroad, and in 1880 was a leading figure in the process of finding $40 million of additional capital for the Northern Pacific Railroad in its time of dire need.

The combination of resources provided by private investors and local communities, the latter having been empowered by the 1869 General Bonding Law to raise money for the purchase of railroad securities, meant that railroad construction in the 1870s completely outstripped demand for railroad services. Thus many new lines were built without any realistic hope of longer-term, let alone shorter-term, profitability; by the later part of the 1870s the bankruptcies of railroads had become commonplace events. The scale of the problem is revealed by the fact that in 1879 alone, some 65 railroads were capitalized and a total of more than $200 million became bankrupt. Adding to the problem were larger numbers of railroads which managed to avoid bankruptcy but were nonetheless faced with the acute financial problem of having to hand over more than half of their operating incomes merely to service the interest on their

outstanding loans. Such was the undimmed optimism of the average American banker and speculator, however, that no one seems to have considered the reasons for the situation, and as a result the stabilization of the railroad market after every crisis and panic was accompanied by a new burst of enthusiasm for the construction of railroads without any real regard for whether or not there was likely to be a profitable outcome for the undertaking.

This tendency was nowhere more evident than in the state of New York that was, admittedly, economically prosperous and highly populated, but by 1880 was criss-crossed by more than 6,000 miles (9655km) of railroad track to which a further 2,000 miles (3220km) were added in the following 10 years. The level of competition between the railroads in the state was most acute in the contest between operators of the major trunk routes. The New York Central and the Erie railroads each included major networks of feeder lines allowing the transport of passengers and freight between outlying areas and the major stations of their central lines, but these major New York operators also faced external competition from the Baltimore & Ohio and the Pennsylvania railroads for traffic to the Midwest. The well-organized and excellently-run Pennsylvania Railroad was expanding very swiftly by the 1880s, and largely to the cost of the other three operators.

The same period also witnessed the emergence of new railroads, for which the sole purpose was the duplication of the route system of an existing railroad, which would therefore be forced to remove the possibility of profit-destroying competition, in a limited

The station of the Pennsylvania Railroad at Richmond, Indiana.

market, by buying out the new railroad at an inflated price and so enriching the shareholders (most generally the directors) of the upstart company. Typical of this process, which was designed solely for personal enrichment, were two events involving Vanderbilt. In 1878 Vanderbilt bought the newly established New York, Chicago & St.

Louis Railroad, which would otherwise have threatened Vanderbilt's Lake Shore route to Chicago; when in 1883 the West Shore Railroad began building a line up the Hudson river valley in direct competition with the New York Central Railroad, Vanderbilt believed that the financial force behind this move into what he believed to be his personal railroad

bailiwick was the Pennsylvania Railroad, to which he responded by purchasing the small but profitable coal-carrying Philadelphia & Reading as the basis for a new venture, the South Pennsylvania Railroad, that would in turn threaten the Pennsylvania Railroad in its own bailiwick.

By 1885 Morgan's reputation as a railroad entrepreneur was paying the penalty of association with such endeavours, and indicated that a major effort was both required and justified to improve the situation. Morgan's answer to the problem was that Vanderbilt and the Pennsylvania Railroad should each purchase the other's competing railroad organizations, Vanderbilt thereby assuming control of the West Shore Railroad, and the Pennsylvania Railroad taking over the South Pennsylvania Railroad. Morgan possessed the financial strength to impose this solution on people and organizations that were decidedly unhappy with it, in the process of which Morgan also took charge of reorganizing the South Pennsylvania, the West Shore, and the Philadelphia & Reading railroads. In the process he became the owner of the South Pennsylvania Railroad to get around the law enacted by the Pennsylvania state legislature to prevent the Pennsylvania Railroad from taking financial control of any competing railroads.

This was the period in which the main weight of new railroad companies and new railroad construction was moving farther to the west and Morgan, in common with several other bankers and financiers with an involvement in the railroad business, found his

This locomotive, a 4-4-0 of the Pennsylvania Railroad, was the first to be fitted with the Westinghouse compressed air brake system. Power-operated brakes of this and other types soon became standard all over the world, and not just in the U.S.A., and transformed the safety of railroad operations for the better.

interests moving in the same general direction. Here Morgan was soon embroiled with new adversaries, many of them with similar ambitions if not quite the same financial power. When trying to expand the Vanderbilt system from Chicago into Iowa, Morgan was checked by Edward Harriman, who had gained control of the Illinois Central Railroad in 1881 and used its steadily increasing prosperity to drive it in the direction of a major expansion. The first clash between the two giants, over the little known Dubuque & Sioux City Railroad, took place in 1886 and resulted in a victory for Harriman, though the two men soon had larger bones of contention to fight over.

In 1893 the writing that had been on the wall for some time finally took a more concrete form, and the Erie Railway collapsed. Faced with the task of restructuring the company, Morgan once more found himself in opposition to Harriman, who gained the upper hand and managed to impose some of his own conditions on the reorganization. Just two years later, one of more than 150 railroads that failed was the Union Pacific Railroad, but the condition of the railroad company's finances, tracks, equipment and other elements of its operation had by this time deteriorated to so marked an extent that Morgan decided it would bring no financial success for him to attempt a resurrection. This opened the way for Harriman, with the financial backing of Standard Oil, to take control of the Union Pacific Railroad. Within five years Harriman turned the Union Pacific Railroad into a highly successful operation; moreover, in 1900, when Huntington died, Harriman paid $50 million to take control of the Southern Pacific Railroad.

In the interim, Morgan had forged an association with Hill to create a common ownership of the monopoly enjoyed by the Northern Pacific and the Great Northern railroads in the north-eastern part of the U.S.A., and had also seen the Chicago, Burlington & Quincy Railroad added to this system. In New England, Morgan extended his control of the New York New Haven & Hartford Railroad by taking control of many of the region's smaller railroads, and also used his influence to check the proposed expansion of the Philadelphia & Reading Railway, which had now developed into a system with 5,000 miles (8046km) of track, until he himself had seized control of it. In the south-eastern part of the U.S.A., where the ruination of the Civil War had been followed by constructors who took state funds but made little or no effort to construct the railroads for which these funds were meant, Morgan revealed a genuine railroad flair in the creation of the 9,000-mile (14485-km) Southern Railway system.

Morgan was also able to complete his control over the network of New York state trunk routes and their associated feederlines, one of the advantages of this being the even distribution of the coal traffic, whose

movement was charged at a standard rate. It is worth noting that Morgan had interests not only in the railroad business, but also in a number of other major industrial areas, as typified by his part in the establishment of the huge U.S. Steel conglomerate. However, an industrial empire of the type controlled by Morgan can by maintained only on the basis of continuous growth, and it was the search for growth in the railroad industry that brought Morgan to a final clash with the other railroad giant, Edward Harriman.

The scene for this showdown was the north-western region of the U.S.A., where the takeover of the Chicago, Burlington & Quincy Railroad by James Hill, a supporter of Morgan, left Harriman with little alternative to the implementation of an extraordinary plan designed to facilitate the entry into Chicago of his own Union Pacific-Southern Pacific system. After Hill had refused to allow the sale of part of the Chicago, Burlington & Quincy Railroad to Harriman, the latter decided to buy control of the Northern Pacific Railroad as a means of securing its Chicago, Burlington & Quincy Railroad holdings for his own advantage. The result was a huge financial battle between Hill, aided by the financial strength of Morgan on the one side, and Harriman, with the financial support of Rockefeller, on the other. A struggle of this type has always provided opportunities for smaller operators to enter the fray in a limited manner to seize crumbs from the table, and in the case of the battle between the organizations of Hill and Morgan and of Harriman and Rockefeller smaller fry sought to take advantage by short-selling the rising

stock of the Northern Pacific Railroad, but then suffered as the stock price continued to rise and there was no more stock available for purchase. This led to a financial panic that was checked only as the two major parties reached an armistice agreement; this led to creation of the Northern Securities Corporation as a holding company in which both parties had an interest. The public was thereby pushed out into the commercial cold, pressure on the Congress then resulting in the February 1888 passage through the Congress of the Interstate Commerce Act. This reversed the effect of the 1886 Supreme Court ruling in the matter of the National Grange, and made illegal the setting up of pools, discriminatory rates, preferential treatment and the full range of other altogether too common abuses. The act also established that rates must be 'just and reasonable', creating the Interstate Commerce Commission to supervise the equitable enforcement of the act's provisions. The Interstate Commerce Commission was not provided with the 'teeth' to enforce its decisions, however: between 1888 and 1905 the 16 rate cases to come before the Supreme Court resulted in 15 victories for the railroads, and the public not unnaturally became wholly disenchanted with the act as a means of controlling the worst excesses of the railroad companies.

The Interstate Commerce Act was just one example, moreover, of the dilatory approach of the federal government to the need for action in a number of railroad-related matters: the standard gauge was not legally established until 1886; the Westinghouse air brake, which made possible huge improvements in operating efficiency as well as public safety, was adopted only hesitantly; and the universal coupling, another device which was eventually to save the lives of large numbers of railroad brakemen every year, was not made mandatory until 1893, which was the year in which air brakes were finally demanded by law as a standard feature. The Northern Pacific Railroad affair of 1901 finally forced the federal government into action. By this time the railroads themselves were not unwilling to have a regulatory framework imposed on them, for the effects of years of unregulated expansion and cut-throat competition were making themselves felt in a decidedly adverse manner, the railroads themselves now being subjected on an increasing basis to the type of abuse they had been all too willing to impose on their customers only a few years earlier. The growth of freight as a major force in railroad economics combined with the availability of rival railroads to make it possible for major users of the railroads for freight movement to demand and receive significant and wholly secret reductions in the freight rates that were advertised. The losers were now the railroads rather than the freight companies.

What was needed, at least in the short term, was the provision of effective teeth for the Interstate Commerce Commission. Thus the Elkins Act of 1903 strengthened the Interstate Commerce Act by making any modification of the published rates illegal, and removed the need for customers to take court action to prove their case. The Hepburn Act of 1906 improved matters still further, enhancing the Interstate Commerce Commission's

powers to investigate and exercise control over all railroad activities, except those of a purely operational nature; the act also enlarged the Interstate Commerce Commission, gave it the authority to impose mandatory maximum rates, and made binding any of the rulings it thought fit to promulgate.

Further regulation of the railroad industry followed in the next decade, for in 1916 the eight-hour working day was legally fixed as the standard, leading in 1917 to further intervention by the federal authorities. The implementation of an eight-hour working day increased the railroads's costs to an appreciable degree, but the combination of increased costs and the Interstate Commerce Commission's refusal to permit an increase in freight rates meant that the entirety of the U.S. railroad system was on the verge of financial collapse in the period that followed the entry of the U.S.A. into World War I. This period, in which the U.S. armed forces were hugely enlarged and prepared for large-scale movement overseas, combined with the introduction of vast numbers of new weapons from a much enlarged American industrial base demanding the delivery of raw materials in quantities that had never before been envisaged: all of this demanded an enormous and rapid increase in the numbers of men needing to be moved by railroad to training camps and then to embarkation ports on the Atlantic seaboard. Moreover, the volume of raw materials that had to be delivered by rail from mining areas and ports to industrial cities, and the redistribution of armaments and supplies that had to be implemented by train from manufacturing centres to camps and

depots all over the U.S.A., all took their toll. So difficult was the process, and so injurious to the U.S.A.'s war effort, that for a period of just over two years, ending in the aftermath of World War I, the federal government felt itself compelled to operate the railroads itself.

The railroads passed back to the operational control of their owners after this interval of governmental control, but the conditions in which the railroads now had to operate were wholly different from those typical of the period before World War I. New forms of transport were on the verge of making major inroads into the market for mass transportation, and this was reflected in the slow but steady diminution of American railroad mileage from its peak of 252,845 miles (406903km) in 1916. This peak, it should be noted, had been reached via interim figures of 53,878 miles (86706km) in 1870, 94,671 miles (152354km) in 1880, 163,507 miles (263132km) in 1890, 193,346 miles (311152km) in 1900 and 240,293 miles (386704km) in 1910. In the period after World War I the overall mileage began finally to drop, initially only slowly, as indicated by the figure for 1930, which was 240,052 miles (386316km).

CHAPTER FOUR
THE HEYDAY & DECLINE OF STEAM LOCOMOTION

RIGHT
This 1945 aerial view of Corbin Yards, Kentucky, looking south toward Knoxville, reveals an important rail terminal, shop and classification point for the vast tonnages of coal being hauled out of eastern Kentucky. On the right is the southbound leaving yard, in the centre the car shop, 26-stall roundhouse and back shop, and on the left toward the top of the picture the northbound departure yard.

OPPOSITE
New track mileage was still coming into existence, but the processes leading to such an event were altogether more advanced than those evident in this illustration of American engineers surveying the Cheat river valley for the Baltimore & Ohio Railroad in the 1840s.

When the federal government took control of the U.S. railroad system toward the end of 1917, it was evident that a new era was about to begin. The giants of the previous era had disappeared or were leaving the scene: never again would the U.S. railroad industry be dominated by men possessing the stature, the vision and the power (for good or bad) of Jay Gould, Edward Harriman, James Hill, J. Pierpont Morgan and Cornelius Vanderbilt. Of these it was perhaps Morgan who had been the most important, for it was he who had made the most effective start in the extraordinarily complex task of restructuring the national railroad system from a hotchpotch of divided and often antagonistic companies into a more cohesive whole, characterized by closer links and a more effective overall organization. It was on Morgan's foundations that an increasing quantity of federal legislation over the railroads began to build from the beginning of the 20th century. This was the result partly of the work undertaken by the Interstate Commerce Commission, and partly a belated recognition within the industry itself that future survival, let alone prosperity, depended

on increasing levels of co-operation instead of the mutual antipathies that had hitherto been the norm for the industry's component companies, which differed widely in terms of size, financial muscle, ambitions and capabilities. This latter was one of the primary reasons that the industry had welcomed rather than fought the standardization of freight rates by the Interstate Commerce Commission. That the right formula had been found was suggested by the fact that, in the period between 1900 and 1913, levels of traffic, turnover and earnings had more than doubled before a depression in 1913–14 was reflected in a modest lessening of traffic but a greater decrease in earnings.

That this was a result, in part at least, of a distinct excess of capacity over demand, was reflected in the period 1914–15 by the fact that some 15,000 miles (24140km) of track were in receivership. The financial situation of the U.S. railroad system had also been weakened by the readiness of some operators to pay more than a realistic figure for the acquisition of interests they coveted: for example, the Pennsylvania Railroad paid considerably too high a figure for a large part of the Baltimore & Ohio Railroad and other north-eastern systems, and was then not in the position to fund the programme that was found to be necessary for the maintenance and replacement of its track and rolling stock. A further consequence of this tendency was that traffic increases, in both terms of passenger and freight, after the outbreak of World War I, pushed the railroads to the limit of their capabilities and in some cases beyond in terms of both financial returns and the safety of their operations. The factor that most strongly typified this failure was the large-scale

breakdown of the logistical system that provided for freight cars hauled over other operators's tracks to be returned to their owners. Increased by an unprecedented percentage, the freight traffic directed to the north-eastern ports from which weapons, and later men, were embarked on ships for transportation over the Atlantic Ocean to Europe was just too much for the railroads of this region to process and handle. The inevitable consequence was a huge concentration of empty cars that could not easily be sorted and returned to their operators, in the process severely hampering the handling of freight cars recently arrived at the ports in the states of New Jersey and New York. The shipment of weapons and other essential supplies were severely affected, and the knock-on effect was also serious as freight operators in other parts of the country began to run short of the freight cars they so desperately needed. This was one of the reasons for the creation during 1917 of the Railroad War Board, whose primary task was the solution of this and other problems. The board achieved so little real success, however, that the federal government was forced, in the interests of national security, to intervene and take over this vital task.

After the event which signalled an almost unprecedented intervention in the affairs of private companies, the federal government's operation of the U.S. railroad system was the subject of great controversy. The proponents of the almost sacrosanct U.S. concept of private enterprise claimed that the control of the railroad by the federal system had led to a considerable deterioration in the system's overall level of efficiency, that the notion of

The Pathfinders
Early Engineers in
the Cheat River Valley

rerouting traffic from the Pennsylvania and the Baltimore & Ohio railroads onto the trunk routes in New York had been wrong in its basic and indeed fundamental features, and that the property of the railroads had been wrongly neglected and was therefore suffering in material terms to the cost of its owners rather than the federal government that had in fact been responsible for the deterioration. The opposing point of view was expressed by the Director General of Railroads, who claimed that the U.S. railroad system's overall level of operating efficiency had in fact been enhanced by the countrywide standardization of operating procedures, and that the federal government's purchase of new equipment, and the compensation it paid to the railroad operators, in fact amounted to a very significant federal subsidy.

There is no clear-cut answer as to which of these two opposing views better reflected the actuality of the situation. However, a fact which cannot be denied is that the inflation of wages and prices in the period from 1914 up to 1920 had a strong and indeed adverse effect on the commercial viability of the American railroad system. This is more than suggested by the fact that while in the period in question railroad operating revenues doubled to $4 billion, the railroad companies's net incomes declined by a factor of five to a mere $100 million.

After World War I, the new commercial realities of the time were reflected in the passing of the Transportation Act of 1920. This restored the railroads to their private-enterprise owners, and at the same time made provision for the allocation of low-interest loans and grants of federal funds to aid the railroad industry in its reconstruction to meet the demands of the period. It is also worthy of note that the act additionally imposed on the Interstate Commerce Commission the task of devising a wide-ranging plan for the consolidation of the U.S. railroad network, not least to improve its capacity for a rapid and effective response to the type of emergency that had led to the takeover of the system by the federal government at the end of 1917. The remit of the Interstate Commerce Commission in this respect was the preparation of a plan that would consolidate the current diversity of many railroad companies, some very large and others very small, into a limited number of large systems, each with about the same earning power. This in itself marked a major transformation in U.S. thinking concerning the railroad industry, for the previous emphasis on private-enterprise competition was now replaced by a concept of relative equality dictated from above. In drawing up its plan, the Interstate Commerce Commission was instructed to allow the railroad companies to keep their existing routes, to ensure that there was an adequate level of competition, and to provide for the preservation of the concept of uniform rates. Denied the power to enforce the mergers that it already thought were necessary as the primary means of streamlining the operations of the U.S. railroad industry, the Interstate Commerce Commission was, in real terms, being ordered to plan a competitive system that had to come into existence under the conditions in which a monopoly existed, and then to bring this system into being with powers that did not include the right to force mergers, only the right to veto any that the industry might consider desirable but the commission did not. Inevitably, therefore, the net result was the continued existence of the current situation.

Even so, the Interstate Commerce Commission did manage to develop the type of plan envisaged by the Congress, but any chances of the plan being brought to fruition were effectively checked by the opposition of the railroad operators. However, the railroad companies then started their own programme of consolidation, often employing cleverly conceived financial manoeuvres that created what were mergers in all but legal name, and thereby denied the Interstate Commerce Commission any opportunity to use its power to veto them, which had been clearly defined in its remit. In the north-eastern region of the U.S.A., for example, the Interstate Commerce Commission thought it would be appropriate to create a fifth trunk route by rearrangements in the current situation, involving the Pennsylvania, the New York Central, the Baltimore & Ohio, and the Erie railroad systems in concert with a consolidation of the Delaware, Lackawanna & Western and the Nickel Plate railroads to create a balance of power between what would now be five major operators. The Pennsylvania and the New York Central railroads would have been the major losers had this arrangement been implemented, but successfully opposed the scheme. What they did not manage to achieve, however, was a commercially and financially viable alternative.

OPPOSITE
Locomotive No. 1223 of the Strasburg Railroad in Pennsylvania.

ABOVE
Locomotive No. 494, a 4-4-0 unit of the Boston & Maine Railroad, is seen at White River Junction.

OPPOSITE
The power of steam locomotion in action is evident in illustrations such as this, which shows locomotive No. 2146 of the Norfolk & Western Railroad.

The Interstate Commerce Commission's recommendations for the consolidation of the U.S. railroad industry was first published in an interim form during 1921. There followed a period of discussion in which the Commission several times asked the federal government, without success, to be relieved of this burden. Further progress was slow, and it was December 1929 before the Interstate Commerce Commission published its final plan. This called for the establishment of a consolidated system of 21 companies, but the whole concept was then rendered irrelevant by the financial collapse of that year.

The period was also marked by a return to the business of railroad operation on the lines of standard American business practice, most notably in a change of ownership for several railroads. New entrants into the field included the Van Swerigen brothers, who purchased a number of railroads, including the Nickel Plate in 1916 and the Erie in 1923. During 1924 the Pennsylvania Railroad used a holding company in its successful attempt to obtain a controlling interest in the Norfolk & Western Railroad, which was a major operator in the coal transport industry at Roanoke in Virginia and, as further proof (if such were needed) that it was doing well for itself, used the same tactic for additional purchases that gave it controlling interests in three other railroads, namely the Lehigh Valley, the Wabash, and the Boston & Maine railroads.

A photograph reveals the 4-4-0 locomotive No. 124 immediately after completion by the Rogers Locomotive & Machine Works of Paterson, New Jersey.

4-4-0 locomotive No. 72 of the Long Island Railroad.

evading the possibility of the Interstate Commerce Commission exercising its veto, that holding companies created by the eastern trunk lines expended $300 million on purchases during 1928–29.

With their positions now immune, to all intents and purposes, from the strictures of the Interstate Commerce Commission, the railroads enjoyed something of a boom period that mirrored the success of the U.S. economy of the period. However, this success also persuaded the railroad companies, by a process of omission if not commission, to ignore the need for effective forward and contingency planning: it was as if the railroads believed that the 'good times' were here to stay, and that there were no clouds at all looming on the horizon. Thus the lessons of 1920 were conveniently forgotten. Though overall route mileage dropped slightly from the maximum level attained in 1916, track mileage increased by some 100,000 miles (160930km) to something in the order of 360,000 miles (579350km) in the course of 1928. Although, with the exception of the holdings of the Van Swerigen brothers, the railroad companies were now operating on a genuinely corporate basis rather than as the particular empires of affluent private individuals, they currently appeared to be teetering on the edge of the types of devastating internecine battles that had led to financial and operating mayhem in the past.

This possibility was then overtaken by an altogether larger crisis, one with national and indeed international and global ramifications. This was the 'great crash' of 1929, one of whose first and most direly affected victims

The use of this financial tactic (one or more holding companies to place actual ownership at one remove) as a means of bypassing the regulations of the Interstate Commerce Commission was also practised by the Van Swerigen brothers. The brothers's holding company was the Allegheny Corporation, which became the vehicle by which the brothers developed a system of 30,000 miles (42280km). So useful was the tactic in

Steam locomotion really came into its own as it worked freight and passenger services in the vast open spaces typified by this stretch of the Wisconsin Central Railroad at Rugby, Wisconsin.

OPPOSITE
This is the 2-8-0 locomotive No. 1207 of the Northern Pacific Railroad hauling freight near Yakima, Washington state.

in the U.S. economy was the railroad industry. In 1930 the revenues of the railroad companies fell by 15 per cent from the level of 1929, and in 1932 these had dropped to just half the 1929 figure. This was largely as a result of the financial and economic crises affecting the economy of the U.S.A., but another factor that has to be taken into consideration is the effect of the motor car. By now this new mode of transport had proved itself fully practical in terms of reliability, and was by the later 1920s highly affordable as a result of the advanced mass-production techniques pioneered and introduced by Henry Ford: by 1928 deliveries of the Ford Model T had reached 15 million. An initial consequence of people abandoning the railroad for the motor car, especially for shorter journeys, had been a 33 per cent drop in passenger miles from the level of 1920, and further major falls were yet to come.

The railroad companies did not fully appreciate the effect that the advent of the motor car and the decline of the economy would have on them, and therefore omitted to take a long, hard look at the very nature of their operations in an attempt to sidestep the problems facing them or to create alternative sources of income. Thus the railroad companies reacted with the solutions that had seen them through troubled times in the past: reductions in wages, the slashing of employee numbers, and the severe trimming of dividends. This is not to suggest that there were in fact any real, guaranteed ways to improve the situation, but the railroad companies signally failed even to look for answers.

In 1932 the federal government set up the National Transportation Committee, which came up with the recommendation that the railroad companies should co-operate in a process to find and trim out duplications of any type that created wasteful competition. In 1933 a new administration was sworn in under the leadership of President Franklin D. Roosevelt, and a compliant Congress soon passed the Emergency Transportation Act, which gave legal force to the recommendations of the National Transport Committee and established the framework for the creation of three co-ordinating committees (eastern, western and southern) to help a newly-appointed federal transport commissioner to implement, as quickly and simply as possible, the changes that had been planned, but at the same time responded to the need to maintain as high a level of employment as possible by limiting the railroad companies's scope for trimming their labour forces.

By this time the railroad companies were themselves fully conscious of the need for drastic and effective action at an industry-wide rather than individual-operator level; another important step, in 1934, was the establishment of the Association of American Railroads to act as a national policy-making body for the industry. This and the Interstate Commerce Commission wasted no time in reaching broad agreement about several measures designed to check the further decline in a situation that represented, for many railroad operators, a real struggle for survival. Traffic levels were still falling, and by July 1938 no fewer than 39 major

railroads (including the Van Swerigen holdings), with more than 25 per cent of the U.S.A.'s total mileage between them, were in receivership. On the direct recommendation of the Association of American Railroads, the Interstate Commerce Commission brought under its direct control all interstate railroad traffic and strengthened its rate parity regime. This latter was not altogether successful, however, for in a not inconsiderable number of instances it effectively limited the competitiveness of the railroads relative to road transport. The Interstate Commerce Commission also proved most useful to the cause of the railroad companies in matters such as facilitating the easing of the railroads's debt obligations, the obtaining of federal loans wherever this was possible, and the fighting of public demand for public ownership of the railroads.

As they began to emerge from the bleakest of periods during the late 1930s, the railroad companies found that their future had been given a rosier tinge by the passage through the Congress of the 1940 Transportation Act, which went still further toward meeting their needs: the long-established requirement for the land-grant railroads to carry federal traffic at reduced rates was removed, water transport was added to the responsibilities of the Interstate Commerce Commission, and it was announced that there were to be a non-competitive national transport policy and fixed new rules for the Interstate Commerce Commission's system of approval for mergers. These last required the Interstate Commerce Commission to take into account

OPPOSITE
A passenger train of the Durango & Silverton Railroad hauled by the 2-8-2 locomotive No. 480 of the K36 class.

RIGHT
During World War II, oil from Wyoming was hauled in vast strings of tank cars, as seen here in this 1944 photograph of a double-header steaming through the canyon of the Wind river, Wyoming.

both the interests of the public and the debt position of the railroads involved. The primary reason for the decidedly gentle and soothing treatment that the railroad companies received during 1940 was the concern of the federal government about World War II, which had started in Europe during 1939, did not as yet directly involve the U.S.A., but was nonetheless spreading steadily and threatening ultimately to force an American commitment. It was abundantly clear, as a result of the lessons of World War I, that should the U.S.A. become involved it would have a pressing need for a comprehensive and integrated national railroad

network that was optimized for the movement of large quantities of raw materials from mines and ports to manufacturing centres at modest speeds, and also for the transport of personnel, weapons and other equipment over long distances at high speeds. Another factor that had to be taken into account was the need to keep the U.S. economy operating on a viable basis for civil as well as military applications.

The U.S.A. was finally sucked into World War II during December 1941 as a result of the Japanese attack on Pearl Harbor and other American interests in and around the Pacific Ocean. The railroads once again became a key

element of a U.S. war effort that expanded in size and capability very markedly and in a notably short time. Apart from a token three-week nationalization of the railroads at the end of 1944, designed to prevent the possibility of labour problems, the privately-owned railroad companies worked extremely capably throughout the U.S.A.'s 1941–45 involvement in World War II. The railroad operators co-operated excellently with the Office of Defense Transportation, and so made unnecessary any repetition of the type of drastic action that had been required in 1917. The movement of war materiel and personnel to port areas and the subsequent extraction of the empty cars worked well, avoiding the congested log jams that had partially crippled the movement of men and equipment to France in World War I.

The railroad operators also revealed the improved level of financial maturity they had attained: rather than using their enlarged profits, derived from the movement of war traffic, to declare large dividends, they used the money to reduce their debt. Between 1940 and 1945, therefore, the railroad companies were able to reduce their levels of indebtedness to such a degree that their annual fixed charges were trimmed by some $80 million. This marked a radical departure for the railroad operators, for debt had been a millstone round their necks right from the beginnings of the U.S. railroad industry, and had severely curtailed their financial flexibility throughout this period of some 115 years. This display of greater fiscal maturity had considerable benefits in the years following the end of World War II, when the railroads's

RIGHT
The ability of the U.S. railroad system to maintain the steady movement of petroleum products to ports on the U.S.A.'s eastern and western seaboards was a major factor in the success of the Allied forces in the European and Pacific theatres of World War II. This is a scene typical of the operations of the Missouri Pacific Railroad, showing hundreds of tank cars moving through a terminal during May 1943.

OPPOSITE LEFT
An express service of the Lehigh Valley Railroad headed by locomotive No. 2102.

OPPOSITE RIGHT
Locomotive No. 328 of the Northern Pacific Railroad.

newly-created financial 'credibility' made it simpler for them to raise the $2 billion they needed for the implementation of a programme of large-scale 'dieselization' that the railroads decided was the right option to replace coal-fired locomotion; this was already in terminal decline for shorter-distance transport, where both electric and diesel locomotion offered significant advantages, and was now under dire threat for longer-distance transport, where diesel locomotion was the

coming force. These threats to steam locomotion for shorter- and longer-distance transport came largely from the cleaner and more economical operation promised by electric and diesel locomotives, but there were other factors in the post-war years that also adversely affected the railroads in general. As just a single example, by 1946 the railroad companies's incomes had already fallen by 10 per cent compared with those of 1944, with the end of the mass of transport required for

war purposes, and the 'slack' had not been taken up by a return of civilian passenger numbers, which were declining dramatically. By 1950 the railroads's share of passenger mileage for journeys between cities, rather than travel in and around them, was under 50 per cent of the national total, with buses currently taking nearly 40 per cent. But the buses's share also suffered from that point as the importance of air travel increased. By 1960 buses and trains were each carrying about 25

per cent of the total, while the airlines's share was 40 per cent; by 1970 the airlines accounted for more than 75 per cent of the total. After the railroads's drastic reduction of passenger services in the early 1970s, even private aircraft was logging a greater number of passenger miles than the railroads. It is worth remembering, though, that all other forms of public intercity transport had been overtaken by the private motor car as early as the 1920s, but it is nonetheless gloomy news for the railroads that by the mid-1970s all forms of public transport combined (and in this the railroads accounted for only a very small proportion) were transporting just a miserable 13 per cent.

The analysis of freight traffic, over the same period, also reveals that there was a steady decline in railroad freight within the context of the total freight business in the U.S.A. From a figure of almost 70 per cent in 1944, the railroads of the freight market declined to 56 per cent by 1950, 44 per cent by 1960, and less than 40 per cent during the 1970s: over the same period, trucks carried more than 20 per cent from 1960, canals and rivers more than 10 per cent by 1970, and oil pipelines almost 25 per cent. Actual freight tonnages moved by the railroads were slightly greater in the mid-1970s than they had been in 1944, but during the period the overall freight tonnage had doubled.

CHAPTER FIVE
MATERIAL MATTERS

BELOW
Construction work in progress on Cut no. 1 west of the Narrows in Weber Canyon, some 4 -miles (6.4-km) west of Echo and 995-miles (1601-km) west of Omaha during the later part of 1868. This area presented some of the most difficult grading in the construction of the Union Pacific Railroad. Successive shelves had to be hacked into the rock, and then pick-axed and blasted down to the desired grade. Rough, temporary tracks were laid to allow the spoil to be hauled away at the lower levels, while two-wheeled mule cars and wheelbarrows accomplished the same task at the higher levels.

OPPOSITE
The Lloyd's Railroad, Telegraph & Express map of the United States of America and Canada reveals the extent of American and Canadian railroad development to a line west of the Great Lakes and Missouri river up to 1863. Published in 1867.

The world's first railroad was the British Stockton & Darlington Railway, which ran its first steam-hauled service on 27 September 1825. But the pioneer U.S. railroads were not far behind, beginning services in May 1830, which made them among the first in the world. Moreover, because of the physical extent of the U.S.A. and the need to connect what were already fairly far-flung farming, industrial and population centres, these early railroads were from the beginning the longest that had yet been planned. Quite naturally, the pioneering American railroad engineers were starting from a basis of no practical experience and, as the concept of the railroad was so new, only the most limited amount of theoretical thinking. They were therefore compelled to develop the most suitable basic railroad construction techniques largely by trial and error, and had also to face problems that were largely unique to the U.S.A. For example, in the absence of any indigenous capability for the manufacture and working of iron in industrially large quantities, the American railroad companies had to import the rail they required, the majority of it coming from the U.K. Another capability that was currently lacking in all but the smallest quantities throughout the U.S.A. was a heavy engineering capability, but this did not long delay creative individuals from drawing up the designs of locomotives and other equipment, which thus came to possess a distinctively American 'flavour' from a time early in the U.S. development of the railroad.

Before considering the process by which the U.S. railroads were established in their specific physical contexts, it is sensible to

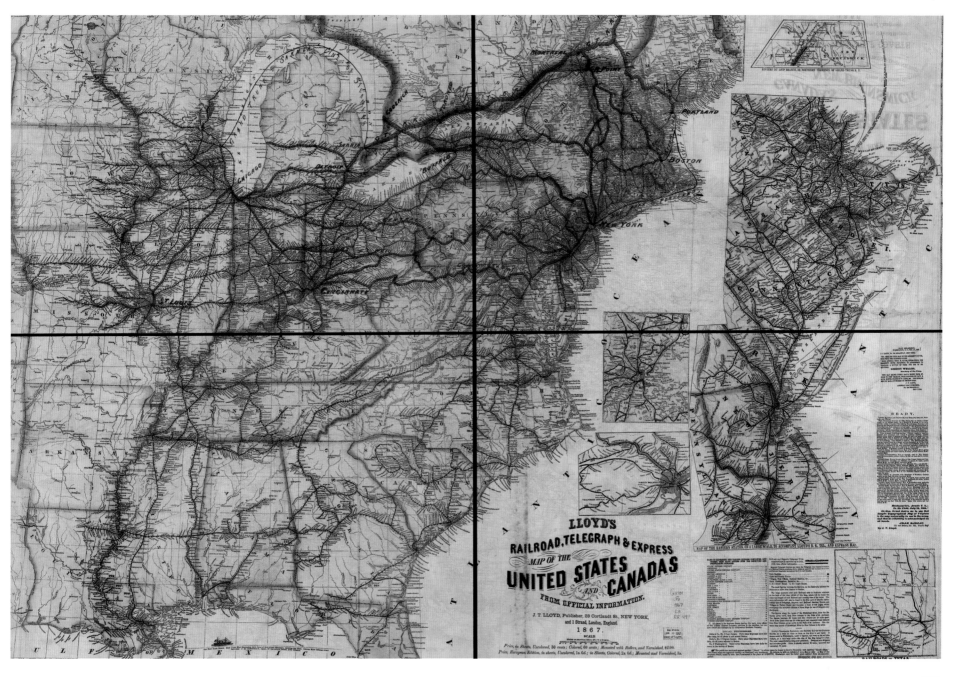

RIGHT
A lithograph by Currier & Ives shows the pioneering Niagara suspension bridge between the U.S.A.. and Canada in 1856.

FAR RIGHT
Men of the Northern Pacific Railroad lay track in western Dakota during 1880. Railroad construction of this period was still based largely on man and animal power, and was therefore extremely labour intensive.

OPPOSITE
Locomotives Nos. 463 and 489 double-head a service of the Cumbres & Toltec Scenic Railroad west of the Cascade Trestle. The nature of the country provides striking evidence of the railroad constructors's need to adopt a winding course to avoid the steepest gradients, even if this meant considerably greater track length.

locomotive and the wear of the track. For example, the tractive effort needed to haul a load up a 1 per cent grade is about five times the requirement on flat track, and a curve of 1° requires an increase of tractive effort in the order of 12 to 25 per cent in tractive effort. (A grade of 1 per cent translates into a rise of 1ft/0.305m over a distance of 100ft/30.48m, while a curve of 1° means that two radii extended inward from the ends of the 100-ft chord of the arc in question constitute the sides of a 1° triangle.) The effects of gradient and curvature are a great reduction in the weight of the load that can be hauled by a given power (the locomotive), or a reduction in the speed it can maintain, or alternatively a combination of both these aspects.

The selection of the route involving the right grades and curvatures is vital to the economics of railroad operation, often needing

consider the basic infrastructure on which the American steam-hauled services operated. The most obvious element is the track, which comprises a pair of parallel rails attached at right angles to large numbers of ties placed at regular intervals. The track has three main functions that are in essence simple to state but in fact require careful consideration if the right technical and economic solutions are to be found. These three core functions are the supporting of the load imposed on it, the provision of a smooth surface for easy movement of the load, and the guidance of the train's wheels.

The line of the railroad should be as flat and straight as can be managed without recourse to expensive preparatory work, for grades and curves increase the burden on the

carefully considered assessment of the cost of avoiding or removing grades and curvatures in relation to the operational savings which should result from so doing. The most important single factor in such an assessment is generally the volume of traffic (current or anticipated): as the amount of traffic increases, the additional operational costs caused by grades and curvatures also increase; therefore the higher the volume of current or anticipated traffic, the greater the financial incentive to undertake the flattening and straightening of the route.

Where it is impossible, for physical or economic reasons, to avoid or remove heavy grades and/or curvatures, such as is often the case in mountainous terrain, it is often necessary to provide additional tractive power (more locomotives) to haul the given load at the desired speed. This additional tractive power can take two forms, either the assignment of extra locomotive capability to an individual train by double-heading with two or more locomotives, or the assignment of helper or pusher locomotives to assist all trains at the most difficult locality, as typified by the approaches to the summit of

a pass through a mountain range.

As a good house must start with good foundations, good track must begin with a good roadbed. This must be firm, well-drained and of dimensions sufficient to support the weight of the track and any trains that pass along it. It may therefore be necessary in places to excavate the original soil to a

carefully calculated depth and replace it with suitable soil or other material brought in from elsewhere. Thus the graded surface, for drainage reasons curved gently downward on each side from the high point along the longitudinal centreline, is covered with a layer of sub-ballast (broken stone of a fairly coarse type) with a flat top and inward-angled sides,

which itself carries the top ballast (broken stone of smaller dimensions), again with inward-angled sides and a flat top somewhat wider than the track that is to be laid on it.

The rails, which in just a few of the earliest railroads were of wood, but in the vast majority of cases of iron and then, definitively, of steel, carry the load which trains (the

OPPOSITE
The 4-8-2 locomotives Nos. 2100 and 2102 double-head a service of the Reading Railway.

LEFT
Work in progress on the construction of the Northern Pacific Railroad's main line. In the background are the prefabricated huts that were moved, as the railhead advanced, to provide accommodation for the work crews.

RIGHT
An early train of the Santa Fe Railway on the celebrated Canyon Diablo Bridge near Winslow, Arizona.

OPPOSITE
Locomotive No. 9 of the Kettle Moraine Railroad at North Cake, Wisconsin.

locomotive and all the cars it hauls) impose on the track, the rails being supported by the transverse ties, the ties supported by the ballast. Thus there are several elements to the equation that must be solved if the track is to be reliable and durable; moreover, the selection of the right combination of materials and design is the subject of extensive research and continuing experimentation. By the end of the period of steam locomotion in the U.S.A., the precise shape and weight of the rails had developed gradually in an evolutionary process to meet operational requirements: at the beginning of the 20th century, rail weighing as little as 56lb/yard (27.8kg/m) was typical, but by 1950 rail weighing as much as 150lb/yard (74.4kg/m) was in service for track designed for the carriage of heavy traffic. The average weight of the rail used for the main tracks of U.S. railroads increased from 83lb/yard (41.2kg/m) during 1921 to 101lb/yard (50.1kg/m) during 1948.

The use of the T-rail (so called as a result of its shape) has been standard in the U.S.A. since about the mid-19th century, this fact reflecting the general appreciation, based on a steadily growing body of experience, that it is

RIGHT
In August 1866, members of the Union Pacific Railroad's railhead crew manhandle metal rails onto the wooden ties that have already been roughly positioned. Such was the speed at which track was generally laid that it was impossible to provide sufficient seasoned timber, so green wood was used and had to be replaced as it started to rot.

OPPOSITE
Dismore & Company's New and Complete Map of the Railway System of the United States & Canada, 1876.

the most practical and economic form of rail. Later in the day of steam locomotion, however, the development of ways to take accurate measurements of the stresses in any portion of the rail under operational conditions, made it feasible to introduce individually small but cumulatively important refinements and improvements in the cross section of the typical rail.

As noted above, the rails are attached to the ties, which keep the rails the proper distance apart and therefore parallel with each other on what is typically the so-called standard gauge of 4ft 8.5in (1.435m). The ties support the rails and transmit the loads carried

Santa Fe Railway's locomotive No. 3880.

Track-laying in Montana during 1887. In conditions such as these, the railroads could push their track forward an amazing distance each day.

in turn by the rails, downward to the ballast, which serves as a cushion (or shock absorber) between the rails/ties and the grade. By the middle of the 20th century there were in U.S. railroads something in the order of one billion ties, of which between 35 and 40 million required changing each year as a result of operational wear and/or natural decay. By this time the latest methods of chemical treatment had on average tripled the life of the typical tie to some 20 years or more, with a figure of

30 years not uncommon. In an effort to cut the degree of mechanical wear on the ties as a result of loads transmitted via the rail, it become standard practice to insert metal tie plates between the rail and the tie to spread the load over a larger area of the tie and so reduce the effect of the rail's base in cutting and/or wearing the tie. Consequently, considerable effort was devoted to the creation of the most effective design of tie plate. Another standard feature of the track's

'life' was the effect of wheel friction, which created the tendency for rails to 'creep' along their length, especially on multiple tracks where the trains generally moved in the same direction on each track. 'Anti-creepers' (in effect small anchors) were therefore applied to the rail, in a fashion that bored against the edges of the ties to limit, if not actually prevent, this movement.

Ballast, usually of crushed rock but sometimes composed of cinders, gravel or

RIGHT
Locomotive No. 150, a 4-4-0 Standard-type unit of the Boston & Maine Railroad, moves out of the operator's engine house at Danvers, Massachusetts in about 1895.

OPPOSITE
Locomotive No. 378 of the Norfolk & Western Railroad emerges from a tunnel straight onto a high trestle bridge.

mine waste and tailings, is employed to support and cushion the ties and thus to assist in keeping them in their right locations. The ballast also serves the purpose of distributing the track loads over the maximum possible area of roadbed. The nature of the ballast also promotes drainage away from the rails and ties, which aids longevity and also enhances the firmness of the track and its ability to offer a ride that is as smooth as possible. With time, the ballast settles and the gaps between the stones become filled with dirt, thus reducing the ability of the ballast to provide ready drainage. It was therefore a constant task for rail maintenance crews to clean the ballast as much as possible, and also to remove grass, weeds and other small items of vegetation growing in it.

As a train enters a curve, inertial factors dictate that its tendency is to continue in a straight line, and therefore fight the lateral movement imposed by the curve. The alteration in the train's movement is imposed by the rail on the outside of the curve. This inevitably imposes great strains on both the rails and the wheels (most especially their flanges) riding on the rails. Although early tracks were laid with the rails at equal heights above the grade, even in curves, it gradually came to be appreciated that trains would continue around curves with safety and greater smoothness if the outside rail was lifted above the level of the inner rail to tilt the train into the curve. This super-elevation helps to equalize the forces resulting from the diversion of the train from straight-line motion. The exact amount of super-elevation was found by trial and error, and its precise nature was very important, as too little meant that too high a percentage of the train's weight and pressure was thrown against the outside rail, while too much threw too much of the

weight and pressure on the inside rail. In deciding the precise degree of super-elevation, the team that designed and created a track would have to assess the weight and speeds of the trains that would operate over the track: high speeds demanded more super-elevation, but it had to be borne in mind that the amount of super-elevation suitable for a fast train might be altogether too much for a heavier but slower train carrying freight rather than passengers. What the creators of new track had to do, therefore, was strike the right compromise between two optimum solutions to create a super-elevation that would be of benefit to high-speed trains with light loads and low-speed trains with heavy loads.

A curve of 2° can be travelled smoothly and safely at 80mph (129km/h) with a super-elevation of 5in (0.127m) for the outside rail, but for the presence of sharper curves or the use of the track by heavier trains, neither of which allows the building-in of so much super-elevation, a reduction in speed in required. Another factor that had to be introduced into the design equation was that a smooth ride demanded that both super-elevation and curve be introduced and reduced progressively, from modest at the entry into the curve, before increasing gradually as the curve was entered fully and then decreasing to the modest figure once more as the curve unwound.

The development of the track, especially in the first half of the 20th century up to the time of the effective demise of steam locomotion, was achieved along two paths, namely the strengthening and improvement of the track to enhance the ride quality, to allow

MATERIAL MATTERS

It was the task of section gangs, such as this team of the Chicago, Burlington & Quincy Railroad, to ride the tracks on a handcar to replace rotten ties, tap loose spikes and tighten bolts. The foreman's daughter occupies the place of honour in this photograph of the 1870s, taken as a memento of the gang's shared sense of responsibility.

The locomotive *Firefly* on what was then the new trestle built by the Union Construction Corps on the Orange & Alexandria Railroad during the American Civil War.

RIGHT
In 1862 President Abraham Lincoln called this trestle of the Richmond, Fredericksburg & Potomac Railroad over the Potomac Creek the 'Beanpole & Cornstalk Bridge'.

OPPOSITE LEFT
In its eagerness to push toward Utah in its race with the westward-building Union Pacific Railroad, the Central Pacific Railroad bridged many of the High Sierra chasms with timber trestles. When the railroad had been completed, the Chinese labourers who had built it were brought back to fill the trestles in with solid earth and embankments. This remarkable photograph was taken at Secrettown Trestle, 62 miles (100km) from Sacramento on the western slope of the Sierra in 1877. Scrapers were not in use as yet for grading, and while dynamite had been invented it was not in general use. The Chinese used picks and shovels, chisels and hammers, black powder, wheelbarrows and one-horse dump carts.

OPPOSITE RIGHT
This picture of a three-tiered trestle and a one-car train was taken in 1887 along the Sheffield & Birmingham Railroad, now the Parrish-Norola section of the Southern Railway's Birmingham Division.

heavier loadings and permit higher speeds; and the creation of track that could be maintained more easily and therefore more cheaply. Progress along both of these paths was greatly facilitated during the first half of the 20th century by the introduction of higher levels of mechanization for tasks as diverse as grading; the laying, levelling and cleaning of ballast; the tamping down of ballast and ties; the cutting and fixing of track; and the

elimination of vegetation from the track. Even the tasks that had been so labour-intensive in the great days of route creation during the second half of the 19th century were aided by the increasing availability of power-operated tools such as augers, drills and devices to drive and pull spikes. Special vehicles were created to ensure the laying of the rails precisely parallel to one another, while the majority of the larger items of track machinery

became self-propelled and capable of work from alongside rather than on the track, thus removing delays to revenue-earning services.

In a country as large and geographically diverse as the U.S.A., there were vast numbers of obstacles that had to be surmounted. By the middle of the 20th century, when the U.S. railroad network amounted to some 225,000 miles (362100km), bridges constituted no less than 3,750 miles (6035km) of this distance.

The first bridges were made, almost inevitably, of wood fastened with iron, but the primary structural medium gradually became iron, then steel, with concrete added in the later stages of the period of steam locomotion. Bridges associated with railroad operations inevitably presented particular design problems, most notably in the need to build in the strength and the resilience to survive the constant imposition and removal of very substantial moving weights, the vibration stemming from the movements of these trains's engines and wheels, and the lateral forces resulting from the sideways motion of the trains.

The nature and interrelationship of these factors varied with the characteristics, especially in terms of length and weight, of the trains that would traverse any particular bridge. Moreover, while a bridge may have been able to cope more than adequately with the trains of the time in which it was designed

RIGHT
River-crossing bridges, built on masonry or stone piers, were slow to build and also expensive, and were therefore more a feature of the older railroads in the eastern seaboard states than of the younger railroads that were pushing their lines into the centre and west of the U.S.A., where wooden trestles were altogether more standard.

OPPOSITE
Locomotive No. 3450 of the Atchison, Topeka & Santa Fe Railway hauls an excursion train over a metal trestle bridge and onto one of the embankments forming each end of the valley crossing.

A train of the Rio Grande Railroad makes its way along the track at the bottom of the Royal Gorge of the Arkansas river with a hanging bridge in the background and, overhead, what was at the time the world's highest suspension bridge.

and built, sooner or later trains of different length and weight would inevitably come into service, demanding from the bridge strengths and capabilities that had not been designed into it from the start. So that safe strain limits were not exceeded, this required that the bridge be structurally strengthened unless the railroad operator was prepared for the newer trains to slow appreciably whenever they approached a bridge of the type in question. This factor was as true of many other types of railroad structure as it was of bridges. Thus it was vital for the design of railroad structures to be wholly consistent and integrated with other phases of operation: to quote just a single example, the introduction of larger locomotives generally required concomitant changes, such as the lengthening of stalls and the raising of roofs in roundhouses, and the strengthening of turntables or the replacement of existing turntables with larger units.

The nub of the matter was that the full extent of railroad operations had to be integrated if they were to operate effectively and economically and so satisfy the requirements of passengers and/or freight operators, and at the same time generate the revenues and the profits required by the shareholders. This need for the maximum possible integration also demanded that every item of major equipment be fully evaluated and tested before its suitability for service was accepted and all of the concomitant changes in other equipment were effected. The experience of railroad operators fully confirms that successful and profitable railroad services were wholly derived from the complete integration of a host of interacting details,

The Baldwin-built locomotive No. 722, a 2-8-0 unit of the Southern Railway, moves onto the Savannah River Bridge near Augusta, Georgia. This is a typical box bridge built up from lattice-work girders.

An early track inspection crew mounted on a handcar and carrying some of the tools of their trade.

each of which had to offer both reliability and efficiency.

The safe and reliable operation of the railroads soon came to depend on the provision of good communications between operating headquarters, way stations, signal towers, yards and other fixed installations, later joined by the trains themselves when the technology made it possible. Such communications were also of great advantage in terms of planning economics for the cost-effective control of operations on an hour-to-hour basis; it was with the development of the electric telegraph that such control started to become a possibility. The telegraphic train order came to be used as a supplement to rules and running rights for train operation laid down in the operating timetable. In a largely successful attempt to standardize and render systematic a basic code of rules and the manner in which operating rules were issued and interpreted, a standard rules code had been implemented by 1889. Some 12 years earlier, the adoption of the first railroad telephone system had begun to make inroads into the way the railroads were operated, and rapidly became indispensable. Another tool that became vital to successful railroad operations almost immediately after its creation was the telegraphic typewriter, which allowed messages to be typed into the system at the sending end, transmitted by telegraph, and automatically typed out at the receiving end.

The railroads's telephone and telegraph systems became closely interrelated over the years, most particularly after it became feasible for the same wires to be used for both types of communication. It was then practical for the same wires to carry two train-dispatching circuits between train-order offices; several message circuits to freight houses, yard offices, passenger ticket offices and other points; a system for messages and conversations; and printing-telegraph circuits.

Perhaps the best-known method of communication between off-line controllers and on-line personnel, most especially the man controlling the locomotive, was the trackside signal. This was used to keep the locomotive engineer informed of conditions on the track ahead of his locomotive. Originally, trains travelling in the same direction were spaced along the track on the basis of time intervals, and meetings of trains travelling in opposite directions were effected either by operating timetables or special instructions issued by the dispatcher and received by a train's crew in the form of written orders. Though this system performed adequately in the sparse days of the U.S. railroad industry's infancy, the increase in traffic density on what came to be the more important lines demanded the adoption of a system that made possible a more effective use of the line's capabilities. This led to the introduction of block signals, which opened the way for the replacement of time intervals by space intervals in the separation of trains. In this system, a railroad line was split along its length into blocks or segments of varying sizes, depending on traffic conditions, and trains were restricted in following or moving against each other into any specified block. As traffic densities increased still further, the manually-controlled block system was replaced by an automatic block system that, by 1950, was standard on more than 105,000 miles (168976km) of U.S. railroad track. In the same year a figure in excess of 90 per cent of all passenger transport was over railroad tracks equipped with block signals.

Reverting to the earliest days of railroad construction in the U.S.A., it is necessary to appreciate that one of the most immediate problems to be overcome by the constructors of the first U.S. railroads was that of moving into almost wholly unknown territory as soon as the railroads started to develop away from the country's longer-established coastal regions. Here the process of basic mapping as a first step and detail surveying as a second became paramount to ensure that the best possible course for the railroad was established.

The process of surveying was undertaken in carefully defined stages. In the first stage, which had to be completed before any further progress was made, the railroad's engineer-in-chief had to make a visual reconnaissance to find and fix the general trend of the direction that the railroad would take. Then followed the second stage, which involved the instrument survey of the proposed route: a lead flagman marked out the approximate route and was followed by the transitman, a team to record the distances and angles involved, and the leveller to measure the elevations and inclines of the selected route. At the same time, this forward planning team was followed by the first construction teams, whose initial task it was to clear trees and undergrowth. On occasion, a topographer was also employed to make a visual record of the

The boring of Northern Pacific Railroad's 9,850-ft (3000-m) Stampede Tunnel in the Cascade mountain range of the Washington Territory was conducted on two levels and from both the eastern and western slopes between 1886 and 1888, the first electric power plant in the west of the U.S.A. being built expressly to bring light to the construction This work also marked the introduction of Ingersoll air-operated drilling equipment to that part of the country.

landscape, including the hills and rivers that might have relevance to the ultimate selection of the route.

Inevitably, of course, this ideal arrangement had to be adapted to particular circumstances and, after the Americans embarked on a serious consideration of how to create transcontinental railroads, the process became altogether more lengthy and considerably more complex, but was still based on the same fundamental processes. When the notion of building a transcontinental railroad was emerging from a theoretical concept toward a practical possibility during the 1850s, the U.S. Army's Corps of Engineers undertook a series of surveys and, after almost a year, produced 13 illustrated volumes of reports on the country its teams had examined: however, the information presented in these volumes was more concerned with the geography of the western regions of the U.S.A. than with the practical matters associated with the establishment of the best route for a railroad.

The course finally adopted for the eastward end of the line was that surveyed by Theodore Judah and his employers of the Southern Pacific Railroad. Even then, however, the course of this first planned route was steadily varied in accordance with the willingness or otherwise of the communities along the way to contribute to the construction costs of the railroad. And while the westward route of the Union Pacific Railroad was generally that of the old Mormon Trail to Utah, the surveyors and construction teams had to bear in mind constantly that trails passable by ox-teams and horse-drawn wagons

Snow was piled high at the side of the track in the Cascade mountain range on 6 January 1893, when two Great Northern Railway officials drove the final spike into a roughly-hewn cross tie to complete a continuous track from the 'twin cities' of Minnesota to Puget Sound. Pomp and ceremony were ignored as workmen on the track-laying rig lowered the last rails into ties. James Hill, the founder of the Great Northern Railway, who pushed the lines across prairies, along river valleys and over the Rockies, was not there for the historic event. As the heavy maul pounded the last spike, cheers rose from the workmen, but these were drowned by sharp cracks of a six-shooter and the shrill whistles of work- train locomotives that reverberated throughout the Skykomish Valley. The site of the impromptu ceremony was near the present western portal of the 7.79-mile (1254-km) Cascade Tunnel that was completed in 1929. The first train over the tortuous switchbacks of the Great Northern Railway's original Cascade crossing arrived in Seattle on 8 January 1893, but it was not until the following June that a regularly-scheduled passenger service was inaugurated between St. Paul, Minnesota, and the Pacific coast.

RIGHT
Locomotive No. 14 of the East Broad Top
Railroad.

OPPOSITE
The fact that the rolling-stock equipment of
one railroad operator often finds it way onto
the tracks of another, for perfectly legitimate
commercial reasons, is indicated by the fact
that this train of the Northern Pacific Railroad
is being hauled by a locomotive of the
Pennsylvania Railroad.

The Northern Pacific Railroad's locomotive No. 398 hauls a short passenger train over this extraordinarily impressive multi-tier wooden trestle bridge some time in 1900. Located between Culdesac and Grangeville, Idaho, the bridge was later replaced by a steel structure.

were often unsuitable for the purposes of railroad operations.

Of the features hampering the advance of the Union Pacific Railroad, one of the most difficult was the Black Hills spur of the Rocky Mountains between Cheyenne and Laramie in the southern part of Wyoming. Grenville Dodge, who had commanded in the U.S. Army's campaigns against the Native Americans in this area during 1865–66, before his appointment as the Union Pacific Railroad's chief engineer, went to the difficulty both of gathering detailed reports on the region and of undertaking his own exploration, but had little success in finding the right type of gap accessible from the east until a chance encounter with some Native Americans provided the breakthrough he was seeking.

During one journey, Dodge and his small party were passing south along the crest of the range from the Cheyenne Pass, while the main body of his command, returning from the Powder river expedition, continued along the trail at the foot of the mountains. Cut off from the main body by a band of Native Americans, Dodge and his party fought their way down from the crest and by fortune found a ridge extending in an unbroken line to the plains below. It was the perfect route by which the railroad could climb into the mountains, and enabled the Union Pacific Railroad to cross over the Black Hills by the pass that Dodge named after his old commander, General William T. Sherman. The summit of the pass, lying at an altitude of more than 8,000ft (2440m), was the highest point reached by an American railroad up to that time.

Moving from the particulars of route-finding in one instance to the generality of laying out any railroad, it should be noted that in the orthodox system (assuming there could ever have been such a system) the chief engineer used the detailed information gathered by the instrument-surveying party for the final determination of the route whose basic line had already been established. This decision might be based on the chief engineer's opinion as the option most likely to provide the easiest course, or on his belief that established towns or the location of physical features such as mountain passes or bridging points on rivers offered the possibilities he thought best for railroad construction. Often, though, the chief engineer might find that he had little room for manoeuvre in the way in

The westbound Oriental Limited prestige service was the first Great Northern Railway train to pass through the newly completed Cascade Tunnel, the date being 12 January 1929. The electric locomotive is shown breaking through a picture of a mountain scene which covered the tunnel's western portal for the opening ceremonies. The tunnel was an extraordinary engineering achievement completed under exceptionally difficult conditions, but the tunnel was deemed too long for trains hauled by steam locomotives.

OPPOSITE
Locomotive No. 4440 of the Baltimore &
Ohio Railroad works its freight train over a
typical river bridge built on stone and
concrete piers, in the process passing a
similar train proceeding in the opposite
direction.

LEFT
This strange-looking 4-4-0 locomotive was
an inspection type with forward platforms and
viewing positions to allow a visual inspection
of the track before the locomotive passed
over it.

which he could reach his decision, for this
might be dictated by the nature or primary
economics of the area, such as a mine in a
mountainous area to be reached, which

required the adoption of the only possible
course regardless of adverse factors.

It was of critical importance that the right
course was chosen for, while it was possible

for poor construction work to be remedied at a
later time, the realization that the wrong
course had been adopted might mean that line
already constructed had to be abandoned and a

A steam-hauled train passes over a long bridge built on piers rising from the bed of a wide river.

LEFT
The Northern Pacific Railroad's locomotive No. 328 passes over the St. Croix river, Wisconsin, on a high trestle bridge.

Though roundhouses almost invariably were of just that configuration in the early days of American steam locomotion, this later changed, as indicated here.

new section built, with very adverse effects on the economics and schedule of the construction programme. The two most decisive elements in the chief engineer's selection of the route were the grades and the curves, which should both be as gentle as it was possible to find.

The severity of grades gave the chief engineer little scope for trade-offs. It is a fact

that there is a low coefficient of friction between a smooth metal wheel and a smooth metal rail, which makes for operating efficiency on the flat, whereas a typical 40-ton car moving at 60mph (97km) rolls to a halt only after about 5 miles (8 km); but this low coefficient of friction also adversely affects the locomotive's tractive effort and imposes a severe limit on the steepness of the gradient

the locomotive can climb before its driving wheels start to slip. Moreover, even if the locomotive can climb the gradient, its tractive power is severely curtailed.

U.S. railroads were generally content to adopt curves that were tighter than those of their European counterparts: in the U.S.A. a curve with a 300-ft (91.5-m) radius was relatively common, but in Europe a main-line

This inspection train of the Atchison, Topeka & Santa Fe is headed by the 4-6-0 locomotive No. 174, which was made by the Brooks Locomotive Works in 1891 and scrapped by the railroad at its Topeka yard in 1926.

curve with a 1,000ft (305m) of tighter radius was decidedly uncommon. The tightness of the curves on U.S. railroads was one of the primary reasons for the development and adoption of the pivoted leading truck and the equalized suspension of the driving wheels typically found in U.S. locomotives. These two features were embodied in the so-called 'standard' locomotive type that was adopted universally in the early years of the railroads.

In practice coinciding with the completion of this first main phase of the development of the U.S. railroad system, there appeared the steam locomotive type that was to remain unaltered for the following half of the century and which would serve as the 'workhorse' of U.S. railroads until virtually the close of the 19th century. The Standard locomotive, as the type came to be called, was not created as such in a single bold technical move, but was rather the result of an evolutionary process characterized by the creation of a number of less successful contenders with differing wheel arrangements. In 1842 Baldwin introduced an interesting eight-coupled freight locomotive, initially for the Central Railroad of Georgia and the Philadelphia & Reading:

this unit combined greater tractive effort through the addition of more driving wheels and improved flexibility to cater for the general irregularity of the track of the period through the mounting of the two front pairs of driving wheels on flexible beams and the use of ball-and-socket couplings to the two rear pairs of driving wheels mounted in a rigid frame.

The most common, indeed the virtually universal, locomotive came to be known as the 'American' type, this having a 4-4-0 wheel arrangement with a leading truck and equalized driving wheels which offered the best possible mix of tractive power and flexibility. The configuration was created in the 1830s, and was soon developed into its increasingly standard form by the addition of a wide firebox for burning wood, the standard fuel of the early days. Other features were the adjustment of the rear of the boiler into a conical shape to fit the firebox, the single large headlamp, the substantial 'balloon-stack' chimney, sandbox and bell disposed along the top of the boiler and smokebox, and the addition of a cab at the rear to provide weather protection for the engineer and fireman. This became the standard locomotive of the railroads that came to criss-cross the U.S.A. from north to south and from east to west.

Whatever the dynamics of the locomotives for which he was planning the track, the chief engineer had to bear in mind the all-important economic fact that track optimized for haulage by being straight and level demands more and therefore costlier construction effort than track that follows the contours of the terrain: straight, flat track

OPPOSITE
Well after the introduction of electric and diesel locomotion, this steam-hauled excursion service passes over a stone-built bridge as it recreates the 'flavour' of an age now long past.

LEFT
This photograph, taken in 1875 some four years after the structure's completion, reveals the bridge of the Baltimore & Ohio Railroad over the Ohio river between Benwood, West Virginia, and Bellaire, Ohio. The high central span was required to provide navigation room for the river traffic on this navigable river, whose water can vary in height quite dramatically.

demands that cuttings be driven through hills and that hollows be traversed with the aid of embankments or viaducts. However, the labour of these tasks was trimmed first by the advent of the steam shovel, which was the initial type of powered construction equipment, and second by the simplification of the task by the appearance of more capable earth-moving equipment: the use of such equipment could lower the cost of major

construction efforts, but could not remove them in their totality.

The art that complemented the scientific and technical skills of the great constructors was an ability to find the right blend in the conflicting factors of minimum construction cost and maximum operational efficiency. The capacity for finding these compromise solutions was in fact typical of U.S. railroad construction during the 19th century. The most

important single principles became the selection of the optimum route and the construction of the track as quickly and as cheaply as possible. Detours were readily accepted for a host of reasons, not least to reach or avoid local communities which showed an unwillingness or a reluctance to help fund the construction effort; the bypassing of obstacles was deemed permissible even if it made the line longer or

less amenable to higher operating speeds. Once trains were running and revenue was being generated, then it was time to improve the route and upgrade the track.

The classic example of this latter concept must be the elimination of the original meeting point of the Union Pacific and Central Pacific railroads at Promontory Point in Utah: in 1904 the Central Pacific Railroad's successor, the Southern Pacific, built a new 132-mile (212-km) line across the Great Salt Lake to miss Promontory Point, lop 44 miles (71km) from the length of the original route, and reduce the number of severe grades and tight curves. Another notable but later improvement of this nature, known as a cut-off, was effected by the Denver & Rio Grande Western Railroad to reduce the distance between Denver and the west via Salt Lake City. The original route involved a lengthy swing to the south via Pueblo, but the 1928 completion of the 6-mile (10-km) Moffat Tunnel between Bond and Dotsero created the Dotsero cut-off, trimming 65 miles (105km) from the route.

In 1929 the Cascade Tunnel, on the Great Northern's line through the Cascade mountain range in Washington state, was completed as the longest tunnel in the U.S.A. This was the second major improvement on this section of the Great Northern's line after a 2.6-mile (4.2-km) tunnel was completed in 1900 to avoid the original switchbacks through the mountains. The line still had severe approach grades, however, and with the competition of the Milwaukee Road on the line to Seattle, the Great Northern Railway began another step in its programme of improvement: this resulted

OPPOSITE
The Union Pacific Railroad's locomotive No. 2709 crosses the Santa Ana river, California, in the course of its last run on 17 March 1954.

LEFT
A Chinese-built Mikado-type locomotive, imported to the U.S.A. specifically for the operation of tourist and nostalgia services by the Boone & Scenic Railroad, heads over a high bridge.

OPPOSITE
A train of the Baltimore & Ohio Railroad is transported by a Brooklyn & Eastern vessel off New York City.

LEFT
A railroad train is prepared for loading onto a special rail-equipped vessel of the same operator for a water crossing too long or deep for the construction of a bridge.

in the 7.8-mile (12.5-km) Cascade Tunnel, the electrification of some 71 miles (114km) of track, and a 10-mile (16-km) reduction in the overall distance through elimination of several miles of snowsheds, older tunnels and grades of more than 2 per cent.

Turning again to the basic processes of creating the U.S. railroad industry in its earliest times, the steps that followed the completion of route planning and surveying were the drafting of plans, the obtaining of rights of way, and the division of the programme into elements whose completion

could be offered to subcontractors.

As practical work on the construction of the railroad was begun, the first task was the grading of the trackway, the task having been simplified as far as possible by the alignment of the trackway in a way that the spoil from any cutting could be used to create the embankments that filled dips and hollows. Culverts were constructed through the base of embankments to provide free passage of lateral watercourses, and on level ground ditches were dug on either side of the graded trackway to keep the roadbed well above the

surface, improving drainage and minimizing the likelihood of snow blocking the track.

With the trackway and associated roadbed laid out, the next task was the placing of the ties which supported the rails. In early days various alternative ideas, including piles sunk in the ground and stone sills laid along the surface, saw a measure of experimentation, but wooden ties were soon accepted as the optimum solution. As techniques improved, it was customary to undertake a chemical treatment of the wooden ties to extend their lives, usually with the pressure application of

very hot creosote. A system of steel ties was developed by the Carnegie company, which was responsible for so much of the steel used in the U.S. railroad industry later in the 19th century, that the company was able to lower prices by an appreciable amount; such ties were used for a time on the Bessemer & Lake Erie Railroad early in the 20th century. Wooden ties offered a number of advantages, however, and were only later complemented (but never supplanted) by concrete ties.

Once the ties had been placed, the rails were laid. Iron rails, weighing just 30lb/yard (14.88kg/m), were standard in the early days of U.S. railroads, but the demands of faster

and heavier trains meant that the weight (and the strength and durability) of the iron rails was increased. Moreover, in the 1870s rolled steel rails became increasingly common. At first, each rail was attached to its ties with just four spikes, but as the weight of trains increased the number of spikes was increased to provide greater support. Before the ready availability of the specialized machinery that allowed a comparatively high level of automation to be introduced, the task of laying track was extremely manpower-intensive. Even so, careful and skilled organization allowed extraordinary results to be achieved: between April and October 1887, for example,

ABOVE
Hauling a train of 33 cars, this is the Denver & Rio Grande Railroad's 2-8-8-2 locomotive No. 3603 near the Moffat Tunnel on the main line near Scenic, Colorado, on the route linking Denver, Colorado, and Salt Lake City, Utah. The whole assembly is negotiating a graded curve on a high embankment.

RIGHT
A New York, Ontario & Western locomotive No. 455 takes on coal from a special overhead coaling gantry.

OPPOSITE
The past preserved: the 4-4-0 Standard- or American-type locomotive *William Crooks* in the museum at Duluth, Minnesota.

Details of the Alco-built 4-6-0 locomotive
No. 328 of the Northern Pacific Railroad.

OPPOSITE
Details of the same locomotive's smokestack,
steam dome and sand dome.

the St. Paul Minneapolis & Manitoba Railway
lengthened its system through Dakota and
Montana by 545 miles (877km) with the aid of
a 10,000-man workforce. A great deal of work
then had to be completed before the road was
fully complete, but the line was already
generating revenue even before these final
stages had been accomplished. Some 20 years
later, the Milwaukee Road had been built
across 2,300 miles (3700km) of Montana,
Idaho and Washington states in just three
years.

The laying of the track was just the first
stage, of course, for the laid track then
required constant maintenance including,
under ideal conditions, a twice-daily visual
inspection of the busiest sections for the
detection, at a stage as early as possible, of
any misalignment or other such faults. One of
the primary reasons for the superiority of the
Pennsylvania Railroad in the last part of the
19th century and first part of the 20th century
was the high level of importance it attached to
intensive track maintenance, complemented
on an annual basis by an inspection of the
whole road.

Despite the efforts of the planning and
surveying teams in the creation of a route that
was as flat and straight as possible, railroad
construction inevitably required that bridges
be constructed to support the track safely over
rivers, gorges and narrow valleys, and also
over depressions too deep for the effective use
of an embankment. As with other aspects of
railroad construction, the U.S. railroad
builders soon developed a distinctive type of
bridge somewhat different from those
employed by the Europeans. Stone arched

While the steam locomotive possessed an undeniable mechanical grandeur, the diesel locomotive offers more economical running and easier maintenance, and at the same time needs only a much smaller infrastructure to support its operations. These are steam and diesel locomotives at Oyster Bay, New York.

bridges, common in Europe, were indeed built for North American railroads in regions in which stone was readily available and durability was considered important. The approach to the Harlem Valley bridge, for example, was supported by stone spans of 60ft (18.3m), and the lines to and from the depot of the Pennsylvania Railroad in Philadelphia were carried by a series of brick arches, each of which spanned one street. However, the very substantial number and widths of the rivers and other gaps that had to be crossed as

the railroads spread from the U.S.A.'s eastern seaboard, together with shortages of the right type of stone and the masons to work it, made such bridges impractical for the vast majority of bridging requirements. The material that was most readily available was wood, and all over the country there were men experienced in the use of this material for major structures. So the wooden trestle bridge became standard all over North America. As it expanded across Maryland, the Baltimore & Ohio Railroad reached Harpers Ferry in 1834 but had to wait

for two years before a wooden bridge could be built across this obstacle, so allowing further progress. An odd feature of this bridge, it is worth noting, is the fact that it incorporated a junction with the branch line to Washington in its centre, above the river. The bridge was soon destroyed by flood waters, however, and the railroad decided that the probability of repeated flood made it sensible to abandon the concept of a wooden structure in favour of a metal bridge, which was constructed in 1852.

Seasoned timber at least two years old

At rest, a steam locomotive possesses a particular resonance of powerful machinery waiting for action, this resonance being compounded of heat, the hissings and low rumblings of the steam-generating system, and the smell of steam, oil, smoke and hot metal.

On a double-deck girder bridge located in Richmond, Virginia, a train of the Chesapeake & Ohio Railroad passes at right angles over a train of the Seaboard Line, itself passing above a train of the Southern Railway.

was the ideal material for the safe construction of bridges, but as the railroads expanded in cut-throat competition into the western regions of the U.S.A., their construction teams had to face the problem that the speed of their advance was outstripping any capacity for the cutting and adequate seasoning of timber along the line of progress. To complete the track and allow the start of revenue-earning services, therefore, they often had recourse to unseasoned timber. As well as providing a somewhat lower level of durability, such timber was highly susceptible to shrinkage and warping. A solution to this problem was found in the so-called Howe truss, which incorporated screws in the joints, which allowed maintenance teams to make compensatory adjustments to offset the timber's natural movement.

So far as the railroads were concerned, the most important advantage of the timber trestle bridge was that its basic simplicity opened the way for construction by a semi-skilled workforce using simple tools and materials that were readily available on a local basis. Thus timber was the standard constructional material in the early period of railroad expansion. What could not be ignored, though, was the fact that while on the one hand the use of timber speeded and made cheaper the process of building the railroad, on the other hand timber structures demanded considerably more maintenance than stone or masonry bridges. Wooden trestle bridges therefore had to be inspected for rot and repaired frequently, and the short life of unseasoned timber also meant that major parts of the bridges needed regular replacement if they were to retain an

adequate structural integrity. For this reason, therefore, wood was gradually replaced by iron as the primary bridge-building material from the 1870s, which also reflected the fact that the railroads had started to reach a certain level of operational and technical maturity, the receipt of growing revenues providing the funds for the use of a material that was appreciated as offering greater long-term advantages.

But it should not be forgotten that it was the adoption of the timber trestle bridge that effectively permitted the huge expansion of the North American railroad system between the 1830s and 1870s. Such bridges were often of considerable size, moreover. By far the longest of them was the 20-mile (32-km) unit built in 1904 to cross the Great Salt Lake as part of the Lucin cut-off in the Southern Pacific Railroad's realignment to miss Promontory Point. This bridge was gradually supplanted by an embankment created by the tipping of earth over the sides, and the same basic tactic was used for the replacement of many other wooden trestle bridges. Considerably shorter, but much more imposing in purely visual terms, was the Great Trestle on the Colorado Midland Railroad's line in the Rocky Mountains. More than 1,000-ft (305-m) long, this was part of the great system of loops by which the track reached the Ivanhoe Pass and carried the line on a curve. The Great Trestle was abandoned in 1900.

Timber was also the primary structural medium used in the building of snowsheds on stretches of railroad running through mountain areas. The object of these, which had

comparatively steeply pitched roofs and extended out from a rock face past the track, was to prevent the line from being blocked by heavy snowfalls and also to protect them from destruction by avalanches. Snow and avalanches represented two very distinct hazards to railroad operations in mountainous regions. A single snow slide could often involve 100,000 tons of snow, so the construction and maintenance of snowsheds were vital to the continued operational viability of railroads. At one stage of its existence, the Central Pacific Railroad had 60 miles (97km) of snowsheds protecting its line across the Sierra Nevada in the eastern part of California.

To return to bridges: the basic feature was the truss, in structural terms a girder created by a framework of individual members. At first, trusses were built up of plates in the form of a box, as employed by Robert Stephenson, the great British engineer, in the classic Victoria bridge over the St. Lawrence river at Montreal. While bridges of this sort were notable for their strength, they were also notable for the high levels of maintenance they required, so American bridge builders generally preferred the suspension bridge, which demanded less in the way of both materials and maintenance. The classic early example of the suspension bridge for the purposes of North American railroads was that at Niagara Falls, which was completed in 1855. But suspension bridges were not built as extensively for railroad service as might at first have seemed likely, for in general they proved torsionally flexible, a problem that was overcome in the Niagara Falls bridge by

RIGHT
A fireman cleans out the ash pan of
locomotive No. 8419 of the Boone

creating the span as two floors trussed together.

As they were cheaper, metal pins in pre-formed holes were preferred to rivets in the construction of iron bridges, and wide gaps were bridged by the use of a series of trusses aligned end-to-end, their junctions supported by masonry or metal-truss piers. With their foundations made from massive wooden piles driven into the riverbed or masonry worked inside a coffer dam from which the water had been pumped, such piers often had as much if not most of their overall length below the water. The size and varying water levels of many American rivers presented particular problems in many cases. During the late 1890s, for example, the Illinois Central Railroad's engineers built a bridge over the Ohio river at Cairo with an allowance of 60ft (18.3m) between the river's high- and low-water points. The bridge over the Mississippi

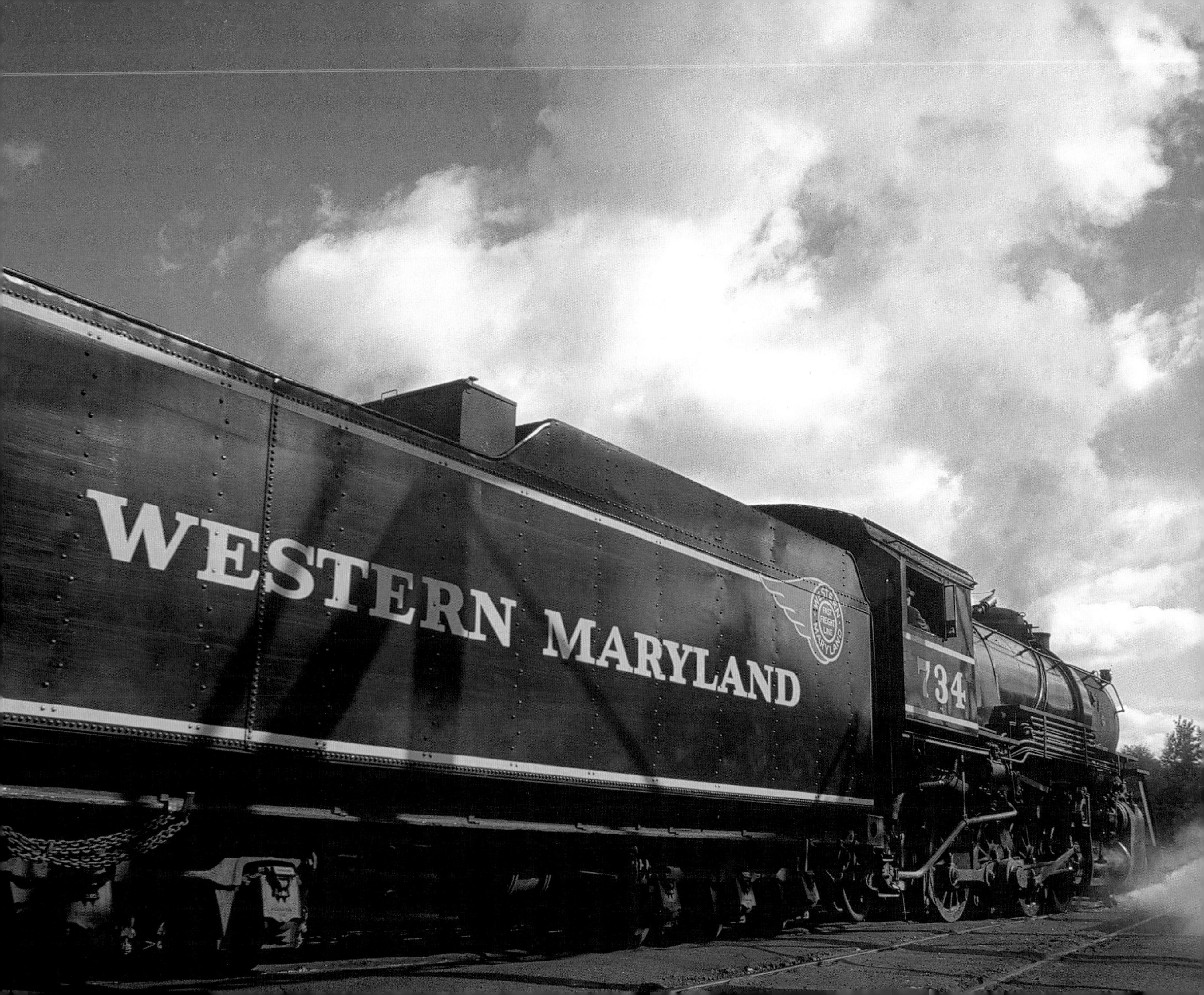
WESTERN MARYLAND
WESTERN FAST FREIGHT LINE MARYLAND
734

The Northern Pacific Railroad's locomotive No. 328 is caught by the camera near Osceola, Wisconsin.

river at St. Louis was based on piers, two-thirds of whose length was under the water.

When it is impractical to use piers, as for instance where it is impossible to build foundations at the right locations to provide support at intermediate points of a bridge's full length, the greater length of the unsupported span requires a truss of greater depth. The extreme example of this is the Metropolis bridge over the Ohio river at Paducah in Kentucky: built by the engineers of the Burlington Northern Railroad, this has a span of 720ft (219m) with a truss height of 110ft (33.5m). Another aspect of using end-to-end trusses is that at crossings where numerous piers can be provided, there is no practical limit to the length of the bridge that can be built. The Huey P. Long bridge of the Southern Pacific Railroad over the Mississippi river at New Orleans, Louisiana, is 4.4-miles (7.1-km) long, yet has a maximum single-span length of just 790ft (241m).

When it was impossible to build adequate piers for a suspension bridge, the engineer had to fall back on an alternative, of which the cantilever bridge was the favourite. This type of structure is based on the use of self-supporting elements built out from the ends to support a smaller girder structure in the centre. Cantilever structures are employed for the widest river crossings, and the longest-span railroad bridge of all, the Quebec bridge of the Canadian National Railway Company over the St. Lawrence river, is such a one. A design fault caused one of the incomplete cantilevers to collapse in 1907, and after work had been restarted

during 1910 the central span was dropped in the river during the first attempt to put it into position in 1916, before it was finally fixed in 1917. Other notable cantilever bridges in Canada include the Lachine bridge over the St. Lawrence river at Montreal and the bridge at Niagara.

The first cantilever railroad bridge to be built in North America, however, was that over the Kentucky river at Cincinnati in Ohio. Here a canyon 1,200-ft (366-m) wide

and 275-ft (84-m) deep channels water whose surface height can change by as much as 55ft (16.76m). To carry the railroad across this obstacle, the engineers started with a pair of 177-ft (54-m) iron piers on masonry foundations in the river, and then added three 375-ft (114-m) cantilever spans to bridge the gaps between the banks and the piers at a height of about 275ft (84m) above the river's mean bottom.

Steam locomotives have a prodigious appetite and thirst for coal and water respectively. The thirst was quenched by the provision of water towers at strategic locations on every longer-distance operator's lines.

RIGHT
Locomotive No. 4442, a 0-6-0 unit of the Union Pacific Railroad, is seen at Las Vegas, Nevada.

OPPOSITE
American railroads were generally happy to have their trains negotiate curves of far tighter radius than were their European counterparts of the same time. Here locomotive No. 484 hauls a tourist train of the Cumbres & Toltec Railroad through the S-bend of the Tanglefoot Curve at Cumbres Pass.

CHAPTER SIX
THE STEAM LOCOMOTIVE

Fabricated in the north-east of England in 1831, the *John Bull* 0-4-0 (later 4-2-0) locomotive operated on the pioneering Camden & Amboy Railroad in New Jersey. The locomotive is now a permanent exhibit in the Smithsonian Institute, Washington, D.C., while the railroad was absorbed into the Pennsylvania Railroad that became a core element of the Pennsylvania Central Railroad and finally Conrail. (See also page 19.)

It was on 9 August 1829 that the first locomotive intended for commercial service in the U.S.A. made its first American run, an event which took place at Honesdale in the state of Pennsylvania on the Delaware & Hudson Canal Company's light track of the 51-in (1.295-m) gauge horse-operated tramway, linking the canal with the mines at Carbondale. This locomotive was the *Stourbridge Lion* (page 15), an 0-4-0 unit built by Foster & Rastrick of Stourbridge, near Birmingham in the midlands of England. The locomotive weighed more than twice the figure promised by the maker when Horatio Allen visited it during the previous year to place the order; consequently its effect on the track was so damaging that it was decided not to put the *Stourbridge Lion* into service as a locomotive, work being found for it instead as a stationary engine. The locomotive had a sister, the *Agenoria*, that had been good enough to perform successfully on the Shutt End Railway near Stourbridge in England for more than 25 years, so it is possible to deduce that the *Stourbridge Lion* would have done well as a locomotive had it been permitted to do so on stronger track.

The two Stourbridge locomotives's driving mechanism was in effect a pair of single-cylinder beam engines, the beams and linkage effectively reducing the stroke of the cylinders from 36 to 27in (914 to 686mm). Loose eccentrics engaged with stops on the rear axle to operate the valves when the engine was running, and there was provision to move them by hand for starting. The basic

design owed much more to William Hedley, the designer of the *Puffing Billy*, than to the designers of the celebrated Stephenson family. In 1829 the *Puffing Billy* had been running for 16 years, so the *Stourbridge Lion* was built to a basic concept that had been well proven in service, but its operating system was designed not to triumph over the direct-drive system, which was that used by

This is a not altogether accurate replica of the *Tom Thumb*, a 0-2-2 locomotive made by Peter Cooper in 1830 for the Baltimore & Ohio Railroad, constructed for the Baltimore & Ohio Railroad's 'Centenary Fair of the Iron Horse' in 1927. (See also page 15 et seq.)

all but the tiniest minority of steam locomotives built after this time; in fact, some 120 years were to pass before locomotives with near-vertical cylinders and complicated transmission systems would supersede the Stephenson concept.

In practical terms, more important history was made on 15 January 1831, the day when the first full-size steam locomotive to be built in the U.S.A. entered service. This was the *Best Friend of Charleston* (page 20), which

hauled services on the U.S.A.'s first commercial steam railway, the South Carolina Rail Road. The *Best Friend of Charleston* can thus be claimed as the real progenitor of approximately 175,000 later steam locomotives manufactured for U.S. service. Designed by E.L. Miller, the engineer of the South Carolina Rail Road, the *Best Friend of Charleston* was a 0-4-0 locomotive manufactured at the West Point Foundry in New York late in 1830; among its technical

features were a vertical boiler, a well tank built as an integral part of the locomotive, four coupled wheels and two modestly inclined cylinders. With the exception of the coupled wheels, none of the locomotive's design concepts was adopted generally, but the locomotive was nonetheless quite successful, even though the limitations of Miller's basic design were recognized. Consequently, the next locomotive to be built for the South Carolina adhered to the same basic concept

181

THE STEAM LOCOMOTIVE

The replica of the *Tom Thumb* is seen near Ellicott's Mill, near Washington, D.C., in a reconstruction of the original locomotive's pioneering run.

only in its mechanical parts, and introduced the first horizontal boiler to be made in the U.S.A. Even so, the original design could handle a train of five cars carrying more than 50 passengers at 20mph (32km/h).

The *Best Friend of Charleston* has one other claim to fame, although this was of a somewhat tragic nature. Annoyed by the noise of steam escaping from the safety valves, the fireman was in the habit of tying down the lever which controlled the valves. In June 1831 he did this once too often and the boiler exploded and killed him. In time, tamper-proof valves became the legally-enforced norm. The locomotive was later rebuilt with a new boiler and re-entered service after it was rechristened, appropriately, as the *Phoenix*. By 1834 the South Carolina Rail Road extended the whole 154-mile (248-km) distance from Charleston to Hamburg, just across the river from the city of Augusta, Georgia; when opened, this was the longest railroad in the world by quite a considerable margin.

In the annals of steam-drawn passenger travel, one of the seminal figures was John B. Jervis, for it was he who in 1832 introduced into the locomotive the concept of the pivoted leading truck or bogie. This had been suggested to him by Robert Stephenson when Jervis visited him in England. A locomotive of which very few details have survived, this little 4-2-0 unit, originally known as the *Experiment* (page 24) but later as the *Brother Jonathan*, was the locomotive in question, and was made by the West Point Foundry for the Mohawk & Hudson River Railroad. Among the locomotive's features was a somewhat small boiler of the Planet type designed by

With its vertical boiler and one-cylinder engine, the *Tom Thumb* was little more than a working toy, yet managed to haul a boat-shaped car carrying the directors of the Baltimore & Ohio Railroad all the way from Baltimore to Ellicott's Mill, then part of the way back before coming to a halt after the breakage of the belt drive for the fan drawing the draught through the firebox.

A bridge constructed in 1852 by Wendell Bollman over the Monorgahela river near Fairmont, West Virginia, reveals the type of truss structure favoured by many of the early railroad pioneers. The bridge was initially a single-track structure but was then revised for the carriage of two tracks in 1912 and remained in use up to the 1930s.

Robert Stephenson, and the provision of space between the sides of the firebox and the main frames (outside the driving wheels) for the connecting rods. The driving wheels were located behind the firebox. None of these latter features became standard, but the four-wheel bogie transformed the comfort of steam-drawn passenger trains and became wholly standard in evolving forms.

The concept of the leading truck was to provide guidance by having two wheels pressing against the outer rail of curves as near as possible in a tangential attitude: for any particular radius or a curve, or even at a kink in the track, the bogie would automatically adopt an angle that ensured that the three contact points between the wheel and the rail on each side would lie correctly on the curve – especially significant on the light, rough tracks of the time. The *Brother Jonathan* demonstrated very clearly the soundness of the principle on which the concept was based, and the leading truck became standard on U.S. locomotives for many years. The *Brother Jonathan* was a successful locomotive in its own right, moreover, and after later conversion to a 4-4-0 layout had a long and productive career.

First chartered in 1827, the first section of the Baltimore & Ohio Railroad was to have been a horse-drawn line, at least over the first section between Baltimore and Ellicott's Mill near Washington. However, once a short length of track had been laid at the Baltimore end, a certain Peter Cooper offered to demonstrate the use of steam traction for the task. Cooper's *Tom Thumb* locomotive (page 181 et seq.) was little more than a proof of concept model with a single-cylinder engine and a vertical boiler. The diminutive machine hauled a single boat-shaped car in which the directors of the Baltimore & Ohio travelled, the event being staged as a race with a horse-drawn vehicle on 28 August 1830.

The 0-2-2 *Tom Thumb* did well on the outward leg of the trip, but lost the battle on the return, when the belt driving the fan used to draw the fire unfortunately broke. Even so, the real victory went to the steam locomotive when the Baltimore & Ohio Railroad's leadership decided to make its operation a steam railroad in the future. The sequel to the trials of the *Tom Thumb* was that the directors of the Baltimore & Ohio Railroad decided to run a competition, open only to American manufacturers, to find the best practical steam locomotive in trials similar to those in which Stephenson's *Rocket* had prevailed in England.

The works of George and Robert Stephenson, of Newcastle-upon-Tyne in north-east England, was once the world leader in the design and manufacture of steam locomotives. The Camden & Amboy Railroad, a predecessor of the celebrated Pennsylvania Railroad, decided in 1830 to order from this manufacturer a small 0-4-0 locomotive based on the Stephensons's well-proven Planet design, bearing in mind that before this time the railroad had relied on horse-drawn services. The resulting locomotive was the *John Bull* (pages 19 and 180), which arrived by sea in Philadelphia during 1831. After further shipment to Bordentown, New Jersey, the locomotive was assembled by the railroad's master mechanic, a young man named Isaac Dripps; here was a man less well known than he should have been as he was responsible for the first use on a locomotive of a headlight, bell and cowcatcher. Although only 22 when appointed, Dripps had had a successful apprenticeship with Thomas & Holloway, which was a manufacturer of steam engines for ships. Dripps went on to become superintendent of motive power to the Pennsylvania Railroad at its Altoona workshops.

The *John Bull* made an initial demonstration run on 12 November 1831, but steam operations did not begin as a regular feature of the railroad's schedule for more than another year, largely as a result of the requirement for the track to be strengthened and improved; the interval was also used for modification of the locomotive. Dripps's cowcatcher was somewhat different from those that emerged later on, for it was carried on its own pair of wheels and as such was a primitive kind of leading truck. The locomotive's coupling rods, with outside cranks, must have been the source of problems, for they were removed, so turning the locomotive from a 0-4-0 into a 4-2-0. A cab was later added, for the 1830s was not a time when crew comfort was considered very seriously. A feature not of Stephenson origin was the circular firebox to a pattern similar to that of Edward Bury, engineer of the London & Birmingham Railway. This item and the 'planet' features were very successful, and the locomotive ran in service until 1866. It even ran to the Columbian Exposition at Chicago in 1893 under its own steam; even more remarkably, the oldest operable locomotive in the World celebrated its 150th anniversary with another run.

RIGHT
The water glass was a simple yet vital item of equipment in all steam locomotives, allowing the driver to see easily and quickly the level of the water in his locomotive's boiler.

FAR RIGHT
Designed by Joseph Harrison and made in Philadelphia during 1836 by Garret & Eastwick for the Beaver Meadow Railroad, the *Hercules* was a 4-4-0 locomotive that turned the scales at some 30,000lb (13608kg) without its tender. The locomotive marked an important step in the development of such machines, for it was the direct precursor of the Standard- or American-type of 4-4-0 locomotive.

FAR RIGHT
Now in the museum of the Baltimore & Ohio Railroad, the locomotive known as the *Atlantic* is in fact the *Andrew Jackson*, seventh of the operator's 1832 Grasshopper-type units, revised to look like the original *Atlantic*. This was the first steam locomotive to enter Washington in the year of its introduction. (See also page 23.)

During 1831, steam trains began to operate on the first part of what would become the New York Central Railroad, namely the 14-mile (22.5-km) Mohawk & Hudson Railroad connecting Albany and Schenectady. The operation had previously run horse-drawn services, but on 25 June it received its first steam locomotive, delivered by water up the Hudson river from the West Point Foundry. The locomotive was the *De Witt Clinton*, which was the third locomotive manufactured by this far-

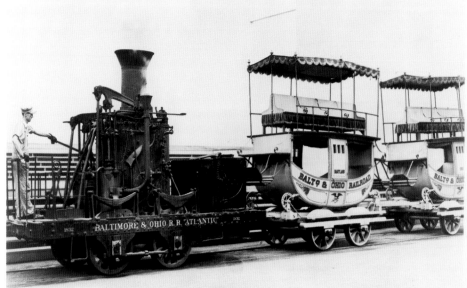

sighted engineering concern, whose previous pair of locomotives had been the *Best Friend of Charleston* and the *West Point* for the South Carolina Rail Road.

The *De Witt Clinton* (page 190) was a design by John B. Jervis, the Mohawk & Hudson's chief engineer and, in common with other early locomotives, required a measure of development before it could run effectively. The boiler was domeless and there was a tendency for water to boil over and enter the cylinders, but this problem was corrected by the addition of a dome; the exhaust pipes also needed some development before they would draw the fire properly. By 9 August all was ready for the first scheduled run, for which five stagecoach bodies mounted on railroad wheels and coupled with chains were the load. However, as the train set off, the slack action of the chains jerked the cars so strongly (particularly those at the rear) that the passengers were thoroughly alarmed. Moreover, the problems of trying to produce sufficient draft for the burning of coal in the firebox meant that wood was burned, and hot embers streamed from the chimney to settle onto and burn the passengers's clothes.

Despite the problems, the train rattled along, averaging 18mph (29km/h) but reaching a maximum of 25mph (40km/h), a hitherto unprecedented speed, one of the reasons for this being that the *De Witt Clinton* was very lightly built. The boiler was so small that there was space for the connecting rods between it and the timber frame as the cylinders were mounted at the rear. In overall terms the performance was excellent, and no damage was caused to the iron-strapped wooden rails, but the

A replica of an early car of the Baltimore & Ohio Railroad, of the type hauled by the Grasshopper-type locomotives and based, quite clearly, on the stagecoach bodies of the time, adapted with seating on the roof under an awning.

OPPOSITE

The *Thomas Jefferson* was the third of the Baltimore & Ohio Railroad's eventual total of 16 Grasshopper-type 0-4-0 locomotives.

LEFT

After the 1836 death of Phineas Davis, of the Davis & Gartner company that built the Baltimore & Ohio Railroad's first Grasshopper-type locomotives, the company became Gillingham & Winans. This continued to produce locomotives for the railroad, and in 1848 produced the 0-8-0 Camel-type to the design of Ross Winans. Some 20 of these locomotives were made up to 1852, but the type had a tendency to come off the rails at anything above very low speeds, and was then adapted by Samuel Hayes into the 'Hayes ten-wheeler'-type with a 4-6-0 configuration. This was more successful, and 10 were made in 1853–54.

locomotive's lightweight construction meant that durability was low, and the locomotive was taken out of service after a couple of years.

With the 0-4-0 Grasshopper units of the Baltimore & Ohio Railroad the steam locomotive in its form with a vertical boiler was developed further than on any other railroad. The Grasshopper designation was derived from the nature of the driving mechanism, which was a further development of that embodied in the *Stourbridge Lion*: vertical cylinders raised and lowered beams connected to a crankshaft, which in its turn was geared to a jackshaft, cranks on the end of this jackshaft then driving the wheels by connecting rods.

The first Grasshoppers were manufactured by the Davis & Gartner company, one of whose founders was Phineas Davis, the watchmaker who had built the vertically boilered *York*, which had won the Baltimore & Ohio

RIGHT
The *De Witt Clinton* (see also page 195) was built for the Mohawk & Hudson Railroad by the West Point Foundry. On 9 August 1831 it made the 17-mile (27.4-km) trip from Albany to Schenectady and back in less than one hour.

OPPOSITE
Lubricating locomotive parts at North Freedom, Wisconsin.

Railroad's locomotive competition of 1831. The company became locomotive builder to the Baltimore & Ohio Railroad and completed the *Atlantic* at its Mount Clare shops in September 1832, a locomotive that was quite successful and which regularly made a daily round trip of 80 miles (129km) between Baltimore and the inclines at Parr's Ridge. Durability was not yet a feature of locomotive design and construction, and together with the *Traveler*, the second Grasshopper also completed in

1832, the *Atlantic* was retired in 1835.

The first unit of an improved model was the *Arabian*, which was delivered in July 1834, and Grasshopper manufacture ended in 1837 after the completion of 16 locomotives. The details of the locomotives were improved, and included advanced concepts such as a fan driven by exhaust steam to draw the fire, a feed water heater and, in the last locomotives, sturdier construction. This meant that the weight of the locomotives virtually doubled

between the first and last units, the latter having the durability and reliability to remain in service for some 50 years, although latterly on switching service. Davis was tragically killed in an accident on the railroad in 1836: the company became Gillingham & Winans on his death.

The company thus came to acquire the name of Ross Winans, a horse-dealer who had been trying to sell animals to the Baltimore & Ohio Railroad at a time when the railroad was

switching entirely to steam locomotion. However, Winans was an astute operator who soon realized that the concept of horse traction was finished in terms of railroad applications, and therefore moved into the locomotive-building business. Winans began as the assistant engineer of machinery for the Baltimore & Ohio Railroad during 1831 and just four years, after buying into the company that had been renamed Gillingham & Winans, took over locomotive building for the Baltimore & Ohio Railroad in the Mount Clare shops from Phineas Davis. The new company completed its predecessor's Grasshopper programme, but by 1837 was ready to produce its own design, the Winan's Crab. With their horizontal cylinders, the Crabs moved one stage further along the road toward what would become the conventional steam locomotive. However, the separate crankshaft gearing and crankshaft remained, as did the vertical boiler. As the drive was geared, the cranks turned in the opposite direction to the wheels, producing what was deemed to be a 'crab-like' movement. The company manufactured two 0-4-0 Crabs, named *McKim* and *Mazeppa*, for the Baltimore & Ohio Railroad, delivered in 1838, and these lasted to 1863 and 1868 respectively.

Out of the Crabs came the relatively enormous 0-8-0 Mud-diggers. A few units of this type, that were essentially prototypes, were built for other railroads, but the definitive model with a proper locomotive boiler was built for the Baltimore & Ohio Railroad. The machinery configuration remained unaltered, however, with the

OPPOSITE LEFT
Headlight of Northern Pacific's No. 328.

LEFT
A Camelback locomotive.

exception of two more axles. The first Mud-digger was named *Hercules*, and another 13 such locomotives were later built between 1844 and 1847. Seven Mud-diggers were rebuilt completely on more conventional lines between 1853 and 1856, losing their names in the process, and the others worked on for many years, the last having been retired in 1880.

The last of these locomotives to be built was the *Mount Clare*, which was rather different from the others. The locomotive was constructed by the Baltimore & Ohio Railroad

itself, had no geared drive, and was inside-connected: the cylinders drove on to a jackshaft mounted between the second and third axles, the jackshaft being connected to the wheels by outside cranks and an additional pair of coupling rods.

A most important niche in the history of the development of the steam locomotive is occupied by the so-called Norris locomotives, for they were built to a basic design that took steam-powered railroad operations one step further along the technical line. William Norris had been building locomotives in

Philadelphia since 1831, although he was by trade a draper. After a few years in partnership with a Colonel Stephen Long, Norris established his own company, and by a time early in 1836 had manufactured seven locomotives. That same year he produced a 4-2-0 locomotive named the *Washington County Farmer* for the Philadelphia & Columbia Railroad. In arrangement, the new locomotive bore some resemblance to the *Brother Jonathan*, having a leading bogie, but the two cylinders were located outside the wheels and frames and the valves were on top

This 4-2-0 Sandusky-type locomotive was built by the Rogers Locomotive Works in 1837 for the Mad River & Lake Erie Railroad. It was among the first of all locomotives to have counter-balanced wheels.

of the cylinders. The driving wheels were ahead of the firebox rather than behind it, a change that increased the proportion of the engine's weight carried on them.

This created what was in effect the final stage before the emergence of the true steam locomotive for express passenger services. Of

earlier British and American locomotives, the *Northumbrian* had possessed the locomotive-type boiler and two outside cylinders, the *Planet* had introduced front-mounted cylinders, the *Vauxhall* had pioneered cylinders outside and at the front, Bury's locomotives had featured the bar frames, and

the *Brother Jonathan* had introduced the leading truck. In the *Washington County Farmer*, however, outside cylinders, bar frames and a leading truck were combined.

Chartered in 1827, the Baltimore & Ohio Railroad was the first U.S. railroad to carry both passenger and freight traffic, initially

The Pennsylvania Railroad's K4-class locomotive No. 5471, named *The General*, is caught by the camera approaching Chicago, Illinois, on 15 August 1939.

using horse-drawn trains. After trials with steam locomotion, this supplanted horse traction in 1834, initially with vertically-boilered Grasshopper units. The railroad reached the Ohio river in 1842, by means of a route that included a series of inclined planes worked by rope, but by this time the railroad

had appreciated the need for greater power than could be provided by vertically-boilered units. The railroad was impressed by the *Washington County Farmer* and requested Norris to manufacture eight essentially similar engines for its own services. The first of these was named the *Lafayette* and was completed

in 1837 as a 4-2-0 unit that was the initial Baltimore & Ohio Railroad locomotive with a horizontal boiler, in this instance in combination with a circular domed firebox, bar frames and, it is believed, cam-operated valves of a type designed by the company's own Ross Winans.

197

OPPOSITE
Locomotive No. 734, a 2-8-0 unit of the Consolidation class.

RIGHT
Locomotive No. 223 of the Long Island Railroad.

The *Lafayette* was followed in 1838 by three more units which, in the practice of the time, had names as well as numbers: these were the *Philip E. Thomas*, *J.W. Patterson* and *Wm. Cooke*, and they were followed in 1839 by the *Patapsco*, *Monocacy*, *Potomac* and *Pegasus*. The last of these to be retired in its original form was the *Pegasus*, in 1863, although the *Philip E. Thomas* was rebuilt as a 4-4-0 unit in 1848 and survived until 1870.

After 1839 the Baltimore & Ohio Railroad bought 4-4-0 locomotives to serve a line that by that time extended 178 miles (286km) from Baltimore. Within the limitation of the low adhesive weight inevitable with just a single driving axle, the Norris locomotive was very successful, operational experience revealing significantly better performance at reduced fuel consumption than could be managed by other locomotives of the period. The Norris

4-2-0 locomotives were also reliable by the standards of the time, and therefore offered the economic advantages of requiring comparatively little in the way of repairs.

It is worth noting that Norris also built a similar locomotive for the Champlain & St. Lawrence Railroad in Canada; this unit has the distinction of being the first true steam locomotive to be exported from the U.S.A. Operational service revealed that the Norris

ABOVE
Valves of a Mikado-type locomotive of the Boone & Scenic Valley Railroad of Boone, Missouri.

OPPOSITE
The 4-6-0 locomotive No. 328 of the Northern Pacific Railroad at Dresser, Wisconsin.

locomotive offered superior hill-climbing capability, which was why the type attracted export orders, including some from railroads in Europe. The first of these to place a contract for a Norris locomotive was the Vienna-Raab Railway, whose *Philadelphia* was completed in late 1837: before being shipped to Europe, the locomotive hauled a 200-ton train up a 1 per cent gradient, which was a remarkable achievement for a

locomotive of the period. The success of the Norris locomotive in service with the Vienna-Raab Railway led to a number of other European orders, most of them from other railroads in the large Austrian (soon to become Austro-Hungarian) empire, but sales were also made to Germany, where Norris locomotives operated on the lines of the Brunswick and the Berlin & Potsdam railways. Among the British railway companies which ordered Norris

locomotives were the Birmingham & Gloucester Railway, which received 15 locomotives; these proved very useful in services which involved progression up the 2.7 per cent Lickey incline at Bromsgrove in Worcestershire.

Demand for the Norris locomotives was so great that the firm decided to maximize its customer appeal by offering them in four standard sizes: the Class C unit had a cylinder bore of 9in (229mm), the Class B unit 10.5in (267mm), the Class A unit 11.5in (292mm) and the Class A Extra 12.5in (318mm), with grate areas of 6.4, 7.3, 7.9 and 9.5sq ft (0.6, 0.69, 0.73 and 0.88m²) respectively for locomotives that turned the scales at 15,750, 20,600, 24,100 and 29,650lb (7144, 9344, 10932 and 13449kg).

The sale of 17 Norris locomotives (nine, three and five Class B, A and A Extra units) to British railway companies, in the period between March 1837 and May 1842, was particularly important, for it marked the true emergence of the U.S.A. as a significant designer and manufacturer of steam locomotives. The concept had been born in the U.K., after all, and British engineering companies had found the export of their locomotives to be a lucrative trade, but this marked something of a reversal of the trend. The five Class A Extra locomotives were used as bankers on the heavy gradients, improvements having been made to reduce what was originally a very high fuel consumption on these duties. All five of the Class A Extra units were converted to tank locomotives, which removed the need to haul the weight of tenders. Steam blown from the

The 4-8-0 Mastodon-type locomotive No. 475 of the Northern & Western.

safety valves and some exhaust steam was turned back into the new saddle tanks. The original iron fireboxes were replaced by copper ones, and a number of items revealing poor workmanship were replaced by items of improved British manufacture. As a result, coal consumption was reduced by 53 per cent in the period between 1841 and 1843. The best of the Norris locomotives remained in service until 1856.

In the U.S.A. in the 1830s, Norris's customers included 27 predecessors of the railroads of the great age of steam in states such as Connecticut, Georgia, Louisiana, Maryland, Massachusetts, New York, North Carolina, Pennsylvania, Tennessee and Virginia. For a time, the success of this pioneering locomotive helped to make Norris the greatest steam locomotive manufacturer in the U.S.A., with a product line that included 4-4-0, 0-6-0 and finally 4-6-0 types in addition to the 4-2-0 locomotives with which he had made his name. However, despite the technical success of his locomotives in Europe, Norris failed to find a lasting niche on that continent: William Norris and his brother Octavius travelled to Vienna in 1844 and set up a manufacturing facility, but the real sales success was gained by other manufacturers who adopted the Norris concept and made considerable sums of money though the sale of several hundreds of such locomotives. The first European builder was John Haswell of Vienna, and others included Sigl of Vienna, Guenther of Austria, Cockerill of Belgium, Borsig and Emil Kessler (later the Esslingen company) of Germany, and Hick of Bolton and Nasmyth of Manchester in the U.K.

By the middle of the 19th century, the American standard type of locomotive had reached the form that was to remain almost universal for 50 years, and can therefore be accorded the unofficial but appropriate designation Standard-type, of which perhaps 25,000 examples were eventually manufactured. As noted above, the 4-4-0 wheel arrangement had been adopted at an early stage, but it was during the early part of the 1850s that Thomas Rogers of the Rogers, Ketchum & Grosvenor company of Paterson, New Jersey, started to produce the locomotives which introduced the definitive configuration that was then widely imitated. The most significant aspect of the concept embodied in Rogers's locomotives, beginning with an early example that was trialled in 1853 but reached its definitive initial form with *The General* of 1855 (page 205), was a lengthening of the wheelbase, which permitted the horizontal mounting of the cylinders at the sides of the smokebox, which was carried on the upper part of the four-wheel pilot truck that had proved so important in enabling locomotives to cope with the irregularities typical of early American track. Another standard feature, by this stage, was the equalizing beams carrying the driving wheels; another feature of the

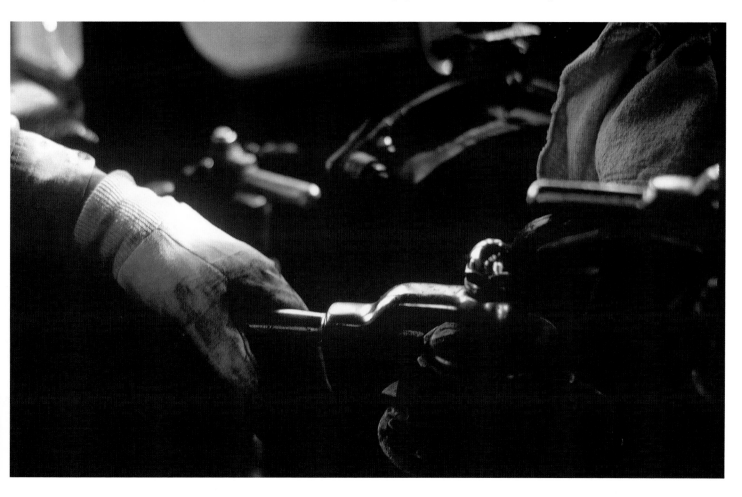

A typical locomotive brake handle.

Rogers design was incorporation of a tapered boiler surrounding the large firebox, which was set at the rear.

Other external features that became typical of American locomotive manufacturing practices stemmed directly from the environment in which the locomotives were intended to operate. A large cab for the engineer and fireman was vital for the protection it provided in the enormously varied climes in which the locomotives operated; a large chimney with a spark-arrester arrangement was essential to avoid the distribution of the sparks that could readily ignite fires in the woods and prairies through which the locomotive travelled; a bell, a headlight and a cowcatcher were required to protect the train and to provide a warning of any animals on the track, while the provision of a large sandbox on top of the boiler provided the capability for the engineer to overcome the problem of slipping wheels on remote stretches of line lacking the possibility of outside aid. The Standard type was also typified by another highly visible and distinctive feature that had no practical value: this was the elaborate decoration comprising bright colours, a trim of highly polished copper and brass, and sometimes flags and/or pictures painted on the side panels. These features were all typical of the early Standard-type locomotives, and later disappeared, largely when the practice of allocating a crew a particular locomotive, in which it could therefore take a special pride, ceased.

So far as its internal workings were concerned, the Standard type of locomotive was based, of course, on the basic principles evolved by the British engineer George

An early 4-6-0 locomotive of the Cape Fear & Yadkin Valley Railroad.

This is *The General*, from a time earlier in the era of the Standard- or American-type 4-4-0 locomotive.

Stephenson and wholly embodied in his famous *Rocket* locomotive of 1829. The hot gases flowing from a firebox passed through an array of tubes inside a boiler to a smokebox. The water in the boiler was heated by the passage of the hot gases through the tubes and formed steam, which was fed into cylinders and, by acting on a piston, powered the wheels by means of a connecting rod. The rotation of the wheels was in turn transmitted to the valves admitting the steam to the cylinders, allowing the spent steam to escape from them. Finally, the exhaust steam was fed into the smokebox to create the draft required for the fire and so maintained the cycle of the complete process.

In the 1850s and 1860s the 4-4-0 Standard type of locomotive was used to haul both passenger and freight trains, of which neither could reach any great speeds, but the appearance of the Wootten firebox in the following decade produced changes that led to generally higher performance. The firebox was designed to burn the powdery residue from anthracite coal that was otherwise wasted, and its revised form, which was wider and shallower than that of fireboxes that had been used up to this time, required modification of the wheel arrangement. One method that was tested was known as the 'camelback' or 'Mother Hubbard': to avoid an unfortunate lengthening of the wheelbase, the engineer's cab was superimposed on the

This is a unit of the Grand Trunk Railway from the days of the Standard or American type of 4-4-0 locomotive.

boiler, with a platform on the front of the tender so that the stoker could feed fuel into the firebox. The cab on top of the boiler had earlier been used by Ross Winans in the locomotives he built for the Baltimore & Ohio Railroad, but in this case the change had been effected to give the engineer a better forward field of vision. In combination with the Wootten firebox, the camelback arrangement was employed in the locomotives of several railroads, and also for locomotives of several wheel configurations.

Although the 4-4-0 wheel arrangement was the norm for the Standard-type locomotives that came into service in virtually every part of North America, locomotives with the 2-8-0 arrangement were built in the U.S.A. from 1866, and proved so successful that some 24,000 such locomotives had been manufactured for service with operators all

over the world by the time the last was completed in 1946. The difference in the capabilities of the locomotives completed for service in different parts of the world is revealed by the tractive effort of the locomotives, which ranged from a minimum figure of 14,000lb (6350kg) for narrow-gauge examples up to 94,000lb (42638kg) for a single locomotive fitted with a booster tender and built for the Delaware & Hudson Railroad during the 1920s. All of these 2-8-0 locomotives were intended for highly economical freight-hauling at modest speed rather than for passenger express services with their higher speeds and considerably high fuel consumption, but were nonetheless used on limited occasions to haul passenger trains on steep gradients.

Now generally known as the Consolidation type, from the name of the first

heavy freight locomotive of this type supplied to the Lehigh Valley Railroad in 1866, because the company had come into being through the consolidation of a number of smaller railroads in the area, the first locomotives having been initially operated to haul trains up the 2.5 per cent gradient of the Mahoney Hill. To make the passage of the locomotives around curves as easy as possible, the two central pairs of driving wheels were flangeless. The connecting rods drove the third axle, the eccentric rods and links of the Stephenson link motion being positioned clear of the leading axles. Otherwise, the concepts that were so successful in American steam locomotives of the 19th century were there in their entirety. A feature that became standard during this period was the casting of each cylinder as a unit integral with half of the smokebox saddle, the bolting together of the two assemblies producing a very sturdy front end.

At this time, Baldwin had begun to make a major effort to standardize locomotive fittings as well as parts, which was useful in the maintenance of locomotives and also helped to reduce manufacturing costs.

The Mogul type of 2-6-0 locomotives, of which the first appeared in 1863, was so called for what was, at the time, its high power. The type was designed as a locomotive with much the same size as a 4-4-0 unit but with one guiding and three driving axles, rather than two guiding and two driving axles, for a theoretical 50 per cent more adhesion and tractive power. The concept was the brainchild of Levi Bissel, a New Yorker who in 1858 had taken out a patent for a new kind of leading truck which

could move sideways as well as swivel, and which was applicable to two- and four-wheel trucks. Inclined planes gave a self-centring action, bringing a combination of flexibility and stability that had hitherto been impossible.

William Hudson, of the Rogers Locomotive Works, Paterson, New Jersey, then developed the principle by replacing the inclined planes with swing links. He also linked the truck springs to the main springs by a large compensating lever in a fashion that ensured constancy of weight distribution on the type of rough tracks typical of freight operations. The Rogers company was the first to build a true Mogul, and over the following 50 years some 11,000 Mogul-type locomotives were built for U.S. railroads, serving as a

Seen at Columbia, South Carolina, in 1916, this is the 4-4-0 Standard- or American-type locomotive No. 2 of the Columbia, Newburg & Larens Railroad.

Locomotive No. 600 of the Baltimore & Ohio Railroad, designed by its own master mechanic, J.C. Davis, and built at its own Mount Clare workshops, was the first 2-6-0 Mogul-type locomotive created and manufactured anywhere in the world for passenger operations and was created to handle trains on the 17-mile (27.4-km) grade between Piedmont and Altamont. When it was exhibited at the Centennial Exhibition of 1876 at Philadelphia, Pennsylvania, the locomotive was still the largest in the world.

RIGHT
Photographed outside the Rochester, New Hampshire, engine house of the Boston & Maine Railroad during 1912, this is the 4-8-0 Mastodon-type locomotive No. 2909 of the L-class.

BELOW RIGHT
1902 photograph of the New York Central Railroad's Twentieth Century Limited prestige service linking New York and Chicago.

BELOW
This Baldwin-made Vauclain-type compound 4-4-2 locomotive was a unit of the Central Railroad of New Jersey.

Valve gear on a 2-8-2 locomotive.

general-purpose type that filled the operational interval between the 4-4-0 passenger and the 2-8-0 freight locomotives.

The Congressional act that sanctioned the construction of the original transcontinental railroad route was signed by President Lincoln on 1 July 1862, and stipulated that the eastward section of the line from California would be the responsibility of the Central Pacific Railroad. The company's initial problem, and indeed the most difficult task of the whole project, was the crossing of the

The builder's plate of the Baldwin Locomotive Works.

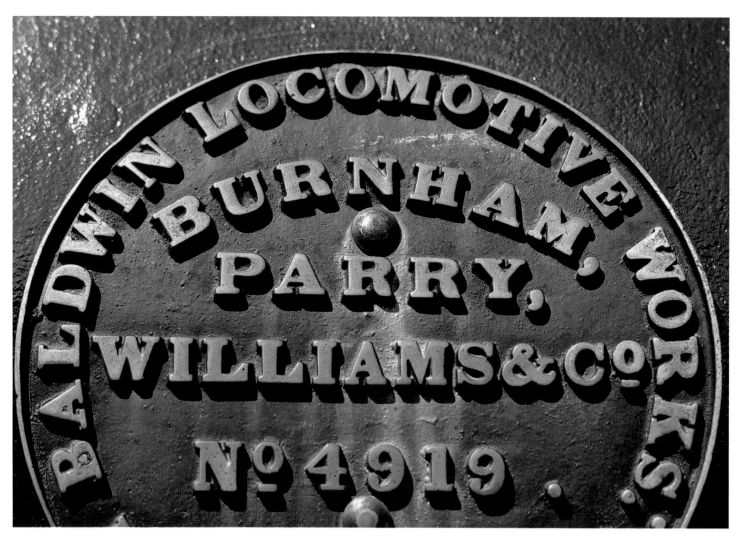

Sierra Nevada mountain range. The grade was held to a maximum of 2.77 per cent, but nothing could be done to alter the fact that the line had to climb from a point virtually at sea level, near Sacramento, to 7,000ft (2134m) at the Summit Tunnel.

The Central Pacific Railroad's first locomotive, a 4-4-0 unit named *Governor Stanford*, was delivered by sea during the summer of 1863. With the railhead moving steadily inland toward the meeting point with the Union Pacific Railroad at Promontory Point in Utah, a distance of some 700 miles (1126km) from Sacramento, the Central Pacific Railroad acquired more and more locomotives. When the rails from east and west met on 28 April 1869, the Central Pacific Railroad numbered in its inventory almost 200 locomotives, mostly 4-4-0 Standard types, but some 4-6-0 units. From 1872 the Central Pacific Railroad began to manufacture its own

The builder's plate of a Baldwin 2-8-2 locomotive.

A Camelback-type 4-2-2 locomotive of the
Philadelphia & Reading Railway.

locomotives at its Sacramento workshops to a design created by the railroad's own master mechanic, A.J. Stevens. To meet the demands of 'The Hill', as the climb to the peak of the Sierra Nevada was generally known, during 1882 Stevens pioneered a 4-8-0 locomotive named the *Mastodon*. This proved very successful and paved the way for the construction of many more basically similar units.

Two years after the introduction of the *Mastodon*, Stevens developed the concept one stage further with the 4-10-0 *El Gobernador*, which was at the time the largest and most powerful locomotive in the world by a

The builder's plate of the Schenectady Locomotive Works, in this instance on a 2-8-0 locomotive of 36-in (914-mm) gauge.

This 4-4-0 locomotive No. 999 is seen hauling the Empire State Express service of the New York Central Railroad.

ABOVE
Among the notable feature of this Vauclain compound 4-4-2 locomotive No. 209 of the Canadian Pacific Railway are the duplex piston rods above and below the cross head and slide bars.

OPPOSITE
28 January 1946: the 2-8-0 locomotive No. 113 of the Long Island Railroad is recorded for posterity at Bethpage, New York. The locomotive had been built in 1916 by Alco/Brooks as the Pennsylvania Railroad's No. 9732.

considerable margin. The most interesting feature was the design of the valves and valve gear by Stevens, each cylinder having two valves in the form of a main valve and a cut-off. The main valve was worked by a single eccentric rocking link, while the cut-off was actuated by a connection with the cross head, whose movement could be varied to alter the cut-off. Originally the double valves were of a rotary type, but more conventional slide valves soon replaced them.

Running revealed that Stevens had attempted too much too quickly, however, and *El Gobernador* was not successful, except as an engine for publicity, and saw little use apart

from switching duties at Sacramento.

The 5,000th locomotive to come from the Baldwin works was somewhat unusual and not notably successful in itself, though it had a strong influence on locomotive design, and possessed the 4-2-2 wheel arrangement known as the 'bicycle' type. The locomotive had been ordered by the Philadelphia & Reading Railway to haul light high-speed trains, most especially on the route connecting Philadelphia and New Jersey. The arrangement, with just one driving axle, was simple, but also offered little adhesive weight. However, it had an interesting device that, through the use of a steam-powered servo-cylinder between the frames, was able to move

the effective central pivot position of the equalizing levers connecting the driving wheels with the rear wheels. In this way the adhesive weight could be temporarily increased from 35,000 to 45,000lb (15876 to 20412kg) to boost starting traction.

Oddly enough, this device was not generally adopted, but another of the locomotive's features did become wholly standard. This was the wide firebox, usually supported by a pair or pairs of small idle wheels underneath. Suitable for virtually any type of fuel, a big grate was essential when burning the anthracite coal which happened to be mined in the area served by the Reading Railway.

Although the Philadelphia & Reading Railway later purchased other 4-2-2 locomotives larger than Baldwin's No. 5000, but generally similar at the conceptual level, the railroad was in the short term incapable of paying for the locomotive, which was therefore recalled for sale to the Eames Vacuum Brake Company, which needed a light but speedy demonstration locomotive. At about this time the now-familiar Westinghouse air brake was coming into general use on North American railroads, obliging other manufacturers of vacuum brakes to find new markets. Both types of brake had fail-safe qualities, but the vacuum brake was very much simpler. On the other hand it had problems associated with the fact that only limited differential pressure was available, and that reduced with altitude, whereas the air brake had at least six times more pressure differential. Though the air brake became standard in the U.S.A., the vacuum brake was in fact more successful abroad.

RIGHT
An Atlantic-type 4-4-2 locomotive of the New Haven Railroad.

OPPOSITE
Prominent on the Canadian Pacific Railway was the 4-6-2 Pacific-type locomotive, developed around the end of the 19th century and beginning of the 20th century for service on main passenger routes. The Pacifics eventually found their way onto all parts of the Canadian Pacific's route system, hauling trains on the transcontinental and local services and occasionally working as a helper in mountainous regions.

So the Lovatt Eames was sent across the sea to Britain where, over a short trial period, it played a small part in persuading several companies to adopt the vacuum brake.

On 10 May 1893 the New York Central & Hudson River Railroad's locomotive No. 999 received national and even international acclaim for hauling the Empire State Express at the speed of 112.5mph (181km/h) down a 0.28 per cent gradient in Batavia in New York state. This represented a world speed record

for steam railroads and indeed an absolute world speed record. Since then, however, there have been grave suspicions that the calculated speed was not accurate: the time of the train between two trackside marks one mile apart was clocked by the conductor, probably with nothing more accurate than his issue watch, and later reassessment of the event suggests that to haul four 55-ton Wagner cars over the distance at this speed would have required some 2,000hp (1491kW), which would have

been virtually impossible for the No. 999 locomotive. More credible, but certainly not fully proven, is the speed of 102.8mph (165.4km/h) over 5 miles (8km), claimed to have been established on the preceding night.

The 4-4-0 locomotive in question was not the result of efforts by a major railroad operator but one Daniels, a New York patent medicine salesman, who had been hired as the New York Central & Hudson River's passenger agent in New York. Daniels

On 12 June 1905 this train reportedly established the fastest train run ever recorded on the U.S. railroad system, covering 3 miles (4.8km) in Ohio in 85 seconds for an average speed of 127.06mph (204.48 km/h).

persuaded the railroad's management to run the exclusive Empire State Express between New York and Chicago during the period of the Colombian Exposition of 1893, the time of 20 hours for the 960-mile (1545-km) distance representing a 48-mph (77-km/h) average speed, which was very high for a route of this length. The service offered considerable comfort as well as high speed, and as such was the precursor of one of the most famous railroad services in the world, the legendary year-round Twentieth Century Limited, that operated daily between New York and

Chicago. The locomotive built especially for the 1893 task was No. 999, which was basically a Standard-type locomotive constructed in the New York Central & Hudson River Railroad's own workshops with slide-valves, Stephenson valve gear, and wheels of 78-in (1.98-m) diameter rather than the 86-in (2.18-m) of the 'record' runs. So celebrated did the locomotive become that it was featured on the U.S. two-cent stamp of 1900.

The song about the man who has become the most famous railroad engineer in American

history, John Luther 'Casey' Jones, wrongly refers to his locomotive as a 'six-eight wheeler'. In April 1900 Jones, an employee of the Illinois Central Railroad, boarded his locomotive, which was in fact a 4-6-0, in Memphis, Tennessee. Departing Memphis for Canton, Missouri, the train was involved in an accident at Vaughan in Mississippi, some 174 miles (280km) to the south of Memphis. The train order system of operation, which was still in extensive use at this time, was adequate for routes on which there were few trains which ran only at low speeds, but was altogether too susceptible to human error when used on major routes, such as this section of the trunk line linking Chicago and New Orleans, on which there was a higher frequency of trains which also ran at a fairly high speed. For whatever reason, most probably the fact that Jones's watch was running slow and he was therefore ahead of the ordered

schedule, the Cannonball Express train ran into the back of another train, halted on the track but not 'protected' by a flagman or signal. Given the distance that could be seen in the light of the single and not very effective headlight of the day, there was no chance that Jones could have seen the train ahead of him in time to halt.

The locomotive was perfectly orthodox by the standards of the period, being a product of the Rogers Locomotive Works of Paterson, New Jersey. No. 382 had outside slide-valve cylinders, inside Stephenson valve gear and a narrow firebox boiler; the locomotive's single most unusual feature was the clerestory cab roof. After the accident, the locomotive was

One of the six driving wheels of Northern Pacific's 4-6-0 locomotive No. 328.

repaired and gave many more years of service in a career that is thought to have involved the deaths of other men. The locomotive was later taken in hand for modernization when the slide-valve cylinders were adapted with piston valves, the original inside Stephenson gear being replaced by outside Baker valve gear; it was also provided with a superheater but unfortunately without the clerestory cab.

The Camelback-type 4-4-2 locomotives, built for the Atlantic City Railroad in the 1890s, had a decidedly unusual appearance but in fact offered excellent performance by the standards of their day, and were to a certain extent ahead of their time. The Atlantic

Locomotive No. 3267 of the Pennsylvania Railroad.

A scene typical of the main-line passenger services operated in the U.S.A. during the heyday of steam locomotion, in this instance by the Pennsylvania Railroad.

City Railroad operated the locomotives to haul the trains carrying passengers from the great city of Philadelphia to the resort cities of the Atlantic coast of New Jersey. The enthusiasm for retreating to the coast, which lies only some 55 miles (88km) from Philadelphia proper, meant that there was intense competition on this lucrative route between the Atlantic City

Railroad, operating from Camden on the other side of the river from Philadelphia, and the Pennsylvania Railroad operating from the city proper. Consequently, in order to compete, the Atlantic City Railroad was obliged to offer great speed in combination with a high level of passenger comfort.

The Atlantic City Railroad offered a 50-

minute service, but during July and August the trains generally ran the distance in less, the lowest recorded time being 46.5 minutes, the average speed of 71.6mph (115km/h) indicating that a 'cruising speed' of 90mph (145km/h) was typical, certainly making the Atlantic City Flier the fastest scheduled train service in the world in its time.

Locomotive No. 5351 of the Pennsylvania Railroad seen at Camden, New Jersey, during 1955 in the dying days of American steam locomotion.

A notable feature of the Camelback locomotives was an early appearance, in a passenger- rather than freight-hauling locomotive, of the wide, deep firebox, which was soon to become virtually standard on passenger expresses. The 4-4-2 layout was ideally suited to the use of such a firebox, which in this instance was chosen so that anthracite could be effectively burned, and was later seen to be admirably suitable for burning bituminous coal and even oil. There were two other interesting features. First was the pair of compound cylinders on each side, driving through a common cross head in an arrangement named for Samuel Vauclain, who headed the Baldwin Locomotive Works. In developing this arrangement, Vauclain's desire had been to profit from the advantages of compound operation without the mechanical complexity of other compounding arrangements: in the Vauclain arrangement, as used on the Camelback locomotives, the high-pressure cylinders, with a diameter of 13in (330mm) and a stroke of 26in (660mm), were mounted above the low-pressure cylinders, which had a bore of 22in (559mm) and stroke of 26in (660mm). A single set of valve gear and a single connecting rod served both cylinders of each compound pair. Though workable, the Vauclain system was maintenance-intensive and was not popular for long.

The second interesting feature was the 'camelback' (alternatively 'Mother Hubbard') cab on top of the boiler for the driver. For obvious reasons, the fireman had to remain in the normal position, where a smaller and less

A freight service on the lines of the Long Island Railroad.

RIGHT
The 4-4-0 locomotive No. 1223 of the
Pennsylvania Railroad's D16b class is seen
on the Strasburg Railroad's line at Paradise,
Pennsylvania.

OPPOSITE
The 4-8-4 locomotive No. 700 of the E1 class
is caught by the camera at speed on 20 April
2001, racing along the bank of the Columbia
river near Plymouth, Washington.

protective shelter was provided. It was appreciated that the arrangement would separate the two members of the crew, but was thought desirable as the engineer would have a much better forward field of vision.

The Philadelphia & Reading Railway (later the Reading Railway) absorbed the Atlantic City Railroad at about this time, and continued the programme of building Camelback locomotives for some years. These gained a fair degree of currency among the railroads of the area, but never extended their reach far beyond this limited market.

Despite the fact that they had first been built for the Atlantic City Railroad, these Camelbacks were not the origin of the designation Atlantic-type locomotive generally applied to 4-4-2 locomotives. The origin in fact lay with some perfectly standard and wholly unexceptional 4-4-2 locomotives, without a wide firebox, produced in 1893 for

OPPOSITE
Locomotive No. 700 of the Spokane, Portland & Seattle Railroad, a 4-8-4 unit built by Baldwin in 1938, is seen outside Wishram, Washington, on 20 April 2001.

ABOVE
The 2-8-0 locomotive No. 2651 of the K8c class is seen with a snow plough near Rigby, Maine, on 7 February 1939.

ABOVE LEFT
The K2-class locomotive No. 2908 of the Erie Railroad is seen heading west near Rutherford, New Jersey.

LEFT
A 2-8-0 K-class locomotive heads a passenger train of the Boston & Maine Railroad about to depart from the North Station of Boston, Massachusetts, in the late 1940s.

the Atlanta Coast Line, an operation that extended south toward Florida along the U.S.A.'s eastern seaboard.

At the time he created the firebox that bore his name, Wootten was the general manager of the Philadelphia & Reading Railway, so it was inevitable that it should be among the first and largest users of the Wootten firebox. The firebox was originally applied to 4-6-0 freight engines with small driving wheels, but for the Atlantic City route, where the Philadelphia & Reading Railway was facing direct competition from the mighty Pennsylvania Railroad, Wootten developed a 2-4-2 fast passenger locomotive in which two small trailing wheels supported the firebox. As well as creating his own type of firebox, Wootten incorporated another innovation designed by Samuel Vauclain of the Baldwin locomotive works: Vauclain's system of compound working was just one of several ways of using the partially expanded steam from one cylinder to work another, usually of greater diameter to allow for the extraction of the maximum possible work from the now-lowered pressure of the steam. The distinctive feature of Vauclain's system was that both cylinders drove the same cross head, thus removing some of the complications.

However, the 2-4-2 locomotives of the Philadelphia & Reading Railway proved to be somewhat lacking in stability at the comparatively high speeds for which they had been designed, and in 1896 Wootten produced a much more significant design using the 4-4-2 wheel arrangement.

Though the 4-4-0 Standard-type locomotive served American railroads with great success from their entry into service in the mid-1850s until late in the 19th century, there inevitably came the time when the growth of traffic and the demands of passengers for faster travel began to make locomotives with just two driven axles obsolete.

The simplest, and therefore the most obvious solution, was the addition of a third coupled axle to create a 4-6-0 locomotive. The best aspects of the 4-4-0 layout, such as the leading truck to guide the locomotive, were retained, but operations with the new 4-6-0 locomotives revealed problems with the stretched 4-4-0 arrangement: there was insufficient space between the ashpan and the rear axle, and the gap between the leading driving wheels and the cylinders, a useful feature on the 4-4-0 and conducive to easy maintenance, became cluttered. Even so, for a time toward the end of the 19th century, the 4-6-0 locomotive was the 'cock of the roost', and manufacture reached some 16,000 units between 1880 and 1910.

There were many types of 4-6-0 locomotive, but one that may be taken as typical of the breed is that manufactured by the Brooks Locomotive Works of Dunkirk in New York state during 1900, most particularly for the Lake Shore & Michigan Southern Railroad. The locomotives were intended for the prestige services operating on the western part of the main line, owned by what was soon to become the New York Central Railroad, connecting New York and Chicago.

The fact that their development fell between two major periods is indicated by the locomotives' s completion to a design

characterized by narrow fireboxes, slide valves and saturated steam, at a time when strides toward the wide firebox, piston valves and superheated steam had already been completed. This meant that the locomotives had only comparatively short first-line careers, for soon after their completion the railroad began to order locomotives of the more advanced type with a 2-4-2 layout. The new locomotives were not without their own problems, however, such as the tendency of the single-axle leading truck to lift from the rails, which allowed the 4-6-0 units to make a limited comeback hauling services such as the Twentieth Century Limited, which was introduced on the New York to Chicago route in June 1902. The service operated over a distance of 920 miles (1480km) between Grand Central Terminal in New York and the La Salle Street Station in Chicago in a time of 20 hours, and included several servicing and locomotive-changing halts. This makes the 48-mph (77-km/h) average speed very respectable, especially as the service also had to run at slow speed though towns such as Syracuse, where the line extended along the main street.

At first the train comprised buffet/library car, dining car and three sleeping cars, of which the last had an observation saloon complete with brass-railed open platform. In overall terms, the comfort offered by the Twentieth Century Limited was comparable to that of the best hotels, and was enhanced by the use of heavy Pullman cars, each of which was 80-ft (24.4-m) long. So popular did the service become that additional passenger capacity had to be provided, making the

longer and heavier trains beyond the capabilities of the 4-6-0 locomotives.

By 1900 the Pennsylvania Railroad had become firmly established as one of the best in the U.S.A., and was a notable operator of large locomotives. Most of these it manufactured in its own workshops at Altoona; the locomotives were distinguishable by the incorporation of a Belpaire firebox, a type that saw little use in North America except on the locomotives of the Pennsylvania Railroad. The railroad's 4-4-0 locomotives accorded with this general trend, and among these the peak of development was attained in the D16 class, which was introduced in 1895. With cylinders characterized by a diameter of 18.5in (470mm) and stroke of 26in (660mm), and operating at a steam pressure of 185lb/sq in (130 kg/cm²), these were substantial locomotives for the period. They had an impressive look to them, not least because the firebox was located above the frames, lifting the boiler to a position that was also somewhat higher than was typical at the time.

Of the two initial subvariants, the D16a class had 80-in (2.03-m) driving wheels for use on the railroad's more level routes, while the D16 proper had 68-in (1.727-m) wheels for service on the railroad's hillier routes. The D16a-class locomotives were soon well known for their high performance, and were therefore used on the railroad's route, fiercely competitive with that of the Atlantic City Railroad, between Philadelphia and the Atlantic coastal resorts of New Jersey. On one occasion, an engineer managed to drive the Presidential Special service over the 90-mile (145-km) trip between Philadelphia and Jersey City at an average speed of 72mph (116km/h).

As well as its power, the class was also notable for its mechanical reliability and durability. It is recorded that one locomotive covered 300,000 miles (483000km) in a period of 40 months without once needing anything other than routine maintenance.

Some 426 of these locomotives were manufactured between 1895 and 1910 in five D16 subclasses. Apart from the two sizes of driving-wheel diameter, the main dimensions were identical. After the introduction of Atlantic- and then Pacific-type locomotives early in the 21st century, the D16 locomotives were displaced from hauling the more prestigious services, but from 1914 enjoyed a new lease of life after slightly less than half their number had been updated in line with the later engines: slightly larger cylinders with piston valves were fitted (still with the inside Stephenson valve gear) and the boiler was given a Schmidt superheater with the pressure slightly reduced. Most of the rebuilt locomotives were of the subclasses with smaller-diameter driving wheels, and these became the D16sb subclass that worked many branch lines, three of them remaining in service until the early 1940s.

In 1901 there appeared the first example of a truly classic locomotive type, which was arguably the most famous of them all. Intended to work express passenger services, the Pacific-type locomotive was built until the end of the steam locomotion period and, by one of those strange but fascinating quirks of history, and even though it was of American design, resulted from the needs of a small nation rather than those of the great American railroad companies.

The country was New Zealand, where A.W. Beattie, the chief mechanical engineer of the Government Railway, recognized the need for a locomotive with a large firebox capable of burning poor quality lignite coal from Otago on New Zealand's South Island. Baldwin, a leading American locomotive manufacturer, recommended a 4-6-0 unit of the Camelback type with a wide firebox above the coupled rear wheels, but Beattie countered with the suggestion for a 4-6-2 that was in effect a 4-6-0 with a large firebox carried by a two-wheel pony truck. The 13 locomotives ordered to this revised design were quickly completed and shipped across the Pacific Ocean, which led to the popular name of the type.

The locomotives were among the first completed with Walschaert's valve gear, which rapidly became ubiquitous. The gear itself was not new, a Belgian engineer named Egide Walschaert having created it as early as 1844, even though a German engineer, Heusinger, had subsequently reinvented it; this application signalled the spread of Walschaert's valve gear from Europe to the rest of the world. The gear provided a good distribution of the steam, but its primary benefit was its mechanical simplicity and the convenience of its installation outside the frames in a location that was readily accessible for such maintenance as was required. In the case of the Baldwin Pacific-type locomotives for New Zealand, Walschaert's gear was disposed to operate outside-admission piston valves, the piston valves themselves being at the cutting edge of

OPPOSITE
An E3-class locomotive of the Pennsylvania Railroad on the lines of the Long Island Railroad.

A K4-class locomotive of the Pennsylvania Railroad.

steam locomotion technology at this time. This class of locomotive therefore came closer than any which had preceded it to marking the definitive form of the steam locomotive, the only fundamental improvements still needing to make an appearance being inside-admission piston valves and superheating.

After some minor modification, these Q-class locomotives gave durable and reliable service, and the last unit was not finally retired until 1957. For the most part, the locomotives hauled services on New Zealand's South Island, but there were occasions on which some of them were shipped over to the North

Island and hauled the Rotorua Express linking Auckland and Rotorua with its celebrated hot springs and geysers.

Though it had been chartered in 1785, with George Washington as its president, the James River Company eventually became the Chesapeake & Ohio Railroad, though in the guise of another of its antecedents, the Louisa Railroad of Virginia, it had operated its first railroad service in 1836. Thereafter, the Chesapeake & Ohio grew quickly and impressively into one of the major 'players' of railroad operations in the east of the U.S.A., receiving its first 4-6-2 Pacific-type locomotive in 1902, only a few weeks after the type had entered service with the Missouri

Pacific Railroad. This was manufactured by the American Locomotive Company (more generally known as Alco), and was in effect the prototype of the magnificent F15 class of Pacific-type locomotives, and as such the first of the standard type of North American express passenger locomotive of the 20th century. The new locomotive was fitted with piston valves, but retained the Stephenson link

valve motion between the frames. There was as yet no superheating, but the size and power of the new locomotive established a benchmark by which others would be judged.

This prototype was followed by another 26 basically similar locomotives in the period between 1903 and 1911. So effective were they that most of them remained in service with the Chesapeake & Ohio into the early

Seen in immaculate condition after being rebuilt in 1924, this is the 4-6-2 K2a-class locomotive No. 916 of the Chicago Great Western Railroad.

1950s, when the railroad switched to diesel-engined locomotion. In the later stages of their careers, the locomotives generally worked services that were less prestigious but just as important to the railroad in commercial terms. It is worth noting, though, that their light weight suited the F15-class locomotives to first-line haulage in areas where there were weaker bridges.

Such was their importance that during the 1920s it was deemed financially desirable to upgrade all the F15 locomotives with the full range of modern features, such as Walschaert's valve gear, superheaters, enlarged tenders, improved cabs, mechanical stokers, new cylinders and, in some cases, even new frames. Moreover, their success paved the way for a number of successor types within the total of 7,000 or so American-built 4-6-2 locomotives. The successors included the F16 class of 1913, with a 34 per cent increase in tractive power with 28 per cent greater grate area, and the

FAR LEFT
Leased from the Pennsylvania Railroad, this is 4-6-2 locomotive No. 3655 of the K4-class run on the Long Island Railroad.

LEFT
The reverse lever of a typical American steam locomotive.

ABOVE
This is the J1-class locomotive No. 3244, a 4-4-2 unit built by Alco in 1909.

Coupled veterans of the Pennsylvania Railroad: the E7-class 4-4-2 No. 8063 (Juanita Shops, Altoona, 1902) heads the D16sb-class 4-4-0 No. 1223 (Juanita, 1906) on a main-line excursion over former Pennsylvania Railroad track now owned by Conrail and Amtrak at Middletown, Pennsylvania, on 23 August 1985. Both locomotives are now owned by the State Railroad Museum of Pennsylvania and are leased to the adjacent Strasburg Railroad, which has rebuilt and operates them The leading engine is numbered 7002 but is in fact No. 8063 masquerading as such, the original record-breaking engine having been scrapped in the 1930s.

F17, with 45 per cent greater tractive power with a 71 per cent greater grate area, in each case for a weight penalty of just 27 per cent in axle load. Once World War I had ended in 1918, there appeared the F18 and F19 classes, which introduced much larger 18-wheel tenders. These 61 4-6-2 locomotives worked all of the Chesapeake & Ohio Railroad's express passenger services until they were supplanted by 4-6-4 locomotives in 1941.

The Pacific-type locomotive's main rival was the Atlantic type. As noted above, the heart of American railroad capability for most of the second half of the 19th century had been provided by the 4-4-0 types of Standard locomotive. Toward the last decade of the century, however, the weight of traffic, in literal as well as metaphorical terms, was pushing the limits of what was feasible with four-wheel-drive on an eight-wheeled

locomotive. With the loads that needed to be hauled still increasing, a change to a 10-wheel layout was inevitable, and for this the two most realistic options were the 4-6-0 and 4-4-2 configurations. The latter was generally more attractive, and came to be called the Atlantic type. The 4-6-0 offered the advantages of six-wheel-drive for greater adhesive weight and traction power, but could accommodate only a comparatively small grate, as this had to fit

between the rear coupled wheels, while the latter had reduced adhesive weight but was able to accommodate a larger grate.

So far as the Pennsylvania Railroad was concerned, the Atlantic represented the better of the options: it was already laying very heavy rails, fully capable of accepting the high-axle loads, while the locomotive was able to burn relatively low-grade coal, to which the railroad had ready access at the right price and

in large quantities. It was in 1899 that the railroad's Altoona workshops completed their first two Atlantic-type locomotives. These made the maximum possible use of the features inherent in the   4-4-2 layout with an adhesive weight of 101,600lb (46086kg) and a grate area of 68sq ft (6.32m²), which was somewhat more than twice the figure for the largest 4-4-0 locomotive currently operated by the railroad. The workshops then delivered a

third locomotive with a grate area of just 55.5sq ft (5.16m²), which became standard for all later Atlantic-type locomotives, as well as for many other types of steam locomotives of this period. Thus the third of the locomotives from the Altoona workshops fixed the mould for the total of 576 locomotives that followed with the same 80-in (2.032-m) driving-wheel diameter, 205lb/sq in (14.4kg/cm²) boiler pressure and 55.5sq ft of grate area.

Within this limitation to the same basic parameters listed above, and also essentially the same overall dimensions, a steady flow of improvement was introduced in the design of successive classes. The three prototypes had

ABOVE
The Pennsylvania Railroad's 4-4-2 locomotive No. 460. This 'Lindbergh Engine', later the only unit of the 83 E6-series locomotives to be preserved, is here seen in about 1937 at Babylon, New York.

ABOVE LEFT
A Hudson-type 4-6-4 locomotive of the Hudson River Railroad in 1950.

fireboxes with Belpaire tops, as was standard in Pennsylvania Railroad locomotives at this time, but the 96 locomotives of the following two production lots had the more common round-topped fireboxes. The Belpaire firebox then reappeared and was retained on all the later Atlantic-type locomotives. The two batches with round-topped fireboxes, as mentioned above, differed from each other only in the diameter of their cylinders, the locomotives of the E2 class having 20.5-in (521-mm) cylinders and the E3 class 22-in (559-mm) cylinders (the railroad planned to operate the E3-class locomotives to work its heavier services). All of these engines had slide valves, but in the next series, whose

manufacture was launched in 1903, piston valves were employed, initially with Stephenson's valve gear but with Walschaert's from 1906.

Some 493 locomotives had been manufactured by 1913, all with a boiler diameter of 65.5in (1.664m). By that time, the Pacific type of locomotive was well established in service, so there was the possibility that the Atlantic type had reached the high point of its service and would shortly begin to decline in importance. Axel Vogt, the Pennsylvania Railroad's chief engineer, was not a man to give up so easily, however, especially when an effective improvement of the arrangement with four driving wheels

ABOVE
A Hudson-type 4-6-4 locomotive of the Lackawanna Railroad.

RIGHT
The 4-6-2 K4-class locomotive No. 1361 of the Pennsylvania Railroad at Tyrone, Pennsylvania, on 21 June 1987.

OPPOSITE
Locomotive No. 1361, a 4-6-2 K4-class unit of the Pennsylvania Railroad, on an excursion service.

Coaling operations on locomotive No. 812, built by the New York Central Railroad and now operated by the Ulster & Delaware Railroad.

The 2-10-2 locomotive No. 2954, possibly built for the Reading Railway, is seen in service with the Chesapeake & Ohio Railroad.

could offer an advantage over the mechanically more complex and also more expensive arrangement with six driving wheels. In 1910, therefore, Vogt arranged for the manufacture of an Atlantic-type locomotive with a different type of boiler, in this instance possessing the same grate area as the earlier Atlantic types in combination with a boiler diameter of 76.75-in (1.949-m), and thus almost as large as that of

the Pacific-type locomotives, and a combustion chamber at the front. The new E6-class locomotive developed a higher power than current Pacific-type locomotives when travelling at a speed greater than 40mph (64km/h). There followed another two E6-class locomotives to an improved standard with superheaters, which further enhanced the performance and also made it feasible to

enlarge the cylinder diameter to 23.5in (597mm). Superheating had been a development by a German engineer, Wilhelm Schmidt, and involved collecting the steam in the normal way but then ducting it through elements inside the fire tubes so that it was superheated to much greater temperatures and pressures before being admitted to the cylinders. With the addition of superheating in

Old and new: the PA-A-1 diesel locomotive No. 1178 of the New York Central Railroad moves away from a train it has just hauled as the J1e-class 4-6-4 steam locomotive No. 5333 moves to take up the load at Harmon, New York, on 27 April 1935.

1910, the E6 developed 2,400hp (1789kW), which for its weight of 110 tons made it one of the most powerful locomotives ever built.

The prototype locomotives were taken in hand for a programme of concentrated development, and after four years work began on a group of 80 E6-class locomotives to a standard, slightly different from those of the prototypes, that included longer boiler tubes. In an impressive feat of engineering, these 80 locomotives were built in the period between February and August 1914, which was the year in which the first of the magnificent K4-

class locomotives of the Pacific type were manufactured.

The production-standard E6-class locomotives assumed the railroad's main express workings on all the flatter parts of Pennsylvania Railroad's system, and during World War I proved invaluable for the movement of heavy loads. After the appearance of the K4s in larger numbers, in the period following the end of World War I, the E6-class locomotives were gradually relegated to working less intensive routes, especially in the state of New Jersey

Meanwhile, the smaller Atlantic-class locomotives were building up a good record of high-speed service, but the capabilities of the type were realized fully only in 1905, when the Pennsylvania Special service between Jersey City and Chicago was trimmed to just 18 hours for an average speed of 50.2mph (81km/h); the 189-mile (304-km) section between Jersey City and Harrisburg was covered at an average of 57.8mph (92.9km/h). It has been claimed that an E2 locomotive exceeded 120mph (193km/h) in the first westbound operation of the Pennsylvania

A 2-8-0 Consolidation-class locomotive of the Lehigh Valley Railroad, which introduced the type in 1866.

The 4-10-0 locomotive No. 4253 of the Pennsylvania Railroad is seen on the Horse Shoe Curve in Pennsylvania in 1938.

Special service, but with hindsight the claim appears to be overinflated. It is worth noting that on the Pennsylvania Special the E2- and E3-class locomotives were each able to maintain the published schedule when hauling 360-ton trains of up to eight wooden coaches, but after somewhat heavier steel coaches had been introduced the timely operation of the service required double-heading by these two classes of locomotive.

The E6-class locomotives could work 800/900-ton trains on the service linking New York with Washington via Philadelphia, but offered their best performance with lighter trains. The most impressive of all the services

worked by the these locomotives was the 300/350-ton Detroit Arrow of five or six steel coaches between Fort Wayne and Chicago. In 1933 this was the world's fastest train service with an average speed of 75.5mph

(121.5km/h) over the 64 miles (103km) between Plymouth and Fort Wayne and 75.3mph (121.1km/h) over the 123 miles (198km) between Fort Wayne and Gary.

The durability and cost-efficiency of the

Atlantic types meant that many of the earlier examples were taken in hand for modernization later in their careers, the main changes being the addition of superheaters and piston valves. This gave the locomotives a new

A class B15 Mogul-type locomotive at Hillsborough, New Hampshire, on the Boston & Maine Railroad.

lease of life, making them suitable for
lighter duties. Five of the locomotives
survived until 1947.

As noted above, the Atlantic-type
locomotives of the Pennsylvania Railroad
did not use the Wootten firebox, but rather the
square-topped Belpaire type for the better
burning of the bituminous coal to which the
Pennsylvania Railroad had easier access than

the Philadelphia & Reading. The latter
therefore retained the Wootten firebox, and in
the course of 1915 added a four-wheel
trailing truck to produce a 4-4-4 type. Apart
from some high-speed machines built for
special services with lightweight trains during
the 1930s, this was the last development of the
four-coupled passenger engine, but the four-
wheel trailing truck in fact fulfilled its true

potential only in other applications.

So far as Pacific-type locomotives were
concerned, presaged by the 2-6-2 Prairie
type with the same early problem of a
leading truck that tended to lift from the rail,
it was the Pennsylvania Railroad that
produced the most impressive examples of the
type, and again the new wheel configuration
was combined with other innovations to create

a peak of steam-locomotive development.

The Pennsylvania Railroad's first real success with the Pacific-class locomotive was the K4 class that appeared in 1914 and was built to the extent of 425 locomotives in the period up to 1928. The K4 did not emerge as a wholly fresh design, however, for the Pennsylvania Railroad already had a relatively long history of operations with 4-6-2 locomotives, those of the K4 class being the core of the railroad's operations right up to the period following the end of World War II.

Generally noted for the conservatism of its approach to engineering matters, the Pennsylvania Railroad was no exception to its own rule when it first approached the matter of the Pacific-type locomotive. Thus in 1907 the railroad ordered a single locomotive of this

OPPOSITE
The cost and availability of heavy freight haulage by steam locomotives was a decisive element in the development of the U.S. economy in the period between 1900 and 1950.

LEFT
Canadian Pacific 2-8-2 Mikado-type locomotive No. 5427 heads a freight train, boosted by a mid-train locomotive, on the open stretches of the prairies near Winnipeg, Manitoba, in 1957.

The mainstay of the Boston & Maine Railroad's freight services up to 1920 were the K-class Consolidation-type locomotives. Even though replaced by larger power units, they still remained in service for lesser services. Here the K8c-class locomotive No. 2726 is seen at Salem, Massachusetts, with a local freight train on 15 August 1941.

type from the American Locomotive Company, later designating it the K28-class unit. By 1910 the railroad believed that it had built up sufficient knowledge through the operation and maintenance of this initial unit to begin the process of creating its own Pacific-type locomotive. The correct nature of the railroad's thinking is evident in the fact that it was soon operating a fleet of 329 K2-class locomotives which, from 1912, were upgraded to a nore current standard by the retrofit of a superheating capability.

During 1913 the Pennsylvania Railroad approached Baldwin for a series of 30 K3-class locomotives, whose primary interest to the railroad enthusiast is that they were fitted with the earliest practical type of mechanical stoker, the 'Crawford', so named for its designer, D.F. Crawford, who was the Superintendent of Motive Power (Lines West). The stoker had been in service with the Pennsylvania Railroad since 1905, and by 1914 the railroad had almost 300 of them in operation, though a mere 64 of them were to

be found in its Pacific-type locomotives. Though later stoker designs were based on the use of a screw-feed system, Crawford stokers brought the coal forward to the firebox through the agency of a series of paddles or vanes, which were oscillated by steam cylinders and feathered, like oars, on the return stroke. The coal was fed into the firebox at grate level, unlike the later types of stoker, which fed the coal onto a platform at the rear for distribution by steam jets.

The prototype Pacific-type locomotive of

The Great Northern Railway's L-class 2-6-6-2 locomotives, built by Baldwin in 1906–07, were true Mallet locomotives of the articulated type, No. 1810, shown here, being an L2-class unit of 1907 vintage. These engines had 20/31 x 30-in (508/787 x 762-mm) cylinders and used saturated steam, though superheaters were applied later to 12 of the original 67 engines. They boasted slide valves and Walschaert's valve gear, and weighed 144 tons. The calculated adhesion factor was 4.78 as a measure against wheel slippage. Between 1922 and 1925 the L-class engines were converted in the railway's shops to O5- and O6-class Mikado-type units with 2-8-2 wheel arrangements.

This is the Chicago, Burlington & Quincy Railroad's locomotive No. 4960, a 2-8-2 Mikado unit of the O1a-class built by the Baldwin Locomotive Works in 1923.

the K4 class was completed in 1914, as noted above, and was immediately apparent as a unit altogether larger than the K2: thus it had 36 per cent more tractive effort and 26 per cent more grate area but only a 9 per cent heavier axle loading. In overall terms the design owed as great a debt to that paragon of the Atlantic-type locomotives, the E6 class, as to the railroad's earlier Pacific-type units.

It is worth noting that the Pennsylvania Railroad was one of the very few North American operators both to desire and almost attain a position of self-sufficiency in the design and manufacture of steam locomotives, and was convinced of the real economic and operational advantages of designing its own locomotives to meet its particular requirements, before building the relevant

number in its own workshops, which also offered an excellent repair and maintenance base. This effort was concentrated at Altoona, where in addition to its design and manufacturing facilities the Pennsylvania Railroad operated the only establishment in North America in which a locomotive could be run up to full speed and power on rollers, with the system's instrumentation providing full

The first locomotive of the Mallet type in the U.S.A. was the Baltimore & Ohio Railroad's 0-6-6-0 No. 2400 *Old Maude* of the O-class, shown in 1905.

The T1a-class 2-8-4 locomotive No. 4005 of the Boston & Maine Railroad. This was an original Berkshire-class unit with a coffin feed-water heater.

information about what was happening inside as well as outside the locomotive on test. Thus the thinking of the designers and the work of the manufacturing team could be evaluated and tested under laboratory conditions so that the right corrections could be implemented and further tested before production was started.

The prototype of the K4-class locomotive was tested at Altoona soon after its completion, but this static yet fully-powered test discovered the need for none but limited changes. Production then began, and by 1923 more than 200 K4s had been completed. At this stage the design was modified to incorporate a power reverse system in place of the original hand-operated screw reversing gear. As they came in for maintenance and repair, the older engines were converted to this definitive standard, and the whole fleet was modified before hand reversing became illegal in 1937 for locomotives turning the scales at any adhesive weight over 160,000lb (72576kg). At the same time, an automatic stoker was incorporated in most but not all of the K4-class locomotives, reflecting what operational experience had revealed – that power had in general been limited more by the strength and stamina of the fireman than by any other factor. The last five K4 locomotives were based on one-piece steel locomotive frames. Another development of the 1930s incorporated in them was the continuous cab-signalling system, in which a receiver on the locomotive picked up coded current flowing in track circuits and translated it into a miniature signal in the cab.

RIGHT
A 36-in (0.914-m) gauge 2-8-2 locomotive
of the East Broad Top Railroad.

OPPOSITE
The Baldwin-built 2-8-2 K36-class
locomotive No. 487 of the Cumbres & Toltec
Railroad.

Signs of the Pennsylvania Railroad's conservative approach were evident in the low evaporative heating surface/superheater size ratio and a decidedly limited boiler pressure. These may have reduced outright performance, but they also obviated the frequency and cost of repair and maintenance. This show of conservatism in the operation of its locomotives did not prevent the Pennsylvania Railroad from undertaking experimental developments, however. Two K4-class locomotives were revised with poppet valve gear, thermic syphons in the firebox and improved drafting, and in this form developed one-third more cylinder power than the 3,000hp (2237kW) of the standard locomotive. Some other locomotives, which became the K4sa class, were revised for greater power in a less dramatic fashion: the firebox and exhaust improvements were partnered by enlarged piston valves with a diameter of 15in (381mm) rather than 12in (305mm). One locomotive was fully streamlined for a time, while others were partially streamlined and specially painted to match the livery of the special streamlined trains they hauled. There were also many sizes and types of tender, some of them dwarfing the locomotive.

In the winter of 1934 the Detroit Arrow was scheduled at an average of 75mph (121km/h) for the 64 miles (103km) between Plymouth and Fort Wayne, a distance covered in 51 minutes, which made the service the fastest in the world for its time. However, the limits of the cylinders of the K4-class locomotives meant that considerable recourse was made to working the Pennsylvania

Railroad's superb Limited services over long, flat routes. However, the operational economy of the K4s meant that it was still a viable option in financial terms, economy in other areas more than balancing such extravagances as the use of two locomotives on one train. On mountain sections of such services, three or even four K4-class locomotives were sometimes required at the head.

On the route between New York and Chicago, the Pennsylvania Railroad's main opposition was the New York Central Railroad. This operated a longer but somewhat easier route that ran beside the Hudson river and Erie Canal to the shores of the Great Lakes, whereas the Pennsylvania Railroad operated on the direct route across the mountains. The New York Central Railroad also developed a series of Pacific-type locomotives, beginning with its first models in 1905, to take advantage of the operator's easier route through the running of heavier trains. A series of New York Central Railroad Pacific-type locomotives culminated in the K5 class that appeared in 1925 (an indication of the work required from them is given by the carriage of 15,000 U.S. gal (56780 litres) of water in their tenders).

The locomotives of the K5 class were very close to the limits of what could be achieved with the concept inherent in the Pacific type. Thus the need for a still more capable and therefore heavier locomotive resulted during 1927 in the introduction of the first locomotive of 4-6-4 configuration, known as the Hudson type after the location of the New York Central Railroad's main line

out of New York. The four-wheel trailing truck permitted the use of a larger grate, and the Baker valve gear, a development of the Walschaert type, was introduced on later models. Another feature of the Hudson type of locomotive, and one that had earlier appeared on the Pacific-type locomotives of the New York Central Railroad, was a small booster engine on the trailing truck to provide additional power for starting.

The original J1 class of Hudson-type locomotives were steadily improved over time, reaching their apogee in the J3 class of streamlined locomotives, and secured enduring fame as the locomotives that hauled the classic Twentieth Century Limited services between New York and Chicago during the latter part of the 1930s. But the New York Central Railroad needed locomotives of still greater power, and this requirement led to the creation of the Niagara type of 4-8-4 locomotives. This was a development of the Mohawk type of 4-8-2 freight engines via the L3-class 4-8-2 locomotives that had shown themselves capable of reaching speeds of more than 80mph (129km/h), even with the relatively small wheels that were standard for freight locomotives.

These were only a very small percentage of the locomotive types, great and small, effective and not so effective, that saw service with the U.S.A.'s still considerable number of independent railroads. To take just one example: on the Milwaukee Road there had been a similar strain of development. First there had been series of 4-6-0 locomotives during the 1890s, and both these

OPPOSITE
The Duluth & Northern Minnesota's 2-8-2
Mikado-type locomotive No. 14.

and the Atlantic-type locomotives that followed them used the Vauclain system of power compounding. In 1907, however, there appeared the first of another type of Atlantic locomotive with the balanced system of compounding. This 1907 pattern had two high-pressure and two low-pressure cylinders, but rather than locating them in pairs one above the other outside the leading truck wheels, the balanced system mounted the pair of low-pressure cylinders inside the frames. From this position they drove the axle of the leading pair of driving wheels, cranked for the purpose, while the high-pressure cylinders drove the leading coupled wheels in the conventional fashion. This type of balanced compounding was more complicated than 'simple' compounding and was also more difficult to maintain, so it never achieved more than transitory popularity with American railroad operators. The fact that balanced compounding was by no means perfect or cost-effective is reflected in the fact that the Milwaukee Road reverted to the Vauclain pattern of compounding on its last class of Atlantic-type locomotives, which appeared in 1908. In 1910 the Milwaukee Road introduced its first Pacific-type locomotives in the form of the units of the F3 class, and these were followed by those of the F4 class during the next two years, then by the units of the F5 class with superheating. Production of the three F-class locomotives totalled 160 units, and the earlier engines were gradually upgraded to the definitive standard with superheating.

After it had opened its route to Tacoma and Seattle on the western seaboard of the

U.S.A., the Milwaukee Road was faced with the problems of satisfying the differing demands of its transcontinental route, of which some parts were electrified and most parts were subject to the most adverse weather conditions, and also of its shorter but considerably more competitive routes, such as those to Milwaukee, St. Paul and Omaha. Until the later part of the 1920s the Milwaukee Road used Pacific-type locomotives on both types of its services, but then in 1929 there appeared a new class of locomotive with a 4-6-4 wheel configuration. The new locomotives soon proved themselves to be very fast: in July 1934 one of them on a special high-speed run on the 86-mile (138-km) line between Chicago and Milwaukee recorded an average of 92.3mph (148.5km/h) on a segment of 65.6 miles (105.6km), and a maximum speed of 103.5mph (166.6km/h).

For the long runs typical of the route to the Pacific coast a more powerful type, the S1 class of 4-8-4 locomotives was introduced. The first of these was delivered by Baldwin in 1930 and, with a tractive force of more than 62,000lb (28123kg) by comparison with the 45,820lb (20874kg) of the F6 class of 4-6-4-type locomotives, was more than capable of hauling the heaviest of passenger trains. In the 1930s the Milwaukee Road introduced its celebrated streamlined Hiawatha services, and for the route between Chicago and Minneapolis with six cars, the American Locomotive Company in 1935 produced the A class of 4-4-2 locomotives, which was able to maintain a speed higher than 100mph (161km/h); its success meant that the Milwaukee Road soon increased the Hiawatha

service first to nine and finally to 12 cars, even though it meant a modest degradation in overall performance. This led to the introduction in 1938 of the F7 class of 4-6-4 locomotives, which was able to haul even a 12-car train at a maximum speed of more than 120mph (193km/h), and was utilized on one of the fastest steam-hauled scheduled services in the world, the section of the route linking Minneapolis and Milwaukee between Sparta and Portage, which was covered at an average speed of 81mph (130.4km/h).

Another outstanding locomotive of the late 1930s was the Atchison, Topeka & Santa Fe Railway's 3771 class of 4-8-4 engines, which were used on the 1,790-mile (2880-km) route linking Kansas City and Los Angeles. These were able to complete the one-way trip in 26 hours, and could be readied for the return journey in only a few hours.

By this stage of the development of American railroads, where a technical peak had been achieved in the development of steam locomotives but the operating railroads were coming under increasing financial pressure through the emergence of other forms of long-distance and high-speed travel, the aspect of locomotive operation that was now in the highest demand was not so much outright performance as the combination of high performance with the minimum possible servicing and maintenance requirements. It is worth noting that the steam locomotive's ability to deliver power and speed had reached the point at which further developments along these dimensions of performance could not be considered as a result of the limitations imposed by the nature of the track.

OPPOSITE
A locomotive of the East Broad Top Railroad
at Rockhill Furnace, Pennsylvania.

LEFT
The 2-8-2 Mikado-type locomotive No. 17 of
the East Broad Top Railroad hauls at freight
train at Orbisonia, Pennsylvania.

RIGHT
Narrow-gauge Mikado-type 2-8-2
locomotives of the Denver & Rio Grande
Railroad.

OPPOSITE
A narrow-gauge Mikado-type 2-8-2
locomotive of the K27 class operated by the
Denver & Rio Grande Railroad.

Another threat to the steam-powered locomotive at this time was posed by the diesel-engined locomotive. This was a comparatively new type, but already it was beginning to rival the steam-powered locomotive in terms of performance and, perhaps more importantly, in terms of instant availability for service when required, without the need for a period in which to light the fire and heat the water to operating temperature.

One of the ultimate expressions of American steam-locomotive development that appeared at this time, was the New York Central Railroad's Niagara type, which was designed with the very high 6,000hp (4474kW) and also a power/weight ratio better than that offered by the railroad's current 4-6-4 locomotives. This objective was achieved by the combination of a number of factors, including the omission of a steam dome to allow the introduction of a boiler of greater diameter, the enlargement of the firebox, steam passages and superheater elements, the use of higher-strength carbon steel, where appropriate, and the introduction of roller bearings. To allow full exploitation of the design's capabilities, driving wheels with diameters of 75 and 79in (1.905 and 2.007m) were supplied. Appearing in 1945, the S1 class of Niagara-type locomotives was used on the route linking New York and Chicago, regularly working the 930-mile (1497-km) stretch from Harmon, where they took over from the electric locomotives that brought the trains out of Grand Central Station, to Chicago. The railroad undertook a very rigorous comparative examination of the performance and operating economics of the S1-class steam

locomotives and comparable diesel locomotives: the six S1 locomotives had availability and utilization rates of 76 per cent and 69 per cent respectively, amounting to the ability to cover 260,000 miles (418420km) per year, while the diesels, which were nearly twice as expensive to purchase, typically offered 330,000 miles (531070km).

Thus there was a limited case for the continued use of the S1-class locomotives, but there were problems with the high-strength/low-weight steel that had been used for the manufacture of their boilers, which soon began to crack. The New York Central Railroad then decided that the reboilering programme that would be required would not offer a good return on the required investment, and abandoned its last steam-powered locomotives in favour of diesel-engined locomotives for its next generation of engines. Within a few years more, virtually every American railroad had followed the same course and the steam-powered locomotive retreated into history.

In parallel with steam-powered locomotives for passenger services, the steady evolution of the same type of locomotive suitable for freight was in progress. As early as 1842 Matthias Baldwin had created the design of a 0-8-0 dedicated freight locomotive for the Central Railway of Georgia. This was too complex in its mechanical details to be adopted by more than a very limited number of operators, but it nonetheless demonstrated that the use of larger numbers of smaller wheels was the way in which an effective freight-hauling locomotive should be designed.

An operator whose services needed considerably increased power was the Central Pacific Railroad, whose line included a steep climb from Sacramento into the Sierra Nevada mountains. In 1882 A.J. Stevens created an effective 4-8-0 design, of which 20 were manufactured for the Central Pacific Railroad. The following year Stevens expanded on this original concept to produce the 4-10-0 locomotive named *El Gobernador*, but the huge engine turned the scales at 65 tons and was thus too heavy for the track of the period and remained a prototype, albeit the largest locomotive in the world, rather than a working engine.

In the last part of the 19th century, Mogul- and Consolidation-type locomotives, of 2-6-0 and 2-8-0 layouts respectively, became the standard types for freight operations. The latter was generally more successful and popular, and among the most powerful of such locomotives at the beginning of the 20th century were two manufactured in 1900 by the Pittsburgh Locomotive Works for the Bessemer & Lake Erie Railroad's iron ore-carrying operation. Weighing more than 110 tons and developing a tractive effort of almost 64,000lb (29030kg), these were created to work the heavily graded line between the railroad's docks at Conneaut and its yard at Albion. Others of the same manufacturer's 2-8-0 locomotives for use on less steeply graded sections of the same operator's line were less massive at a weight of 79 tons or slightly more, with a tractive effort of 38,400lb (17420kg).

The principal advantage offered by the eight-coupled layout was the concentration of the weight on the driving wheels, which provided greater adhesion and thus improved tractive effort. An indication of the popularity of the type in the early part of the 20th century was the series of orders, totalling 680 units, placed by the government of the U.S.A. for locomotives of the type for military service in France during World War I. Such was the manufacturing effort devoted to this high-priority programme that by a time early in 1918 no fewer than 30 locomotives were being completed every day. By this time, still larger locomotives were being adopted for regular use.

There was not the same speed requirement for freight as there was for passenger locomotives, so two-wheel leading trucks were standard even though some operators did prefer four : the Pennsylvania Railroad, as just a single example, during 1918 introduced the first of an extensive series of 4-8-2 locomotives for fast freight duties. The series reached its peak in 1930 with the M1a class, whose units each weighed 342 tons, including the tender, and offered a tractive effort of 64,550lb (29280kg).

More commonly used was the freight locomotive counterpart of the Pacific-type passenger engine. This was the Mikado type of 2-8-2 configuration, and was the single type of freight locomotive manufactured in the largest numbers: production totalled some 9,500 units compared with the manufacture of about 22,000 2-8-0 locomotives. The Atchison, Topeka & Santa Fe Railway took the process one step further in 1903 with the introduction of its 2-10-2 locomotive, which used the trailing truck to give greater

flexibility on the railroad's sections over mountainous terrain, characterized by steep grades and tight curves.

The Mikado type of 2-8-2 steam locomotives were manufactured in considerably greater numbers than any other type of steam locomotive in the 20th century and, like the Pacific-type locomotive, the first examples were built for narrow-gauge operation on a gauge of 42in (1.067m). The initial order for 20 engines was placed with Baldwin in 1897 by the government of Japan, so the origin of the name is more than obvious. The task facing Baldwin, when it was tasked with designing and building this type, was the production of an eight-coupled freight locomotive capable of generating an adequate head of steam on coal of inferior quality, which was all that the Japanese could obtain at that time. Baldwin decided that the best approach to the problem was a deep firebox of considerable volume with a grate of large area, which dictated the incorporation of an additional pair of pivoted carrying wheels at the rear, so creating the 2-8-2 layout.

The Mikado-type locomotives were otherwise typical of the design and manufacturing standards prevalent at the end of the 19th century, and thus incorporated inside Stephenson's valve gear and outside slide-valve cylinders. Unusual features were the copper cap of the smokestack and the inside bearings to the rear truck, plus Japanese-specified ancillary equipment such as the buffers, screw-couplings and vacuum brakes then used on the Nippon Railway. Automatic couplers of U.S. pattern replaced the original units in the 1930s.

The locomotives were very reliable and successful, to the extent that the Japanese were encouraged to build large numbers of additional locomotives of the same type in their own facilities, the last of them emerging from Japanese workshops as late as 1962. The Japanese also built a number of locomotives for standard-gauge operations during Japan's occupation of much of China during the 1930s and 1940s.

Large numbers of Mikado-type locomotives were also manufactured for a host of American operators, and so many of them were still in service during World War II that an effort was made to change the name from 'Mikado' to 'MacArthur', after General Douglas MacArthur, who was supervising Allied operations against the Japanese in the South-West Asian theatre of war. The effort never really got off the ground, and during the war the MacArthur name was current only for the locomotives built for operation in the regions liberated from Japanese control.

From the use of a trailing truck with two wheels it was natural to evolve toward one with four wheels, so that a firebox of greater size could be supported. During the mid-1920s eight- and 10-coupled locomotives of this layout were created. The 2-10-4 configuration was known to American operators as the Texas type, as the first such engine was built to the order of the Texas & Pacific Railroad in 1925, and to Canadian operators as the Selkirk type, being first used in this mountain region of western Canada from 1929. The 2-8-4 freight locomotive was first used by the New York Central Railroad in 1925, which led to the general use of the designation Berkshire

A Denver & Rio Grande Railroad excursion train hauled by a 2-8-2 locomotive of the Mikado type.

Captured for posterity on 8 August 1991, this is the A-class 2-6-6-2 locomotive No. 1218 of the Norfolk & Western (built at Roanoke in 1943) crossing the Ohio river bridge at Kenova, West Virginia.

A 2-8-2 locomotive of the K36-class, latterly of the Denver & Rio Grande Western Railroad, rests at Osier, Colorado.

This Atchison, Topeka & Santa Fe Railway heavy-duty freight locomotive, of the 2-10-4 type, was purchased from the Baldwin Locomotive Works as a unit of the 5000-class. Its tender carried 20,000 U.S. gallons (75708 litres) of water, and each of the five coal tenders had a capacity of 23 tons of coal.

Locomotive No. 2903, a 4-8-4 unit of the 2900 class with driving wheels of 80-in (2.03-m) diameter, was used for heavy fast-freight services on level territory and also for heavy passenger services.

type, after the mountain range of that name in the western part of Massachusetts.

Certainly numbered among the largest non-articulated freight locomotives must be the 4-10-2 and 4-12-2 engines manufactured by Alco for the Union Pacific Railroad and delivered for service from 1926. The four-wheel pilot trucks allowed the use of three cylinders, which maximized the power that could be obtained without resorting to articulation. Weighing 350 tons, the 90 examples of the 4-12-2 type each delivered a tractive effort of 96,600lb (43820kg) and could work 3,800-ton trains at an average speed of 35mph (56m/h).

Largest of all steam locomotives, however, were the articulated units. The particular articulation system employed for locomotives used on American railroads was that developed by Anatole Mallet in France in the later part of the 19th century. This was based on a single boiler supplying steam to two sets of cylinders. This steam was used first by two high-pressure cylinders and was then delivered to two low-pressure ones. The main feature differentiating the Mallet system from other compound systems, however, was the employment of two sets of driving wheels on separate chassis: the leading chassis was arranged so that it could turn and swivel, thus improving the ability of the whole locomotive to negotiate curves without problem.

The Frenchman, Anatole Mallet, took out a patent in 1884 for a locomotive with a hinged front part. He seems to have had it in mind to use his concept mainly in connection with small tank engines intended specifically for sharply curved local and industrial railways. The idea that his patent would be the basis of the largest, heaviest and most powerful locomotives ever built would have seemed strange, had he known, but this is what indeed happened.

The Baltimore & Ohio Railroad had a problem taking heavy trains up the Sand Patch incline, which was 16-miles (26-km) long with a 1 per cent gradient. There were sharp 7° curves (with a radius of 275 yards/250m), which limited the number of driving wheels that could be used on a locomotive with no provision for hinged articulation. The idea developed by the Baltimore & Ohio was to replace the two 2-8-0 helpers, currently necessary to move a 2,000-ton train up the incline, with a single articulated locomotive. Hindsight suggests that the solution had been obvious from the start, but at the time the proposal to introduce a relatively novel concept from Europe, where it was seen as a solution to small-scale problems, must have seemed like wishful thinking; but the management of the Baltimore & Ohio clearly had confidence in its assessment, at least as far as initial development was concerned, and approached the American Locomotive Company for the first Mallet compound locomotive designed and built in the U.S.A. The result was a turning point in U.S. locomotive history.

Numbered 2400, this locomotive marked the appearance of another innovation for U.S. railroad practice, and was in fact destined to have an effect on locomotives even more significant than the Mallet articulated arrangement. It was the first major locomotive of American design and manufacture to feature outside Walschaert valve gear, one set working the inside-admission piston valves of the high-pressure rear cylinders, the other having the slightly different arrangement appropriate to slide valves, which are inherently outside-admission. This straightforward mechanism, offering simplicity, accessibility and sturdy reliability, was responsible for a first-class sequence of valve operation, and rapidly became the standard arrangement for the considerable majority of North American steam locomotives. Another feature introduced on No. 2400, and which later became standard, was the steam-powered reversing gear, the arrangement of four valve gears raising the effort required to a level that was effectively beyond the capacity of manual operation. Moreover, the mechanisms of straight two-cylinder engines later became so large that a power-operated reverse became general for all but the smallest locomotives.

In general terms the Mallet principle can be assessed as producing a normal locomotive with a powered leading truck, for the frame of the rear high-pressure engine has the boiler attached rigidly to it. If deemed necessary, the large low-pressure cylinders can be located ahead of the smokebox, with no limit on their size. The pivoting arrangements for the forward engine are relatively uncomplicated, and comprise a hinge at the rear and a slide at the front.

Delivered in 1904 and popularly known as *Old Maude* (page 253), the 0-6-6-0 No. 2400 remained a one-off locomotive, but proved most prolific in terms of offspring, whose total extended into the thousands. These descendants included, with almost no exceptions, the largest, sturdiest and most potent reciprocating steam locomotives ever built. Thus, within just a few years, the Mallet type of articulated locomotive had became very popular with operators running heavy freight services. As the number of driving wheels was increased from 12 to 16 and even 20, leading and trailing trucks were added to enhance riding qualities and, later, to provide adequate support for a larger firebox. The most popular layout for Mallet-type locomotives in North America was 2-6-6-2, but the largest of all were the 4-8-8-4 Big Boy units delivered to the Union Pacific Railroad from 1941. At 354 tons, these were the heaviest steam locomotives ever made. They were not the most powerful, however, but the Big Boy units were fast and operationally efficient and, like the preceding Challenger-type 4-6-6-4 units, could haul express freight trains at up to 50mph (80.5km/h). Nothing excelled the Big Boy locomotives on the Union Pacific Railroad's route through the mountains between Ogden and Cheyenne, where they ensured timely delivery of fruit trains between Ogden and Green river, where Challenger-type locomotives took over. Like the later Mallet-type locomotives operated by other American railroads, both of these Union Pacific Railroad types dispensed with compounding when the low-pressure cylinders had become so large that they could no longer be installed and the valves had become inadequate to deal with the volume of steam.

Many variations on the theme of the Mallet type eventually made an appearance.

In 1914, for example, the Erie Railway received the first of three 2-8-8-8-2 Triplex Mallet locomotives, of a pattern developed by Baldwin and carrying a second set of low-pressure cylinders on the tender, for service as helpers. The addition of extra cylinders, without extra steam-generating capacity, was a factor that militated against the general success of the Triplex concept, however. A 2-8-8-8-4 unit with a larger boiler and slightly smaller cylinders was delivered to the Virginian Railroad, but this suffered the same type of limitation as the Erie's Triplex unit. The same lack of overall success attended the 2-10-10-2 units of the Atchison, Topeka & Santa Fe Railway; rebuilt to this configuration from earlier locomotives, these were characterized by jointed boilers. More successful, though, were the 10 examples of a 2-10-10-2 type that the Virginian Railroad bought, despite its unhappy experience with the Triplex, to help 6,000-ton coal-carrying trains up an 11-mile (17.7-km) stretch of 2 per cent grades in the Allegheny mountains.

Two other operators which enjoyed considerable success with Mallet-type locomotives in mountainous terrain were the Denver & Rio Grande Western Railroad, which operated locomotives of the articulated type on its difficult main lines in the Rockies, and the Southern Pacific Railroad that developed a cab-first locomotive for service in the Sierra Nevada mountain section of its line linking destinations in the states of California and Nevada. Their use of oil rather than coal as fuel made it possible for 4-8-8-2 locomotives of this type, of which 195 were completed between 1928 and 1944, to run

backward in an unusual arrangement with the tender trailing, the engineer thereby enjoying an unhindered forward field of vision.

As noted above, the Mallet was the largest type of steam locomotive ever built in North America, and it was also among the last of the breed to be manufactured. In the period following the end of World War II, American railroad operators turned quite swiftly to the use of diesel-engined locomotives, but the Norfolk & Western Railroad, involved primarily in the movement of coal from the mining area of Kentucky and West Virginia, tried to improve its locomotives to offer operational availability and efficiency equal to that of diesel-engined locomotives. The Norfolk & Western designed and built three new models in its own facilities: the J-class 4-8-4 locomotives were delivered from 1941 as units optimized for the working of prestige passenger services at 100mph (161km/h) or more, while the A and Y classes of 2-6-6-4 and 2-8-8-2 articulated locomotives, dating from 1936 and 1948 respectively, were optimized for freight-hauling service, the A-class units at speeds of up to 70mph (112.6km/h) and the Y6-class for heavier loads at lower speeds. The real advance with these and the Y6b type, the final development of the Mallet concept, was the complete rationalization of maintenance, so that less than an hour was needed for a total inspection, refuelling and lubrication between runs: significantly, the maintenance cost of the Y6b was 37 per cent lower than that of the preceding Y5-class locomotive.

Even so, the Norfolk & Western Railroad was unable to stem the apparently inexorable

progress of the diesel-engined locomotive. The Y6b was manufactured up to 1952, but the Norfolk & Western had itself contracted for the delivery of 75 diesel-engined locomotives by 1957. The operator's last steam locomotive, and the last such engine completed for any main-line railroad in the U.S.A, was an 0-8-0 switcher, completed in 1953. Finally, the difficulty of maintaining a fleet of steam-engined locomotives, after the rest of the national industry had switched to diesel power, inevitably caught up with the Norfolk & Western, and in 1960 the operator ended steam operations with a final run by a Y6b locomotive on 4 April of that year.

By 1905 the Mallet articulated locomotive was an established fact on North American railroads. The type offered considerably

The 2-10-4 locomotive No. 900.

greater power than conventional locomotives, but did not remove altogether the requirement for greater tractive effort in the provision of helper services on notably severe grades. And while the limitations of drawbar strength obviated any huge increases in tractive effort in the hauling of heavy trains, greater power could be used effectively in the matter of pushing heavy trains.

This fact led to the design and manufacture for the Erie Railway of the Triplex (triple Mallet) type of articulated locomotive. The specific demand was for a powerful type to remove the expensive need for several helpers to move heavy trains up Gulf Hill, one of the most difficult features of the railroad's Susquehanna Division. The design was created by Baldwin as a compound Mallet with three rather than the

more standard engine units. To this extent the Triplex can be regarded as a 2-8-8-0 Mallet to which an 0-8-2 steam-powered tender was linked. The forward and rear units were driven by four low-pressure cylinders, while the central unit was powered by two high-pressure cylinders: all the cylinders had the same bore and stroke. The forward engine disposed of its exhaust straight up the smokestack in the standard fashion, but the rear engine had a separate exhaust at the back of the tender. The heat of the exhaust was used to warm the feed water by the simple expedient of passing the exhaust steam through a heater underneath the tender before it was vented.

In purely nominal terms, the tractive effort of the Triplex was somewhat greater than that offered by the Union Pacific

Railroad's Big Boy locomotives. This was not realized in practice, however, for the design team failed to provide the locomotive with the ability to generate sufficient steam. With only a low speed envisaged, the boiler was in theory large enough for the task, but experience revealed that a mere half of the exhaust steam, and that at very low pressure, became available at the blastpipe: this was insufficient to produce enough smokebox vacuum to ensure good steaming.

The Triplex's overall weight of 853,050lb (386943kg) made it the heaviest of all steam locomotives. Only four Triplex locomotives were manufactured, three of them for the Erie Railway and the fourth, a slightly different unit, for the Virginian Railroad. The first of the Triplex locomotives, which was named the *Matt H. Shay* after one of the Erie's senior

The Mallet-type locomotives Nos. 2175 and 2186 of the Norfolk & Western at Bluefield, West Virginia.

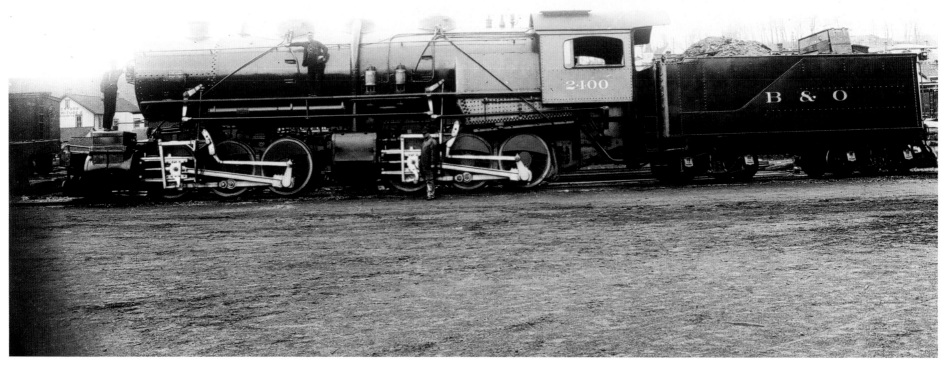

ABOVE
The Mallet-type 0-6-6-0 locomotive No. 2400 of the Baltimore & Ohio Railroad.

OPPOSITE
A Big Boy-type 4-8-8-4 locomotive of the Union Pacific Railroad at Scranton, Pennsylvania.

engineers, set a world record when it was first evaluated: on this occasion, it hauled a 17,600-ton train of 250 wagons along a line that trended uphill and included a number of 0.9 per cent grades over its length of 23 miles (37km). The average speed of this prodigious effort was 13.5mph (21.7km/h). Despite their apparent potential, the Triplex locomotives were never wholly successful in service, and

the last of them was retired in 1925, in the process terminating a fascinating attempt to maximize the capabilities of steam locomotion. This is perhaps a pity, for there was nothing technically wrong with the concept embodied in the Triplex, which was defeated by detail problems and lack of steam-generating capacity, both of them failings that could have been overcome.

The Mallet type of articulated steam locomotive, with more than 16 driving wheels, had not been generally successful in the period up to 1918. However, the Virginian Railroad had a major problem with the working of heavy loads over its routes across the Appalachian Mountains; Baldwin had sold the operator a 2-8-8-8-4 Triplex locomotive similar to the three operated by the Erie

OPPOSITE
The Union Pacific Railroad's Challenger-type 4-6-6-4 steam locomotive No. 3985 banks a diesel-hauled service outside Junction, Oregon.

Railway, but which had been found to possess insufficient steam-generating capability. The Virginian Railroad's Triplex locomotive therefore introduced features designed to improve this deficiency and therefore make possible a more effective employment of its three sets of power-generating machinery. But these still proved inadequate for the task and the Virginian Railroad made the sensible decision to have its Triplex divided into two smaller but more effective locomotives in the form of a 2-8-8-0 and a 2-8-0 unit.

Even so, this left the Virginian Railroad with the problem of how to deliver very heavy loads of coal from the coalfields across the mountains and down to the ports of the coast at Norfolk. The primary difficulty, toward the beginning of the loaded run, was the 2.11 per cent grade from the loading facility at Elmore in West Virginia to the summit at Clark's Gap. The problem became more acute in World War I, when the Virginian Railroad was faced with the need to deliver ever larger quantities of coal to stoke the U.S.A.'s booming industries; consequently, in 1917 the railroad decided to risk another attempt at using large Mallet-type locomotives. This time the order went to the American Locomotive Company, which was contracted to design and manufacture a batch of vast 2-10-10-2 locomotives. The result was a genuinely excellent locomotive type, the 800 class, of which the first examples were delivered in 1918.

At a superficial level, the locomotives did not look huge, largely as a result of their comparatively small tenders, but some of their details indicate the extreme nature of the design. The low-pressure cylinders were the largest ever to enter service on a locomotive, and were typified by a diameter of 48in (1219mm). The locomotives had an adhesive weight 14 per cent greater than that of the Union Pacific Railroad's Big Boy locomotives, and their tractive effort was 40 per cent more than that of the Big Boys as steam was admitted to the low-pressure engine at starting. In overall terms, the power was less than that of the Big Boys, as the locomotives were designed for low-speed freight hauling, but the 800-class locomotives achieved with ease all that was demanded of them, were reliable and comparatively easily maintained, and remained in service with the Virginian Railroad for 30 years up to the final decline of steam locomotion.

A typical 5,500-ton coal train was generally headed by a single 2-8-8-2 locomotive, which was able to handle the whole route, apart from the 2.11 per cent grade, where the locomotive's efforts were supplemented by those of two 800-class locomotives working as pushers to permit the whole assembly to chuff uphill at a ponderous but steady 5.5mph (9km/h).

At the technical level, the 800-class locomotives were interesting in that they combined two different types of valve in their workings: the high-pressure cylinders had conventional piston valves, while the great low-pressure cylinders featured slide valves that now seem somewhat old-fashioned. However, they were perfectly acceptable for the lower temperatures typical of the lower-pressure part of the system, and offered the advantage of being simpler to maintain.

The 800 class is believed to have been the only successful locomotives with as many as 20 driving wheels, and what it certain is that the Mallet concept was nowhere else pushed to such an extreme. The task of moving very heavily laden trains up to Clark's Gap was nonetheless reflected in the decision of the Virginian Railroad, after the 800-class locomotives had been in service for only a few years, to switch this section of the track to electric locomotion. The 800-class locomotives were then given less demanding tasks, in which they remained viable into the 1940s.

Appearing five years after the 800 class, the 4300 class of 4-8-2 Mountain-type locomotives of the Southern Pacific Railroad illustrate in classic form the difference between tractive effort and power. While locomotives with a high tractive effort are often categorized as being powerful, this is basically misleading. This can easily be seen in the 4300-class locomotive, a 4-8-2 developed from a 4-6-2 type: while the addition of two more driving wheels produced a greater tractive effort, the power (based on the size of the firebox) was nonetheless limited, as there was still only one pair of wheels to support the firebox. High tractive effort is essential in movement up steep grades, whereas high power is only useful. This was a factor that was of particular significance to the Southern Pacific Railroad, whose eastward trains from Sacramento faced the difficult climb into the Sierra Nevada, the ascent to Summit Pass over a distance of 80 miles (128km) rising from about sea level to 6,890ft (21000m).

During 1923 the Southern Pacific Railroad contracted with the American Locomotive Company for the first of an eventual 77 4-8-2 locomotives, of which the later units were built by the railroad. The design was essentially orthodox except for the incorporation of a cylindrical Vanderbilt tender, while a booster engine was fitted to drive on the rear carrying wheels to produce additional tractive effort. The locomotives were very successful, and while a 12-wheel tender was standard, some of the earlier locomotives had tenders with eight wheels.

The Mallet-type locomotives were not the only haulers of heavy loads to appear in the first stages of the 20th century. By this time the technology of locomotive design and manufacture had progressed considerably since the failure of early ten-coupled locomotives, such as the Southern Pacific Railroad's *El Gobernador* of 1883. Another operator facing a major problem shifting heavy loads under adverse geographical conditions was the Atchison, Topeka & Santa Fe Railway, which faced the daunting task of hauling freight trains over mountains on its services to and from destinations in the state of California. One of the most adverse of these points in the Atchison, Topeka & Santa Fe system was the approach to the Raton Pass, which was characterized by a 3.5 per cent incline. The railroad procured two large Decapod 2-10-0 locomotives for service as pushers to aid conventionally hauled services up this very daunting incline, and they proved themselves equal to this specialized task. The only significant problem was that when running back down, after boosting a train up

the incline, the Decapods suffered from a lack of guiding wheels to complement the limited tracking capability of their long and rigid wheelbases.

After reflecting on the problem, the Atchison, Topeka & Santa Fe contracted with Baldwin for the design and manufacture of the world's first and therefore history-making class of 2-10-2 locomotives. This, generally designated as the Santa Fe type for obvious reasons, was subsequently manufactured in very large numbers (up to 2,200 units for American service alone) during the following 40 years. The original locomotives, of which the first was delivered in 1903, were especially interesting in their arrangement as 'tandem' compound locomotives, in which each high-pressure cylinder shared a common piston rod with the relevant low-pressure cylinder. As might be imagined, this raised the spectre of maintenance difficulties with regard to the packing of the glands between each pair of cylinders, but the problem had been foreseen and a small crane was therefore provided on each side of the smokebox. Even so, there remained problems and the Atchison, Topeka & Santa Fe soon decided, after initial experience with these 900-class locomotives, never again to buy a locomotive, regardless of size, with anything but two cylinders.

Before the problems of maintenance in so complex a locomotive became fully evident, though, the Atchison, Topeka & Santa Fe took the extraordinary step in 1911 of rebuilding 20 of the 900 class of 2-10-2 locomotives into 10 examples of the 3000 class of 2-10-10-2 articulated locomotives, at the time the most powerful in the world. The 3000-class

conversions were not successful, however, and were thereupon taken in hand during 1915 for reconversion to 2-10-2 standard. This reflected the major change that had been effected in the senior management of the Atchison, Topeka & Santa Fe Railway, which decided at this time to undertake the major process of converting all of the railroad's compound locomotives, some 1,000 units in all, to a simple propulsion standard.

The 2-10-2 locomotives featured at the top of the priority list for this conversion process, which proved so successful that after the end of World War II these long-serving and effective locomotives, used for general freight haulage as well as helping, were joined by more modern locomotives of the same basic type. This meant that as the period of steam locomotion on American railroads drew to a close in the later 1940s, the Atchison, Topeka & Santa Fe still had a total of just under 300 2-10-2 locomotives on strength.

Despite the fact that it was finding itself increasingly unhappy with the reliability and maintenance problems of its most advanced locomotives, such as the units of the 900 class, the Atchison, Topeka & Santa Fe Railway nonetheless took the apparently senseless decision to move one step further and introduce, after its fairly complex locomotives, some very complicated ones indeed. An early result of this process was the 1300 class of just two extraordinary 2-4-6-2 compound locomotives of the Mallet type, which were manufactured by Baldwin and delivered in 1909. The locomotives had been schemed for the working of fast passenger traffic, and for this reason were built with 73-in (1.854-m) wheels, which were even larger in diameter than those installed on a Mallet-type locomotive. Other features of the design were a low centre of gravity, a complex boiler that was long, thin and based on the use of a corrugated firebox, and plate stays in place of the more orthodox staybolts. Moreover, the boiler was in two sections, with a separate forward chamber working as a heater for the feed water.

The locomotives featured a superheater, as was becoming standard during this period, but the Atchison, Topeka & Santa Fe went a stage further along this road and added a reheater, basically similar to a superheater but disposed to apply still more heat to the steam after it departed the high-pressure cylinders but before it reached the low-pressure cylinders. The net result was a small advantage in thermal efficiency, though the cost of maintaining the reheaters proved greater than the saving on their use.

Quite apart from the maintenance difficulties that they revealed, the locomotives of this Mallet type were found in operational service to have another disadvantage, namely an excessive degree of 'flexibility', which made them uncomfortable at higher speeds. This manifested itself in a tendency toward strong oscillations, consequently ways to reduce the front engine's degree of freedom had to be found before these articulated locomotives were deemed suitable for service in anything other than the working of slow freight trains.

During 1915 the two locomotives were revised by removing their front engines and front boiler stages, much improving them for service as simple two-cylinder 4-6-2 units whose potential for high speeds could finally be realized. Despite their general unhappiness with the two 2-4-6-2 locomotives, the Atchison, Topeka & Santa Fe still saw a possible advantage in yet more advanced Mallet-type locomotives, and ordered a small number of 2-6-6-2 articulated locomotives with still more complicated flexible boiler arrangements: the front stage of the boiler was fixed to the leading chassis and was actually hinged to the rear part. In an effort to make the concept workable, concertina connections and ball-and-socket joints were used to join the two parts of the boilers, but neither of these was effective.

This is only one aspect, albeit the core one, of steam locomotion in the U.S.A., for there were many types of locomotives other than those that worked main-line passenger and freight services. Some of these were efforts to extend the life of steam as a practical form of motive power, a typical example being the use of steam turbines, which a small number of railroads experimented with in and around the time of World War II. One such aspect of turbine development was the 6-8-6 geared turbine locomotive that the Pennsylvania Railroad tested in 1944: this saw a limited amount of operational service but had no long-term effect on the decline of steam power. Another way in which steam was applied to railroad operations was in the form of the generation of electricity powering motors on the driving axles. Experiments along this line were undertaken in 1938 by the Union Pacific, in 1947 by the Chesapeake & Ohio, and in 1952 by the Norfolk & Western railroads.

An earlier type of locomotive, based on the use of geared transmission, was created for the specific task of operating on the extemporized railroads associated with the logging industry. The story of the unique Shay locomotive is centred on the Lima Locomotive Works located in the state of Ohio. This had been established as the Lima Machine Works, the builder of machinery for a number of purposes, but in 1880 decided to switch to the manufacture of steam locomotives and in the process changed its name. The initial product of the renamed company was an unusual steam-driven flatcar designed by Ephraim Shay, a man whose primary experience was in the timber, and more specifically, the logging, industry. The first Shay locomotives were completed with vertical boilers, but the type soon switched to horizontal locomotive-type boilers, although these were offset from the locomotive's centreline to balance the engine, which was of a two- or three-cylinder inline design with vertical cylinders. The engine drove the axles by means of a fore-and-aft pair of longitudinal shafts, universal joints and bevel gears.

In its basic form, the Shay locomotive had a pair of two-axle trucks, but was designed to facilitate the addition at the rear of more trucks driven in the same way. Shay locomotives of the three-truck type were common, and there were also limited numbers of four-truck locomotives. Whatever its precise form, the Shay locomotive had all its wheels driven, was very flexible longitudinally, and provided a high degree of reliability and strength because of its structural

The tender of a J4-class 2-8-2 locomotive takes on water at the engine yard of the Radnor Roundhouse at Nashville, Tennessee.

Steam perfection: Norfolk & Western power. Left to right: J-class 4-8-4 No. 604; Y6b compound 2-8-8-2 No. 2147; A-class 2-6-6-4 No. 1212.

and mechanical simplicity. It was therefore capable of hauling useful loads in applications such as logging, in which the Shay's ability to work successfully on highly uneven temporary tracks was also a major asset. These same characteristics also made the Shay locomotive a 'natural' for railroads with very steep grades and curves of small radius. Over a period of 65 years from 1880, some 2,770 were delivered, but sales fell off after 1920 and the last of the breed was completed in 1944. By this time, it should be noted, the emphasis of

the Lima Locomotive Works had shifted from manufacture of the essentially small Shay locomotive to the design and construction of very large and powerful steam locomotives of the conventional type. Thus Lima came to rival the previous two giants of the American steam locomotive industry, Baldwin and the American Locomotive Company.

The Shay locomotive, it should be noted, incorporated a number of important features, other than its basic layout, with varying numbers of flexible powered trucks. For

instance, the boiler was short and of a considerable diameter in its centre, but tapered sharply toward its front and rear in a fashion that ensured the minimum alteration in the boiler's water level at the firebox end, despite the inclination of the locomotive on steep grades. This meant that they could work on 10 per cent grades without problem; moreover, their longitudinal flexibility also meant that they could make their way round curves with a radius as small as 25 yards (23m) without danger of derailment.

OPPOSITE
A Y6b-class locomotive of the 2-8-8-2 Mallet type, hauling a heavy freight service of the Norfolk & Western, takes on water somewhere in Virginia during October 1951.

LEFT
Until suppressors were fitted in the smokestacks of steam locomotives, steaming through wooded areas was a potentially dangerous operation as hot smuts could set trackside grass, bushes and even trees on fire.

The Lima Locomotive Works promoted the saleability of its Shay locomotives by creating a full range of units available in any gauge, in weights from as little as 50,000lb (22680kg) up to 320,000lb (145152kg), and with grates suitable for the burning of fuels as diverse as coal, oil and waste wood from logging operations. Last but certainly not least, the Shay locomotives were very reliable and, should they break, were also easy to repair, even in the most primitive of maintenance and repair facilities. Optimized for heavy haulage under the most adverse of operating and geographical conditions, often exacerbated by dire weather, the Shay locomotive had a typical maximum speed of only 12mph (19.3km/h). Their low cost, easy maintainability and very modest speed has made surviving Shay locomotives ideal for the operation of steam-train services in a number of tourist locations.

The chain-driven Robb was another type of steam locomotive, this time with a tilted boiler but again optimized for use by the logging industry, and was developed in Canada for construction from 1903 to run on timber tracks. Two other unusual types of locomotive were the Heeler and Climax, also for the logging industry: the former had a V-cylinder arrangement and was driven by a central shaft and universal couplings, while the latter had a combination of chains and gears.

These were all very specialized, but within the standard railroad operations there were large numbers of smaller steam locomotives to undertake more mundane but nonetheless vital support tasks. Such, for

example, were the vast numbers of 0-6-0 and 0-8-0 switching engines that were employed to make up trains in the classification yards: these were often obsolete engines past their prime and relegated from the main lines to the yards, but many were purpose-built for the bigger railroads.

By the 1920s the writing was beginning to appear on the wall and the continued viability of steam locomotion was now in doubt. Electric locomotion had made its first appearance in the later part of the 19th century for commuter services, and in the early 1920s the threat of the diesel engine began to develop as an alternative to steam for longer-distance routes. Both of these power sources were still in their comparative infancies, however, so its maturity rather than its obsolescence meant that steam locomotion still had a future, albeit a limited one.

This goes a long way to explaining the continued development of steam locomotives, which reached its apogee in the period between the two world wars with a number of truly classic examples of engineering.

A concise account of the Southern Pacific Railroad's A class of 4-4-2 Atlantic-type locomotives is difficult, due to the fact that the type's operator ran it on three systems, organized as completely separate entities. These were the Southern Pacific Railroad proper, on which there ran 75 locomotives, built in the period between 1902 and 1911; the Southern Pacific de México, and the Texas & New Orleans, the latter often known as the 'Cotton Belt' Railroad. Both of the latter were made necessary because the governments of Mexico and Texas had each enacted legislation

that made it very difficult for non-Mexican and non-Texan railroads to operate on their territories. However, the Southern Pacific Railroad managed to get round these rules by creating entirely autonomous operations in the two regions.

The situation is further complicated by the fact that there were five separate 4-4-2 classes (the A1, A2, A3, A5 and A6) and their various rebuildings, which often meant that the locomotives within any one nominal class sometimes differed from each other more than from the locomotives of another of the original classes. These modifications included, among the most obvious changes, the types of tender used, circular-section Vanderbilt tanks of different sizes and capacities, standard 'box'-type tenders, and tenders with semi-circular tanks. Other changes incorporated in the rebuilding programme were improvements to the ports, passages and valve timing, and Walschaert valve gear in place of the original Stephenson.

The definitive pattern, if such a description can in fact be used with any real degree of accuracy, was the A6 class of 1925. The class resulted from a rebuilding programme, undertaken by the Southern Pacific Railroad at its own workshops in Sacramento, of four of the 51 A3-class locomotives originally manufactured in the period between 1904 and 1908 by the American Locomotive Company and Baldwin. Further complication is added to the story by the fact that these locomotives were renumbered using the numbers initially allocated to A1-class Vauclain-type compound locomotives that had already been scrapped.

Seven other A3-class locomotives were modified to the same standard but did not receive the new class designation.

The most important factor in the success of the 4-4-2 locomotives was the incorporation, from the start, of an excellent firebox, notable for its high volume (a result of its considerable depth) and the useful width of grate that could be installed above the two rear carrying wheels. One adverse factor, however, was the limited adhesion dictated by the use of only four driving wheels, but this was overcome in the rebuilt locomotives by the addition of a booster engine driving the rear wheels. Booster engines were particularly popular with the Southern Pacific Railroad, and over the years appeared on more than 300 4-8-2, 2-8-4, 4-8-4, 2-10-2 and 4-10-2 locomotives. The addition of such an engine was the most important alteration made to the rebuilt Atlantic-type locomotives, and boosted the nominal tractive effort by a useful 11,500lb (5216kg). It was designed to cut out once the speed had reached 10mph (16km/h), leaving the locomotive to operate as a 'pure ' 4-4-2 unit when working the operator's prestigious Daylight express services a high speed.

The locomotives were also used for other tasks, and when the load was greater than could be handled by a 4-8-2 on its own, a 4-4-2 was operated as a helper on steep grades, especially those on the west-coast route linking Los Angeles and San Francisco.

In 1927 there appeared several classes of locomotive with the 4-8-4 wheel arrangement that was arguably the best of all such configurations. The first of these new types was the Northern Pacific Railroad's A class of Northern-type locomotives. Other early operators of 4-8-4 locomotives were the Canadian National Railway (Confederation-type), the Delaware, Lackawanna & Western Railroad (Pocono-type), and the Atchison Topeka & Santa Fe Railway. Eventually, some 40 North American railroads used 4-8-4 locomotives, and the type was also operated in other countries. The first of these latter was Australia, where the South Australia Railway was the initial operator.

The need for the 4-8-4 was found in the tractive effort/grate area imbalance in the preceding 4-8-2 type of locomotive. So far as the Northern Pacific Railroad was concerned, this presented problems, inasmuch as the locally mined coal it used produced a large amount of ash, a fact that demanded the incorporation of a large firebox supported by a four- rather than a two-wheel rear truck. The firebox adopted for the Northern Pacific Railroad's 4-8-4 locomotives measured 13ft 6in (4.1m) by 8ft 6in (2.6m), which was considerably larger than the firebox of any 4-8-4 locomotive operated by other railroads. The Northern Pacific Railroad found its new locomotives to be so effective that it not only continued with the 4-8-4 formula for all its later steam locomotives for passenger services right up to 1943, but also kept to the basic design of the A in a number of subclasses.

The first 12 locomotives were manufactured for the Northern Pacific Railroad by the American Locomotive Company, and with the exception of their wheel layout and huge fireboxes were very typical of American locomotive practice of the time. A booster engine was installed to provide an additional 11,400lb (5170kg) of tractive effort for starting. It is interesting to note that the next 4-8-4 locomotive to operate on the Northern Pacific Railroad's lines was a special engine ordered in 1930 by the Timken Roller Bearing Company to demonstrate its product for the axles of steam locomotives. This locomotive proved successful when trialled on the lines of a number of railroads, thus generating sales for Timken. The Northern Pacific Railroad bought the locomotive in 1933 after it had completed its programme for the original purchaser, and specified Timken bearings for all its later locomotives.

If there is any one class and type of locomotive that can be deemed typical of North American steam locomotive design, manufacturing and operating practice in the 20th century, it was the O1 class of 2-8-2 locomotive, first ordered from Baldwin by the Chicago, Burlington & Quincy Railroad in 1910. The operator had received 70 such locomotives by the end of the following year, which allowed it to make significant improvements in its operations, which had become severely overtaxed through the combination of increasing traffic and obsolescent six-coupled locomotives that had been its mainstay up to this time. The class was produced by Baldwin up to 1923, the Chicago, Burlington & Quincy receiving 133 of them.

Improvements were effected steadily in the light of operating experience, and the total included both coal- and oil-burning examples. The O1-class locomotives were in no way innovatory, but were thoroughly reliable and

OPPOSITE
A diesel helper boosts a steam-pushed freight service of the Denver, Rio Grande & Western Railroad up the grade to the Cumbres Pass near Chama, New Mexico.

LEFT
The 2-8-4 Berkshire-type locomotive No. 765 of the New York, Chicago & St. Louis Railroad, better known as the 'Nickel Plate Road', dead-heads (reverses) its excursion train.

RIGHT
Magnificent though they were to see, hear and smell, steam locomotives were dirty to operate and also fouled the areas through which they ran, so with the advent of diesel and electric propulsion it was inevitable that the railroads should cast their eyes in the direction of the new systems, especially as these latter offered the prospect of lower procurement and operating costs.

OPPOSITE
Norfolk & Western's A-class 2-6-6-4 locomotive No. 1225 hauls an eastbound train through the New River Gorge at Ripplemead, Virginia, in September 1951.

just what the operator required for the maintenance of a regular and unexciting network of services over a region of the U.S.A. that was predominantly flat. Ultimately is was only the superior economics offered by diesel locomotives that persuaded the Chicago, Burlington & Quincy Railroad to retire its O1-class steam locomotives.

Another major force in the regional

railroad network of the Midwest was the Wabash Railroad, which had its headquarters in St. Louis, Missouri, and served destinations such as Chicago, Kansas City, Omaha, Toledo and Detroit with a 4,000-mile (6440-km) route network. In 1943 the Wabash Railroad found that it urgently needed new and more capable locomotives for its passenger services, which were suffering from the railroad's current use

of predominantly elderly locomotives with driving wheels of only 70in (1.778m), generally considered too small for passenger services. In the middle of World War II, however, there was no way that the railroad was going to be able to purchase entirely new locomotives, so it adopted a simple yet effective expedient, namely the reconstruction of six K5-class 2-8-2 locomotives into P1-

OPPOSITE
Single-role railroads, such as those associated with the lumber industry, demanded the creation of specialized steam locomotives that remained in unglamorous but effective service long after the steam locomotive had been relegated to the scrapyard by more prestigious main-line operators.

LEFT
A Shay-type locomotive of the Sugar Pine Railway at Jamestown, California.

class 4-6-4 units, supplemented after the war's end by another rebuilt 2-8-2 locomotive, in this instance a K4-class unit. The task of rebuilding was undertaken by the railroad's own workshops at Decatur, Illinois.

The 2-8-2 locomotives had originally been manufactured in 1925 by the American Locomotive Company to a standard typical of the time, with a three-cylinder machinery arrangement. This was changed to a two-cylinder arrangement when the locomotives were rebuilt, and other changes included three rather than four main axles, driving wheels of 80-in (2.032-m) diameter, two- rather than one-axle rear trucks, and roller rather than plain bearings. The P1-class locomotives were completed in a semi-streamlined form of notably handsome overall appearance, and

RIGHT
The designers and several operators of steam locomotives tried to fight the advent of diesel-engined locomotives for main-line services in several ways. Once such effort was the S2 class of 6-8-6 locomotives for the Pennsylvania Railroad, created and made by Baldwin in 1944 with a direct-drive propulsion arrangement based on a Westinghouse steam turbine.

OPPOSITE
Locomotive No. 2903 was built as a 4-8-4 Northern-type unit of the Atchison, Topeka & Santa Fe Railway's 2900 class.

RIGHT
The Santa Fe-type 2-10-2 locomotive No. 979 of the Atchison, Topeka & Santa Fe Railway.

OPPOSITE
Originally numbered 5, this Shay-type locomotive of the Cass Scenic Railroad of West Virginia began life as an engine of the Birch Valley Lumber Company, Tioga, West Virginia, during 1922. The Mower Lumber Company at Cass, West Virginia, acquired the engine in 1943 and renumbered it No. 4. Shay No. 4, along with No. 7, expanded the present-day No. 5's lineage by representing a typical example of the Lima-built C70-class locomotives built for West Virginia logging companies during the 1920s.

were often used to work prestige services such as the Blue Bird and Banner Blue between St. Louis and Chicago. As expedients, the P1-class locomotives proved difficult and expensive to maintain, and the Wabash Railroad switched to diesel operations soon after the end of World War II.

Several times, an altogether larger concept of steam locomotive was needed by the major

operators of long-distance services to haul trains at high speed. One such operator, of course, was the Union Pacific Railroad, which during the 1920s began to seek a new type of locomotive, powerful and preferably economical, to handle the growing volume of traffic on its routes. At this time the railroad's main locomotives were 2-10-2 units of limited adhesive power, allowing the haulage of light

loads at comparatively high speeds, and 2-8-8-0 Mallet-type compound locomotives of considerable tractive power, allowing the haulage of heavy loads but only at low speeds.

A solution was possible with a 12-coupled locomotive based on the use of a new concept, the lateral motion device developed by the American Locomotive Company as a means of allowing a long-wheelbase locomotive to

RIGHT
The Saginaw Timber Company's No. 2 locomotive, seen here at North Freedom, Wisconsin, is typical of the type of locomotive designed and built primarily for the logging industry.

OPPOSITE
Pacific White Cedar Company's No. 120 at Powers, Oregon.

negotiate sharp curves. The Union Pacific Railroad now planned a locomotive of this type on an altogether larger scale than anything that had hitherto been tried, and then only in places such as Bulgaria, the Dutch East Indies and Germany. The resulting type, ordered from the American Locomotive Company and first delivered in 1926, was the 9000 class, which was more than twice as massive as any previous 12-coupled locomotive.

The machinery was based on a three-cylinder arrangement, as the piston thrust that would be required by two-cylinder machinery was not thought feasible at the time; trials proved that the 9000-class locomotive was able to haul the same weight as the Mallet-type locomotives at considerably higher speeds and with much reduced fuel consumption, giving it the best of both worlds. By 1930 the Union Pacific Railroad had received 88 examples of this sole class of 4-12-2 locomotive. All was not plain sailing, however, for a number of more advanced features had been incorporated into the design and had caused a number of problems.

The length of the fixed wheelbase was no less than 30ft 8in (9.347m), and to ensure that this could negotiate comparatively tight curves the leading and trailing coupled wheels had provision for 1 inch (25mm) of lateral movement to each side of the centreline. Originally, the first of the locomotives to be completed had flangeless wheels on the central driving axle, but the latter locomotives had wheels with thin flanges.

A wheel arrangement especially associated with the New York Central Railroad

is the 4-6-4 layout. After the railroad had completed the manufacture of its final Pacific-type locomotive, a K5b-class unit delivered in 1926, its design team embarked on the creation of a somewhat larger locomotive to satisfy what were anticipated to be the railroad's requirements in the not too distant future. As its starting point, the team planned greater tractive effort for starting, greater cylinder power at higher speeds, and a combination of static and dynamic loads optimized for a useful reduction in the impact loads on the operator's track. Translation of these factors into specific design features suggested the need for a larger firebox, and a four- rather than two-wheel trailing truck to create a 4-6-4 configuration. Evident in the basic design were some of the concepts of the Lima Locomotive Works, but the order to manufacture the J1-class locomotives, which later received the type designation Hudson, was allocated initially to the American Locomotive Company, though some later contracts brought the Lima Locomotive Works into the manufacturing programme.

The first J1a-class locomotive was delivered to the New York Central Railroad in February 1927, though the American Locomotive Company already had similar locomotives in production for a number of other American railroads. The J1a was of notably impressive appearance, the use of a two- rather than one-axle trailing truck being largely responsible for the nice balance that was immediately evident. At the locomotive's front, curved casings, one on each side of the smokebox's base, were braced by diagonal bars and accommodated the air compressors

and boiler feed pump, and unusual curved casings ahead of the cab faired the boiler mountings.

The first J1a-class locomotive soon revealed excellent performance, generating a flurry of orders, mainly for the New York Central Railroad itself but including 80 for three of the railroad's wholly-owned subsidiaries, including the Boston & Albany Railroad, which received 30 locomotives of three J2-class subvariants which, because the operator had steeper gradients on its lines, had driving wheels of slightly smaller diameter. The New York Central Railroad's 145 locomotives were also completed in a number of subvariants between J1a and J1e, differentiated by features such as Walschaert or Baker valve gear, the latter having no moving parts and therefore needing less maintenance.

From the very beginning, these Hudson-type locomotives were notable for the working of heavy trains at high speeds: a typical maximum figure was a 1,270-ton train of 18 cars hauled at an average of 55mph (88.5km/h) on the flatter parts of the operator's route network.

The last J1- and J2-class locomotives were completed in 1932, but production was resumed in 1937 after the New York Central Railroad had contracted for 50 more Hudson-type locomotives, in this instance of the improved J3 class. Unlike the earlier examples of the J-class locomotive, these units included a combustion chamber in the firebox, a tapered boiler barrel to give a greater diameter at the front of the firebox to permit an increased boiler pressure, cylinders changed in

ABOVE
The stock-in-trade of preserved steam locomotives in now the hauling of excursion trains for steam enthusiasts and for visitors to theme parks and scenic areas. This is the Saginaw Timber No. 2 locomotive, a 2-8-2 unit, at North Freedom, Wisconsin.

OPPOSITE
An excursion train in the markings of the Denver & Rio Grande Railroad.

size from 25 x 28in (635 x 711mm) to 22.5 x 29in (572 x 737mm) and, as the most obvious feature, disc driving wheels. The last 10 of these 50 locomotives were enclosed in a streamlined casing designed by Henry Dreyfus. It is worth noting that of all the streamlined casings used on American locomotives, this was the first to work with, rather than against, the natural shape of the locomotive, the working parts of which were left exposed.

Operational experience soon confirmed

that the J3-class locomotives were both more efficient and more powerful than the J1-class units: at a speed of 65mph (105km/h) the J3 was 20 per cent more powerful than a J1. The locomotives could haul 1,125-ton trains over the 147-mile (236-km) route linking Albany and Syracuse at a scheduled speed of 59mph (95km/h), and could also attain 60mph (97km/h) with a 1,640-ton train.

The New York Central Railroad's most prestigious service was the Twentieth Century

Limited, between New York and Chicago, and the advent of the J1-class locomotive allowed the route schedule to be fixed at 20 hours, which was set at 18 hours in 1932 and 18.5 hours in 1936, after the advent of the J1e-class locomotive. This was finally set at just 16 hours in 1938 after the arrival of the J3. After World War II the Hudson-type locomotives were replaced on the New York Central's heaviest services by Niagara-type 4-8-4 locomotives, but the last of the excellent

RIGHT
Something of the mass and complexity of late-generation steam locomotives can be gauged from this photograph of the Y6b-class 2-8-8-2 Mallet-type locomotive No. 2185 in the final stages of its manufacture at the Norfolk & Western's Roanoke, Virginia, workshops on 21 May 1949.

OPPOSITE
Locomotive No. 2197 was a late example of the Mallet-typeY6b class of 2-8-8-2 locomotives designed, built and operated by the Norfolk & Western.

The impression conveyed by the Mallet type of articulated locomotive was often one of enormous brooding strength, which was very much the case with the massive Mallets designed and operated by the Norfolk & Western in the last years of steam locomotion as a major force in American main-line operations.

Hudsons was not taken out of service until 1956.

An operator of the Pacific class of locomotive for its most important passenger services since 1906, the Baltimore & Ohio Railroad began a service linking Washington and Jersey City during 1927, and to operate the route began to acquire its eventual total of eight classes of Pacific-type locomotives. The 20 P7-class units were more than half as powerful again as the original P-class locomotives, were manufactured by Baldwin, and featured water scoops and automatic stokers as standard. In 1928 there appeared a 28th locomotive from the railroad's own Mount Clare workshops, but this was an experimental unit used for the evaluation of features including a water-tube firebox and camshaft-operated poppet valves. The latter proved unsuccessful and were replaced by Walschaert valves in the following year. The water-tube firebox was more successful, and, though not adopted for other locomotives, was retained in this 28th locomotive until its retirement in 1945.

Between 1937 and 1940 one of the P7-class locomotives was operated in streamlined form to haul the Baltimore & Ohio Railroad's Royal Blue service, and in 1946 another four of the locomotives, already rebuilt with cast locomotive beds, roller bearings and provision for a larger 12-wheel tender, received streamlined casings to work the Cincinnatian service.

Although most American railroads saw the working of commuter trains as a task for locomotives which had seen their best years in the haulage of prestige services, the

Pennsylvania Railroad always preferred to operate its commuter services with purpose-designed locomotives from its own design teams and workshops. Typical of this breed was the G5s-class of 4-6-0 locomotives, of which the first entered service in 1923. The parent railroad received 90 of these locomotives (the designation 's' standing for superheating) from its Juanita workshops in the period up to 1926, the design owing much to the E6 class of 4-4-2 locomotives dating from 1910, which yielded useful savings in matters such as design and tooling. Wholly new, however, were the driving wheels with a diameter some 15 per cent smaller than those of the E6-class locomotives.

Only one feature of the design was not fully in accord with the typical North American practices of the time, and this was the use of a Belpaire firebox. Dating from 1864, when it was designed by a Belgian engineer, this represented an attempt to increase the surface area and volume of the firebox without impinging on the volume for the water to circulate around it. The Pennsylvania Railroad was the only North American operator to make extensive use of this firebox.

Another operator of the G5s-class locomotive was the Long Island Railroad, which was a subsidiary of the Pennsylvania Railroad. Unlike larger operators, which could afford to subsidize their commuter services with the revenues of their profit-making freight operations, the Long Island Railroad had to be profitable solely with commuter operations. In the period between 1924 and 1929 the railroad received 31 G5s-class locomotives, which

operated the railroad's longer services right into the 1950s, leaving shorter services to electric locomotives.

Quite naturally, all locomotives have to reflect the conditions in which they are designed to operate, and particular conditions often lead to the creation of specialized locomotives often notable for a special feature. This is certainly the case with the AC4 class of 4-8-8-2 locomotives designed for the use of the Southern Pacific Railroad on one of the world's most taxing routes. This was the Overland Route which, as noted above, was completed eastward from Sacramento in the state of California to Promontory Point in Utah, where in May 1869 it linked with the Union Pacific Railroad's westward advance across the U.S.A. From Sacramento the Southern Pacific Railroad's services have to climb over the Sierra Nevada via the Donner Pass at an altitude of some 7,000ft (2134m), and although the original 2.77 per cent grade had been reduced to 2.42 per cent by the later 1920s, the climb was still a formidable undertaking in the days of steam locomotion. The curves were still very tight in places, and the threat posed by snowfalls and snow slides meant that a considerable mileage of snowsheds had to be maintained in tip-top condition, lest snow sweep away a train or even part of the track.

An early attempt to create a locomotive optimized for the task was the unsuccessful *El Gobernador*, after which the Southern Pacific Railroad decided to try the Mallet type of compound locomotive, in 1909 ordering from Baldwin two 2-8-8-2 locomotives that were, at the time, the most powerful units in the world

Locomotive No. 5000 was the first of the Atchison, Topeka & Santa Fe Railway's 5000 class of 2-10-4 Santa Fe-type engines. This unit was built by Baldwin and delivered to the operator in 1930.

Locomotive No. 3878 was a unit of the 2-10-2 3800 class of Santa Fe-type locomotives built for the Atchison, Topeka & Santa Fe Railway, in this instance during 1924, with driving wheels of 63-in (1.60-m) diameter.

Another classic locomotive operated by the Atchison, Topeka & Santa Fe Railway, in this instance in the 1930s onward, was the Baldwin-built 3460 class of 4-6-4 Pacific-type locomotives. This is No. 3461.

and able to haul 1,300-ton trains over this route.

A problem that still remained was the difficulty of maintaining the crew at a reasonable level of comfort so that it could work effectively. Oil had been used as fuel in place of coal for some years on this route, and this suggested a means to provide the crew with sufficient oxygen. Based on the original idea of an engineer of the North Pacific Coast Railroad, this was to make the crew cab into a sealed unit that would be located at the front of the locomotive rather than its rear, as was standard with the open cabs of coal-fired locomotives requiring easy access to the tender.

The Southern Pacific Railroad took the concept to Baldwin, which manufactured an

This is the Atchison, Topeka & Santa Fe Railway's 3460-class locomotive No. 3465, a Pacific-type 4-6-4 unit built by the Baldwin Locomotive Works in 1937, with 84-in (2.13-m) diameter driving wheels and a tender capacity of 20,000 U.S. gallons (75708 litres) of water.

No. 3461 was a brother of No. 3465 in the Atchison, Topeka & Santa Fe Railway's 3460 class.

RIGHT
This is the Atchison, Topeka & Santa Fe Railway's 3450-class locomotive No. 3456, a 4-6-4 Pacific-type unit built by the Baldwin Locomotive Works in 1923, with 79-in (2.01-m) diameter driving wheels.

BELOW
No. 3450 was the first, and therefore the 'name' locomotive of the Atchison, Topeka & Santa Fe Railway's 3450-class of 4-6-4 Pacific-type locomotives. It was built by the Baldwin Locomotive Works in 1923.

initial series of 15 2-8-8-2 cab-first locomotives that were otherwise quite similar to the earlier 2-8-8-2 locomotives, other than the incorporation of a system, worked by compressed air, to drive the oil fuel up from the tender and forward into the burners. By 1913 the railroad had received 46 of these locomotives, which were later modified from compound to simple working.

In common with the other Mallet-type locomotives of the period, the boiler of these Southern Pacific Railroad locomotives was manufactured in two parts: the rear section, which incorporated the firebox, was wholly conventional, while the separate front section had its own fire tubes and tube plates, which

Seen at Omaha, Nebraska, No. 9000 was a 4-12-2 locomotive of the Union Pacific class, built in 1926 by the Alco-Brooks company for the Union Pacific Railroad, with driving wheels of 67-in (1.70-m) diameter. The locomotive was retired to the California State Fair grounds at Pomona, California, in the course of 1956. The photograph reveals activity associated with the breaking-in of the locomotive soon after its completion.

ABOVE
The Union Pacific Railroad introduced the
FEF2 class of 4-8-4 passenger and freight
locomotives during 1939.

OPPOSITE
Small, unglamorous but wholly essential
were a range of locomotives that provided the
yard services which facilitated main-line
services. Typical of the breed are saddle tank
shunters such as the Brooklyn Eastern
District Terminal Railroad's 0-4-0T No. 15.
This was built by H.K. Porter in 1917 for the
Mesta Machine Works of Homestead,
Pennsylvania, and then passed to the Toledo,
Lake Erie & Western before serving with the
BEDT. The locomotive is now with the
Strasburg Railroad painted as 'Thomas the
Tank Engine'.

acted as a feed-water heater. Once they had
reached a sufficient level of development,
more modern single-stage boilers with a
combustion chamber replaced the earlier
arrangement.

The first 46 locomotives, completed by
the end of 1913, as noted above, were of the
basically similar MC2, MC4 and MC6
subclasses. In 1911 there followed 12 Mallet
Mogul cab-in-front 2-6-6-2 (later changed to
4-6-6-2) locomotives for the working of
passenger trains, but these were switched to
freight work after only a few years as they
were found unsuitable for passenger speeds.

In 1927 the Southern Pacific Railroad
experimentally converted a single MC6-class
locomotive to simple working, which proved
so successful (in terms of operational
efficiency as well as reduced and simplified
maintenance) that the railroad ordered 10

AC4-class 4-8-8-2 locomotives worked by
four high-pressure cylinders. Further orders
placed with Baldwin increased the total of
AC-class locomotives to 185 units through the
delivery of seven batches in the period up to
1944. The earlier MC-class locomotives were
all altered, in the period between 1928 and
1937, to simple working as the AC1, A-2 and
AC3 classes, and the two original MC-class
locomotives were adapted to the same
standard as AC1-class units. Other
conversions were effected, and by the later
1930s the Southern Pacific Railroad had some
257 locomotives of this effective cab-in-
front type.

On the essentially flat route linking
Chicago, Illinois and the 'twin cities' of
Minneapolis and St. Paul, Minnesota, there
was intense rivalry between three operators,
and this produced the fastest services ever

hauled by steam locomotion. The three were
the Chicago & North Western, with a 408-mile
(657-km) route that its '400' express services
covered in 400 minutes for an average speed
of 61.2mph (98.5km/h), the Chicago
Burlington & Quincy, with a 427-mile (687-
km) route, on which the operator ran its
diesel-powered Zephyr lightweight trains of
stainless steel construction, and the Chicago
Milwaukee St. Paul and Pacific Railroad. This
last decided in the mid-1930s to compete with
special steam locomotive and train sets able to
provide a 63.4-mph (102-km/h) average speed
over its 412-mile (663-km) route. For the first
time in steam railroad history the way was
clear for a railroad to contract for the design
and manufacture of locomotives intended to
operate on a daily basis at a speed of more
than 100mph (161km/h).

The resulting type, from the American
Locomotive Company, was the A class of oil-
fired and highly streamlined 4-4-2
locomotives. Although only four were
produced (two in 1935, with the third and
fourth following in 1936 and 1937
respectively), these were each capable of
generating more than 3,000hp (2237kW) in
the cylinders and could reach 110mph
(177km/h). The capabilities of these superb
locomotives is attested by the fact that while
they were designed to haul a six-car train on a
schedule of 6 hours 30 minutes, they were
soon hauling a nine-car train on a 6-hour
schedule on the Hiawatha service.

The design of the locomotives was only
slightly out of the ordinary, oddities being a
drive on the front rather than rear axle, and
the use of a tender with a six-wheel leading

RIGHT
The Southern Pacific Railroad's 4-6-2 Pacific-type locomotive No. 2472 passes through Jack London Square, Oakland, California.

OPPOSITE
The Southern Pacific Railroad's 4-6-2 Pacific-type locomotive No. 2473 hauls a service near Pinole, California.

truck and a four-wheel trailing truck. The design team also devoted considerable effort to creating reciprocating parts that were as light as possible without loss of strength, and that the most precise balancing was achieved.

Its service with these four locomotives were so successful that in 1938 the Chicago Milwaukee St. Paul & Pacific Railroad ordered six more high-speed steam locomotives, in this instance to a wholly conventional but nonetheless streamlined design. These 4-6-4 locomotives were F7-class units and, while not intended to attain the sustained speeds of which the A-class locomotives were capable, were more versatile and capable of undertaking conventional as well as express passenger operations; this was because their attributes included high speed in combination with the ability to haul heavy loads. A speed of up to 120mph (193km/h) was made possible by the use of large-diameter driving wheels, while the heavy haulage capability stemmed from the reversion from oil to coal firing the haulage of heavy ordinary expresses.

Trials revealed that the F7-class

locomotives's very high speed could be maintained with a 12-car train weighing 550 tons; in fact, the capabilities of the F7s were in every respect exceptional. The last examples of each of these two classic classes were retired in 1951.

Despite the geographical limitations seemingly indicated by its name, the Chicago, Burlington & Quincy was one of the major steam railroads and in fact operated to virtually every major destination lying to the south and west of its stated operating region. These operations encompassed virtually the complete gamut of activities between high-speed express services and low-speed freight haulage. The railroad's demand for a diversity of locomotive types was therefore considerable, and during 1930 Baldwin delivered eight O5-class 4-8-4 locomotives, optimized for the heavy freight role, and in 1937 followed with another 13 such locomotives. Designed for coal-burning operation, the locomotives were not in any real way remarkable, but did possess Baker valve gear and the possible complication of a Worthington feed-water heater. A power reverse and mechanical stoker were standard. The O5-class locomotives were eminently reliable and effective, and the railroad's own workshops later boosted the fleet with the manufacture of an eventual 15 O5A-class locomotives that introduced a number of improved features, including disc rather than spoke driving wheels and Timken roller bearings on the axles and the pins of the valve gear. Some of the locomotives were later revised to burn oil rather than coal.

Introduced to service with the Chicago &

A 2-10-2 Santa Fe-type locomotive, No. 3937 of the Baldwin-built 3900 class, heads a heavy freight train of the Atchison, Topeka & Santa Fe Railway through the Cajon Pass, California.

RIGHT
Locomotive No. 614 of the Chesapeake &
Ohio Railroad heads a passenger train at Port
Jervis, New York.

OPPOSITE
A Lima-built 4-8-4 locomotive.

OPPOSITE
A Swedish 4-6-0 locomotive of the Belfast &
Moosehead Lake Railroad.

LEFT
The Pennsylvania Railroad's 4-6-2
locomotive No. 5411 of the K45 class heads
a service passing through a town in New
Jersey during the mid-1930s.

North Western Railroad in 1938, the E4-class
locomotives occupy a particular niche in
American railroad history as the first steam
locomotives to be displaced from their
designed task by diesel-electric locomotives.

Attractive and well-streamlined units, these
locomotives were designed in 1935 to haul its
operator's express services between Chicago
and Minneapolis-St. Paul in competition with
those of two other operators. The first

company to offer an express service on the
route was the Chicago & North Western with
its '400' trains, using refurbished locomotives
and rolling stock rather than new equipment,
though it soon had to respond to its rivals's

RIGHT
The impressive frontal aspect of the Union
Pacific Railroad's locomotive No. 9000, a 4-
12-2 unit that was built by Alco in 1926. It
was the first unit of a new class designed for
the operation of heavy trains in
transcontinental services.

OPPOSITE
The Southern Pacific Railroad's locomotives
Nos. 2472 and 4449, 4-6-2 and 4-8-4 units
respectively, are seen at night at the
operator's Santa Clara yard.

introduction of more advanced equipment by
the acquisition of new locomotives.

This was the genesis of the E4 class,
which was intended to compete most directly
with the Chicago Milwaukee St. Paul &
Pacific Railroad's steam-drawn Hiawatha
service, rather than the Chicago, Burlington
& Quincy Railroad's Zephyr service with
special diesel-electric trains. The E4-class
locomotive was designed by the American
Locomotive Company, which was contracted
to manufacture nine high-speed 4-6-4
locomotives for delivery in 1938. The
railroad then decided that it would adopt
diesel haulage for its 400 service, and the E4-
class locomotives were found alternative
employment on the section of the
transcontinental route which the railroad
operated between Chicago and Omaha.
The last of the locomotives was retired in
the 1950s.

Responding to the need for a capability to
work ever-heavier trains in the mid-1930s, the
Union Pacific Railroad decided that the time
was ripe to progress from its hitherto standard
4-8-2 passenger-haulage mainstays toward a
more potent type. The task of designing the
required locomotive was allocated to the
American Locomotive Company, which
responded with a 4-8-4 type of which an
eventual 45 were delivered. The first 20,
delivered in 1938, were of the FEF1 class with
12-wheel tenders, followed in 1939 with 15
examples of the FEF2 class, with a 14-wheel
tender as well as larger wheels and cylinders;
finally in 1944 there came the final batch of
10 FEF3 locomotives that were essentially
similar to the FEF2s, apart from some changes

in the materials which reflected the fact that the U.S.A. was currently embroiled in World War II.

The design of these 4-8-4 locomotives was a result of the design team's adherence to the concept of evolutionary development rather than a technical leap into the dark. Thus the standard features included two outside cylinders (ensuring the simplest, most reliable and most easily maintained machinery possible) and the 4-8-4 or Northern type of wheel arrangement. The rounding of curves with so long a fixed wheelbase was facilitated by the adoption of Alco's lateral motion device on the leading coupled wheels. Despite possible temptations toward the incorporation of complicated features (including a streamlined casing), the design team and the railroad decided to resist, with the result that the FEF-class locomotives were notable for their uncluttered appearance. That the design team and the railroad were not behind the times, when it came to the matter of introducing more modern features when they served a useful purpose, is attested by the fact that the attractions of a one-piece cast-steel frame prevailed over the older notion of a built-up frame, and that a static exhaust steam injector instead of a steam-driven mechanical water pump and feed-water heater was incorporated.

The most advanced feature, and one that was largely responsible for the overall success of the FEF-class locomotives, was the main motion, in which the design and manufacture of the tapered coupling and connecting rods were pushed to the limit of what was, at the time, state of the art. The pulling and pushing

OPPOSITE
Seen at Klamath Falls, Oregon, this is the 4-8-4 locomotive No. 4449, a GS4- class unit of the Daylight type, built by Lima in 1941 with a fully enclosed cab. The type hauled high-speed prestige services and was completed in a striking livery of orange, red and dark grey.

LEFT
A 4-8-4 GS5-class locomotive of the Southern Pacific Railroad's Daylight type.

LEFT
This is a Daylight-type 4-8-4 locomotive in its definitive form hauling a Southern Pacific Railroad streamliner service between San Francisco and Los Angeles in 1936.

Steam locomotion was always a dirty business, and grimy locomotives were a common sight on long routes and during gusty conditions.

motions of the connecting rods were transmitted to three out of the four pairs of wheels by separate sleeve bearings, rather than the main crankpins, which was the system that was conventional at the time. Thus the separate knuckle-joints in the coupling rods were replaced by adding a fork at each end of the centre pair of rods, thus combining the roles of crank- and knuckle-pins. The result was a genuinely excellent locomotive that was apparently capable of reaching 100mph (161km/h).

After World War II there was a period when supplies of coal were adversely affected by strikes, and the FEF-class locomotives were then adapted to burn oil. Over a long period of service, lasting to 1959, virtually no other modifications were deemed necessary or even desirable.

The heaviest services ever handled on a regular basis anywhere in the world during the era of the steam locomotive were worked by the M3-class 2-8-8-4 Mallet-type locomotives of the Duluth, Missabe & Iron Range Railroad, which received its first such Yellowstone-type unit in 1941, shortly before the U.S.A.'s entry into World War II as a result of Japanese attacks on American bases round the Pacific Ocean. The particular task assigned to these mighty locomotives was the movement of wagons carrying iron ore from the mines some 70 miles (113km) to the port of Duluth on the southern shore of Lake Superior.

The bulk transport of a single commodity, such as iron ore, coal and wheat, is a task to which the railroad is admirably suited, and its concentration on this task, at a time when the

The American steam locomotive reached a peak in the second quarter of the 20th century with the adoption of streamliner casings for the locomotives operated on high-speed prestige passenger services. The casings, highly polished and open completed in a striking livery, reduced drag and thus boosted the locomotives's ability to maintain a high speed, and were also 'instant advertising' for the operating company.

demand for steel and iron was increasing by leaps and bounds, proved very profitable for the Duluth, Missabe & Iron Range Railroad. It was therefore well able to afford the very best in custom-designed equipment, whose reliability and operating economy in turn boosted the operator's profitability.

The movement of loads as heavy as those represented by large quantities of iron ore demanded both great tractive effort and great adhesive weight, which in the case of the M3-class locomotives, each turning the scales at 1,138,000lb (516197kg), were 140,000 and

565,000lb (63504 and 256284kg) respectively. The Duluth, Missabe & Iron Range Railroad took delivery of its first eight M3-class locomotives from Baldwin in 1941, as noted above, and in 1943 there followed another 10 units of the M4 class that differed only is the replacement of some materials by others less vital to the war economy.

The 2-8-8-4 wheel arrangement was pioneered in locomotives for the Northern Pacific Railroad during 1928, which was the reason it was called the Yellowstone type. This operator burned low-quality coal mined right

on its line, so the locomotives had large grates, measuring up to 180sq ft (16.72m²) in some cases and therefore one-fifth larger than those of the Union Pacific Railroad's Big Boy locomotives. The Duluth, Missabe & Iron Range Railroad could use higher-quality coal from Pennsylvania, and this made it possible to reduce the grate area of the M3- and M4-class locomotives to 125sq ft (11.61m²). Even so, the Duluth, Missabe & Iron Range's locomotives had a somewhat greater tractive effort than that of the Big Boys, the figure being the greatest ever recorded for a steam

OPPOSITE & LEFT
A streamlined 4-8-4 locomotive of the   J-class heads an express passenger service of the Norfolk & Western in the late 1940s.

locomotive without compound machinery, but wholly necessary for the working of loads three times heavier than anything that could be handled by the Big Boys, though only over relatively flat terrain.

In the period of steam locomotion, the Duluth, Missabe & Iron Range Railroad shifted something in the order of 50 million tons of iron ore per year, which in practical terms was somewhat less than 365 days due to the fact that Lake Superior freezes in winter. An average requirement was 200,000 tons or more per day, and one of the M3- and M4-class 2-8-8-4 locomotives could move an 18,000-ton train of 190 wagons carrying 13,000 tons of ore. The operation of trains as heavy as this could have presented problems, but the Duluth, Missabe & Iron Range was fortunate that in loaded condition its trains moved generally downhill, the maximum uphill grade being 0.3 per cent.

The braking of very heavy trains was clearly beyond the capabilities of any standard braking system, so the wagons of the Duluth, Missabe & Iron Range Railroad incorporated a special differential system in which an additional, larger brake cylinder was brought into operation automatically when the wagon was loaded with more than twice its own weight of ore. Despite the provision of superb track with heavy rails on deep ballast, the economical operation of the railroad was enhanced by a limitation to a maximum speed of only 30 and 35mph (48 and 56km/h) respectively for trains with loaded and empty wagons.

As diesel locomotion started and then began to mature as a viable alternative to steam during the 1920s and especially the 1930s, many railroads attempted to shrug off the upstart as a 'flash-in-the-pan' phenomenon, with a number of useful but specialized applications but without the capability to overthrow steam locomotion. All of these operators were proved wrong, but that which came the closest to maintaining the viability of steam locomotion was the Norfolk & Western Railroad. Headquartered at Roanoke in Virginia, the Norfolk & Western had a 645-mile (1038-km) main line that linked Columbus in Ohio with the port city of Norfolk in Virginia, and also possessed branch lines that made it possible for the railroad's services to reach virtually every major mine in what was at the time one of the world's greatest coalfields. Finally, even the Norfolk & Western was forced to concede defeat in the battle between steam and diesel locomotion, and with this the age of steam locomotion on the U.S.A.'s main railroads can be said finally to have ended.

That the Norfolk & Western Railroad was able to put up so determined a defence of steam locomotion is an eloquent testimony to the excellence of its locomotives. The overriding care of the Norfolk & Western was to wring everything possible out of well-proven steam locomotion to enhance its capabilities, and at the same time reduce its disadvantages. In this task it was aided by its long experience with the concept of steam locomotion, its purchase of only the best equipment, and the meticulous care it lavished on its track, premises, tools and equipment. This allowed the railroad to maintain the highest possible levels of operating economy without any sacrifice of quality; the railroad's approach to high-quality steam locomotion is no more evident than in its magnificent J class of 4-8-4 express passenger locomotives, which the railroad itself both designed and built.

At the end of the 1930s the railroad's technical management team decided that the time was more than ripe for the railroad to procure a new class of locomotive based on thinking more advanced than that embodied in standard 4-8-2 design of the U.S. Railroad Association, on which the railroad's current locomotives were based. Well-versed in the history and technology of steam locomotion, the technical team appreciated the fact that current technology could be little improved in matters such as the locomotive's thermal and mechanical principles, but also appreciated that there could be ways in which profitability would be enhanced by a reduction in the time and cost involved in maintenance and servicing. For this reason, the technical team decided to adopt roller bearing for the axles and every aspect of the motion; there were also some 200 other bearings (including one for the bell!) that were lubricated automatically by a system whose oil capacity of 29 U.S. gal (110 litres) was sufficient for 1,500 miles (2400km) of steaming. Another lubricator fed high-temperature oil to the steam cylinders, as was the normal practice, but the same system was expanded to provide lubrication for the steam cylinders of the water and air pumps, and for the motor of the mechanical stoker. In overall terms, this removed the need for the separate inspection and filling of a number of smaller systems as the mechanic had merely to inspect and fill one major system. Other elements of the basic design included two-cylinder machinery with Baker's valve gear, whose simplicity enhanced reliability and reduced standard maintenance requirements, and very large tenders (with two three-axle trucks) to enlarge the distance that the locomotive could cover before having to halt for replenishment of water and fuel.

These features, together with the more advanced elements of current structural thinking, such as one-piece cast frames instead of built-up units, meant that the J-class locomotive, of which the first was delivered in 1941, was capable of running 15,000 miles (24000km) per month and on average required repair at a major facility only once every 18 months.

During the period in the 1940s and early 1950s, in which the diesel locomotive generally prevailed over the steam locomotive to gain superiority on the railroads of the U.S.A., the rise of diesel and the decline of steam power were generally reflected in the facilities used to maintain and repair the locomotives. The up-and-coming star of diesel locomotion was clearly seen in the new facilities, which had of necessity to be constructed for their maintenance and repair, but steam locomotion was operating on the legacy of a system that had already lasted more than a century of evolutionary growth with cyclic ups and down. Thus virtually every steam locomotion depot in the U.S. was in a state of sad decline, with old building in a poor state of repair and equipment that was also old and wearing out.

On the Norfolk & Western Railroad, however, things were altogether different, its

locomotives new and its depots in excellent condition. Thus a J-class locomotive could be serviced, greased, lubricated and cleared of ash, and its tender filled with water and coal, in less than one hour, the result of this efficiency being enhanced profitability. It is interesting to note that the Norfolk & Western's shareholders were receiving 6 per cent on their money, while the shareholders of the neighbouring Pennsylvania Railroad, which now operated only electric and diesel locomotives, were receiving just 0.5 per cent.

It was not a situation that could last, however, for as more and more U.S. railroads switched to diesel and electric locomotion the number of companies able to supply equipment and components applicable only to steam locomotion were declining rapidly. In 1960 the Norfolk & Western Railroad bit the bullet and finally conceded that the era of steam locomotion was over, and the J and all other steam locomotive classes were retired. In overall terms it is arguable whether or not the J-class locomotives represented the pinnacle of the art in terms of 4-8-4 locomotion, but not in dispute at all is the fact that they possessed the highest tractive effort and were the last steam locomotives for main-line passenger operations to be manufactured in the U.S. The 14 J-class locomotives were built at the Norfolk & Western's facility at Roanoke, and comprised four completed in 1941, one in 1942, six in 1943 and the final three in 1950. The 1942 unit had a booster engine on the trailing truck, and the six from 1943 initially operated without any streamlining, though this was added after the

end of World War II. The locomotives recorded a maximum speed of 110mph (177km/h) on test and were capable of 90mph (145km/h) in service, despite the fact that they had driving wheels that were comparatively small by express passenger locomotive standards. The test speed, incidentally, was recorded with a 1,000-ton load in the form of a train of 15 cars. This translated into the development of some 6,000hp (4474kW) in the cylinders, making it perhaps a little surprising that point-to-point times were not smaller. The fact is, however, that the Norfolk & Western Railroad's main line extended through some fairly hilly country, with grades of up to 1.6 per cent, so the performance of services such as the Powhatan Arrow, which took 15.75 hours to cover the 676 miles (1088km) between Norfolk and Cincinnati, Ohio, represented an average speed of 43mph (69km/h), which was quite respectable in the circumstances.

Finally, it is worth recording that the Norfolk & Western also operated as a 'bridge road', its 4-8-4 locomotives hauling express services such as the Tennessean and the Pelican (the original Chattanooga choo-choos) between Lynchburg and Bristol on the route linking New York with Chattanooga in Tennessee and points still farther to the west.

The name 'Big Boy' is aptly used to describe the 4-8-8-4 locomotives that possessed a combination of size, weight, power and strength that was unrivalled in any other steam locomotive ever built, although they were exceeded in some of these characteristics, on an individual basis, by other locomotives of American manufacture. In

ABOVE
Seen at Chicago, Illinois, on 24 June 1941, this is the Pennsylvania Railroad's locomotive No. 6100, a 6-4-4-6 unit.

RIGHT & OPPOSITE
The 'Yellow Belly' was a streamlined Hudson-type 4-6-4 locomotive of the Chesapeake & Ohio Railroad.

overall terms, however, it can rightly be said that the Big Boys represented the apogee of steam locomotive design, manufacture and operation.

The origins of the type can be discerned in the recovery of the U.S. economy during the late 1930s, as remedial financial measures (including much greater spending on defence matters) boosted industry and so helped the nation overcome the last stages of the great depression that followed the financial crash of 1929. In 1940 the Union Pacific Railroad approached the American Locomotive Company with a request for a locomotive design able to handle trains, somewhat heavier than those currently the norm, across the routes of its mountainous Wyoming Division in the region between Cheyenne and Ogden in the states of Wyoming and Utah respectively. At this time, the grade on the route extending west from Cheyenne was 1.55

A Norfolk & Western Railroad 4-8-4 locomotive of the J class heads an express passenger service in the late 1940s as the days of main-line steam locomotion were drawing to a close.

per cent on Sherman Hill, while the maximum altitude attained was 8,013ft (2442m) at Sherman Summit. East from Ogden, the crossing of the Wasatch range had to be effected via a climb of 60 miles (97km), much of it at a grade of 1.14 per cent, as the route climbed from 4,300ft (1311m) to 7,230ft (2204m) at Altamont. Consequently, the task that the Union Pacific Railroad set the American Locomotive Company was the design of a locomotive able to work 3,600-ton

trains, without assistance, on this latter section.

The design, which resulted from what was in effect a joint enterprise between the engineering teams of the American Locomotive Company and the Union Pacific Railroad, was completed in only six months, the Union Pacific Railroad ordering no less than 201 of the resulting behemoths at a unit price of slightly more than a quarter of a million dollars. The first of the new

locomotives was delivered to Omaha in September 1941.

Meanwhile, the Union Pacific Railroad was much occupied with the tasks that had to be completed before the new locomotives could enter operational service. These included the strengthening of the track by the replacement of the current type of relatively light rails by new steel rails weighing 130lb/yard (65kg/m); the installation of new turntables with a diameter of 135ft (41.15m) at Ogden and Green river; and the realignment of many of the route's curves. This last was required not to allow the new locomotives to pass along the curves, for they were in fact amazingly 'flexible' in this respect, and could cope with curves of a radius as small as 95 yards (87m), but to avoid the possibility of the long overhangs touching trains passing in the other direction along the parallel track: on a

curve of 145-yard (133-m) radius, the front of the boiler of a Big Boy locomotive moved sideways some 2ft (0.60m), whereas on good alignments the maximum speed was some 70mph (113km/h).

In design and engineering terms, the Big Boy locomotives were wholly orthodox, though on a truly massive scale. Modern features, including cast-steel locomotive beds

and roller bearings, were adopted without further consideration and, with the exception of a single unit that for a time burned oil, the whole class burned coal. The locomotives are on record as developing 6,290hp (4689kW) in their cylinders, using 100,00lb (45360kg) of water and 44,000lb (19958kg) of coal in the process. Operational experience gradually revealed that the Big Boys were in fact capable

'Railroads on Parade' at the New York World's Fair in August 1940: left and right respectively are the Delaware, Lackawanna & Western Railroad's partially streamlined 4-6-4 locomotive No. 1651 (No. 1940) and the Pennsylvania Railroad's fully streamlined 4-6-2 locomotive No. 3768.

This 4-6-4 Hudson-type streamlined locomotive was used to haul the New York Central Railroad's Empire State Express service in the 1930s.

This 4-6-4 Hudson-type locomotive is seen in 1938 at Alco's works as it emerges after being streamlined as one of the units used to haul the New York Central Railroad's Twentieth Century Limited prestige service linking New York and Chicago.

of working loads somewhat heavier than those for which they had been designed, and in combination with the regrading (to a maximum of 0.82 per cent) of some of the worst parts of the line on which they operated, this allowed them to haul trains of up to 6,000 tons, even up Sherman Hill.

Capable and huge as they were, the Big Boy locomotives were eclipsed in terms of sheer power by the 2-6-6-6 Allegheny-type locomotives of the Chesapeake & Ohio Railroad, which introduced these H8-class units in 1941. As was so often the case in the development of ever more capable steam locomotives for service in the eastern half of the country, the primary spur for their development was the need to haul increasingly heavy loads of coal across the major barrier represented by the Allegheny Mountains. Coal was the driving force of U.S. industry in the period up to the end and following World War II, so its delivery, as cheaply as possible and in vast quantities, was one of the most decisive elements in the U.S. economy at this time. As a result, there was intense competition in the railroad's fight to transport coal quickly and economically.

Designed and manufactured by the Lima Locomotive Works, the first of the H8-class locomotives was delivered to the Chesapeake & Ohio Railroad in December 1941. Though optimized for power rather than speed, and therefore massive rather than streamlined, the H8 was thoroughly representative of the locomotive engineer's art and science for its time, and despite its unique 2-6-6-2 wheel configuration, was wholly successful right from the start.

The U.S.A.'s demand for coal rose dramatically at this time, as already booming heavy industries were spurred to greater efforts after the U.S.'s December 1941 entry into World War II. The Chesapeake & Ohio Railroad received no fewer than 59 of the monster locomotives in the period up to 1948, and another eight units of the same class were also delivered to the Virginian Railroad.

The H8-class locomotives were most notable for their huge power, as noted above, and as power, in the steam locomotive, is related directly to the size of the fire, the critical factor in the locomotive was its firebox. This was a truly vast item, its size and weight made possible by the incorporation of the unique three-axle truck under the locomotive's rear. The grate's area was 11 per cent smaller than that of the contemporary Big Boy locomotive of the Union Pacific Railroad but, as it was not located above the rear driving wheels, was considerable deeper. Moreover, the Chesapeake & Ohio Railroad had an advantage in being able to burn higher-quality coal from the West Virginian mines in its locomotives than was possible for the units of the Union Pacific Railroad. As a result, the H8-class locomotives could steam at a higher rate, and high power yields high speed as well as a heavy pull. Even so, it was some time before these massive locomotives were available in sufficient numbers for use in tasks other than the passage over the Alleghenies. About one in three of them were completed with the steam connections that permitted their employment on passenger work, and here their ability to attain 60mph (97km/h) was a useful feature.

In their bread-and-butter work, however, the H8-class locomotives remained unexcelled in the era of steam locomotion. On the eastbound climb from Hinton in West Virginia to the 2,072-ft (631-m) altitude of the summit represented by the Allegheny Tunnel, it was standard practice to use one H8 at each end of the train weighing 11,500 tons and comprising 140 wagons. Here the H8-class locomotives were very usefully served by the fact that they had a high adhesive weight, on which hauling capability is wholly dependent: this amounted to 471,000lb (213646kg) on the six driving axles, corresponding to an unprecedented axle load of 86,350lb (39168kg), an increase of some 37 per cent over that of the preceding H7a class of 2-8-8-2 locomotives.

Such loads were possible only because of the superb permanent way and track that the Chesapeake & Ohio had built and now maintained at a very high level of perfection. To accommodate the H8-class locomotives, however, the railroad had first to complete a fairly large programme of track strengthening and tunnel enlargement. Another factor in the locomotives's successful operations was their completion with relatively large driving wheels, of 67-in (1.701-m) diameter, to reduce the chances of railhead failure: the imposition of too great a load on wheels that are too small is almost inevitably a tendency for the wheels to sink in, causing the running surfaces to fragment.

So long as it was already well proven, every feature of the latest locomotive engineering practice was applied to the H8-class locomotives, not for the sake of any desire for modernity as such, but rather to

The Baltimore & Ohio Railroad's streamlined 4-6-2 locomotive No. 5304 heads the Royal Blue express service passing through New Jersey in about 1940.

The striking livery of streamlined locomotives, right into the late-1940s, often included features such as white-painted wheel rims echoing the whitewall tyres of cars of the period.

improve efficiency and reliability. These features included cast-steel locomotive beds with integral cylinders, roller bearings on all main axles, Worthington feed-water heaters, Baker's valve gear, and very sophisticated counterbalancing of the reciprocating parts; all of these made an effective contribution to the locomotives's smooth operation and reliable running. Older features were not forgotten when they could play a useful part: a fully adequate supply of sand was ensured by the incorporation of four large sandboxes, situated two on each side of the boiler's top, which

could be dispensed just ahead or just behind each driving wheel; there were also steam jets to wash off the sand, thereby keeping the train wheels rolling with minimum friction on clean smooth rails. Other notable features, and indeed a trademark of the Chesapeake & Ohio Railroad, were the 'flying pumps', both brake pumps being located on the front of the smokebox. The H8-class locomotives were Mallet-type units, of course, and in the fashion of this type had the headlight fixed to the leading articulated engine so that its beam illuminated the section of track onto which the

whole locomotive was moving. The tender was slightly unusual in having a three-axle leading truck and a four-axle trailing truck, and the complete assembly of the locomotive and its tender was just able to fit itself onto the line's existing turntables, which had a diameter of 115ft (35.05m).

Despite the capabilities offered by these huge steam locomotives, the Chesapeake & Ohio began the process of replacing the H8-class locomotives with diesel-engined units in 1952, when the most recently delivered engines were still only four years old. By

1956 all 60 of these magnificent pieces of engineering had been discarded.

A type to be regarded almost as the express passenger counterpart of the same operator's Big Boy freight locomotives, the Union Pacific Railroad's Challenger class of 4-6-6-4 locomotives were the largest, heaviest, strongest and most powerful locomotives that ever worked express passenger services on a regular basis. The creation of the class reflected the practicality of the articulated locomotive, i.e. the locomotive with a hinge in its middle. Locomotives of this type were introduced at a comparatively early stage of locomotive history, but it was not until narrow-gauge railways became popular in the later part of the 19th century that locomotives of this pattern were manufactured in any numbers.

There were many types of articulated locomotive, but the only one that gained any real currency was that created by the French engineer, Anatole Mallet, who was also an early devotee of compounding. Several two-cylinder compound locomotives were built to his design from 1876, following which Mallet proposed in 1884 an articulated locomotive design in which the rear set of driving wheels was mounted in the main frame (supporting the firebox and the rear part of the boiler) and the front set in a separate frame hinged at its rear to the front of the main frame. The front of the boiler rested on the hinged frame, and a sliding support was fitted to make it possible for the boiler's front to swing across this frame as the locomotive rounded a curve. The high- and low-pressure cylinders drove the rear and front sets of wheels respectively, and

this ensured that the whole of the high-pressure steam system was retained on the rigid part of the locomotive, with hinged pipes used to transport low-pressure steam to and from the cylinders mounted on the articulated forward frame.

While most of the Mallet-type locomotives built in Europe were designed for operation on narrow-gauge railways, those that were produced in the U.S.A. from 1903 were the result of the desire for maximum adhesion, and resulted from the difficulties of designing a practical locomotive that combined six driving axles and a rigid frame. Articulation offered the prospect of evading this problem, and the first Mallet-type locomotive manufactured in the U.S.A. was an 0-6-6-0 unit built for the Baltimore & Ohio Railroad. At the time of its debut this was the world's largest locomotive, and even as the size of locomotives increased, it was always a Mallet-type unit of American design and manufacture that was the largest in the world.

While the early Mallet-type locomotives made and used in the U.S.A. were operated primarily for banking, there was a gradual change in emphasis and they soon came to be used on an increasing basis for regular operations. Here the most limiting single factor was found to be their use of huge low-pressure cylinders and the tangle of steam pipes associated with them, which rendered the locomotives unsuitable for steaming at speeds above 40mph (64km/h), at which there developed oscillations of the front frame, resulting in heavy wear to the locomotive and also to the track.

During 1924, the Chesapeake & Ohio

Railroad ordered 20 locomotives of a 2-8-8-2 type with four simple expansion cylinders. The main reason for this was the fact that the railroad's loading gauge could not accommodate the large low-pressure cylinders of a compound locomotive, but the change showed that adequate steam piping was feasible and that Mallet-type locomotives were indeed capable of operating effectively at higher speeds. Even so, considerable work had to be done before flexible joints, suitable for carrying high-pressure steam to the leading cylinders, became available. The development of these joints opened the way to a renewed American enthusiasm for the Mallet-type locomotive with four simple cylinders, and over the following years the advent of a succession of improvements allowed a steady improvement in the capabilities of the locomotives, so that they could be used effectively first for main-line freight services and then, in some instances, for express passenger work.

Among the changes that transformed the capabilities of the Mallet type of locomotive were valves of longer travel, more complete balancing of the moving parts and, most importantly as they removed the tendency toward oscillation that had so bedevilled earlier Mallet-type locomotives – the way in which the leading frame was connected to the main frame and the manner in which the lateral movement of the leading wheels was controlled.

The developments paved the way for the Union Pacific Railroad's procurement, in the period between 1918 and 1924, of 70 compounded 2-8-8-0 locomotives with 59-in

RIGHT
A FEF-class 4-8-4 locomotive, No. 844, heads a Union Pacific Railroad train leaving Sacramento, California.

OPPOSITE
Locomotive No. 4278 was a 4-8-8-2 unit of the Southern Pacific Railroad's AC6-class, notable for its forward cab. This example is seen at the head of a 109-car train at Santa Barbara, California.

(1.500-m) driving wheels. These were used for high-intensity but moderate-speed operations; when in 1926 the railroad found itself in need of locomotives suitable for freight services at higher speeds, it procured a class of 88 three-cylinder 4-12-2 locomotives with 67-in (1.702-m) driving wheels. This was the first class to have this particular wheel arrangement, one of only a few with three-cylinder engines of American design, and the only one manufactured in any numbers. The locomotives were very successful even though their long rigid wheelbase and heavy motion limited them to a maximum speed of 45mph (72km/h), but competition demanded a 12-coupled engine offering higher speed.

Operating experience with these

compound Mallet-type locomotives led the railroad to convert them to simple expansion, in which form they were so effective that in 1936 the Union Pacific Railroad contracted for a class of 40 simple-expansion locomotives with a 4-6-6-4 configuration and driving wheels with a diameter of 69in (1.753m). This was the Challenger class, with a leading truck that offered much better lateral control than a pony truck, while the two-axle truck under the firebox made possible the incorporation of a firebox with a very large grate.

The locomotives worked on many parts of the Union Pacific Railroad system, mainly for the hauling of fast freight services. However, the last six locomotives were completed for passenger services with a larger tender carried

by a two-axle leading truck and five other axles in place of the freight locomotives's smaller six-axle tenders.

In 1942, so much more traffic was being carried by the U.S. railroad system, largely as a result of the movements of men and equipment as well as raw materials for the nation's war industries, that there was a demand for more freight capacity and therefore a large number of locomotives. The manufacture of Challenger-class locomotives was therefore resumed, and the Union Pacific Railroad then received another 65 of these excellent units in the period up to 1944. In these later locomotives a number of changes were incorporated, most notably an increase in the size of the grate from 108 to 132sq ft (10 to 12.3m²), the use of cast steel rather than built-up frames, and an increase in boiler pressure in concert with a reduction in cylinder for no change in the tractive effort.

A more fundamental change from the earlier engines was in the pivot between the leading unit and the main frame. In the earlier engines there were vertical and horizontal hinges, but the new engines used the arrangement pioneered in the Big Boys without a horizontal hinge. The vertical hinge was now designed to transmit a load of several tons from the rear to the front unit, so balancing the distribution of weight between the two sets of driving wheels, and in the process reducing the front driving wheels's tendency to slip in the manner that had been a problem with the earlier locomotives. In the absence of a horizontal hinge, the rises and falls of the track were now catered for, as in conventional locomotives, by each axle's own springs.

The Union Pacific Railroad owned its own coal mines and as a result all of the Challenger-class locomotives were completed as coal-burners; but in 1945 five units were converted to oil-burning for employment on passenger trains on lines in the states of Oregon and Washington. Smoke was found to obstruct the driver's field of vision, so the locomotives were then fitted with smoke deflectors. In 1952 the supply of coal was interrupted by a strike and a programme was set in motion for the rapid conversion of other coal-burners to oil, but the strike ended after the completion of only eight locomotives.

The advent of diesel-powered locomotives finally ended the careers of the Challenger-class locomotives in 1958. It is worth noting that several other American railroads also acquired locomotives with the 4-6-6-4 arrangement of wheels, most of them similar to the Challenger in broad terms.

There were many other classes of steam locomotive, but it is with types such as the J, Big Boy and Challenger types that any description of the larger types of American steam locomotive most fittingly ends

CHAPTER SEVEN
ROLLING STOCK

RIGHT
The levels of comfort that prevailed in the passenger cars of American railroads in the 19th century could extend between the genuinely spartan and the opulently sybaritic. This upper end of the scale can be gauged from this illustration of a purpose-built Pullman standard car of the type completed for wealthy private individuals such as the 'railroad barons' and the leading lights of the coal, steel and financial businesses.

OPPPOSITE LEFT
An advertisement highlights the level of comfort available on the Pullman hotel cars of the Chicago & North Western Railway.

OPPOSITE RIGHT
This is the interior of one of the earliest Pullman passenger cars of the Union Pacific Railroad.

The complete train hauled by the locomotive is the combination of cars and/or wagons, whose practical and economic task is the accommodation of the payload, be it people or freight. The two main forms of car have traditionally been those created for the movement of passengers and of freight. The former has declined in importance by comparison with the latter since World War II, even though the latter has also suffered from the inroads made by road and air transport. In earlier times, passengers were of greater importance in the economics of railroad operation. Yet then as now, the lot of the passenger was not always a happy one. The passengers who embarked on the first service of the *De Witt Clinton* on the Mohawk & Hudson Railroad in 1831 soon discovered the pitfalls of early railroad services: some were cast from their seats by the shock of starting, as the 3-ft (1-m) chains connecting the cars jolted taut, and most were soon having to prevent their clothes from catching fire as embers streamed onto them from the locomotive's smokestack. Any stop, such as those inevitably needed to replenish the water that the locomotive required as the

'raw material' for the steam that powered its workings, caused the unbraked cars to shunt forward into the braking engine, and after a drenching during the watering process the

passengers still with the train extemporized wooden buffers to jam between the cars. The journey then proceeded more smoothly, but possibly ended with the passengers

had made it feasible to build longer frames, the stagecoach-type bodies that had been used for the earliest services were replaced by the coach layout that was so much better that it became standard and remains so, albeit with steady streams of improvements. However, despite the fact that the passengers were now

carried inside coaches, railroad travel was still dirty, noisy and uncomfortable, and could also be dangerous. The quality of the ride was then enhanced by the development of cast-iron wheels that were more regular in shape than the hand-crafted ones that been standard up to that time. Spark-arresters in the smokestack

wearing very badly burned clothing.

Clearly, important improvements had of necessity to be made before passenger travel by train could be considered endurable for anything but its novelty factor. Travel on the outside of a car clearly possessed ramifications altogether different from travel on an open horse-drawn wagon, and inside seating quickly became the norm. Stagecoach suspension was equally inadequate, and as early as three years after the *De Witt Clinton*'s pioneering journey Ross Winans patented a method of supporting long cars on a four-wheel truck (or bogie) located under their ends. This improvement facilitated running on uneven track, and also the negotiation of curves. Once the use of independent trucks

The 4-8-4 locomotive No. 614 of the Chesapeake & Ohio Railroad eases round a curve at Salisbury Mills, New York.

Lady passengers enjoy a sing-song on board a Pullman car of the Atchison, Topeka & Santa Fe Railway in the early days of the 20th century.

helped to limit the amount of ember that escaped and could land on the passengers and also, it should be noted, on the adjacent farmland or woodland to cause dangerous and costly fires; any derailment or emergency stop was also likely to cause a fire as kerosene lamps and wood stoves, used to provide light and heat, were dislodged from their mountings.

Discomfort and danger were compounded by any number of inconveniences. For many years it was not possible to obtain through tickets covering more than one railroad, for example, and there were no baggage handling or onboard refreshment facilities. It was only after the expansion of the railroads had started to create competition for the passenger trade that railroads saw the commercial necessity of

351

RIGHT
A wooden passenger car of the Great
Northern Railway.

OPPOSITE
The 2-8-2 locomotive No. 40 of the Valley
Railroad near Essex, Connecticut.

keeping or boosting their market share through the improvement of the passenger's lot. Safety also began to improve as the authorities started to consider the overall implications of railroad transport.

Much was achieved in the elimination of unnecessary dangers, especially in the quarter of a century following the end of the Civil War in 1865. Improvement of the way through the

introduction of heavier iron and then steel track combined with an appreciation that regular maintenance was required to reduce the possibility of sprung rails, which could pierce the bottoms of the carriages with dire results, and of derailments. The introduction of the Westinghouse vacuum brake and the Janney automatic coupler (page 365) made starting and stopping more predictable. The

replacement of stoves and kerosene lamps by steam heating from the engine and gas or electric lighting respectively served to reduce the tendency for accidents or other untoward incidents to cause fires. Outside the railroad train itself, improvement in signalling concepts and the spread of the telegraph also had their effect on reducing accident rates.

The development most appreciated by

passengers, however, was probably the radical improvement in the design of the cars and their internal fittings. Here the name of George Pullman became synonymous with the highest level of comfort. It is worth noting, though, that Pullman was not the first to develop a sleeping car for the provision of night-time accommodation, the first recorded sleeping car having made its appearance in the mid-1830s on the Cumberland Valley Railroad in the state of Pennsylvania. In this arrangement, stagecoach passengers arriving at Chambersburg late in the night were carried in an overnight train to Harrisburg to meet the connecting service to Philadelphia. But this and other early attempts at creating effective overnight accommodation on trains were based on simple berths without bedding. It was in 1853 that Pullman found himself on a sleeper car of this type while travelling between Buffalo and Westfield. The wooden berths were uncomfortable, but Pullman also decided that the single most limiting factor in the provision of comfortable sleeping accommodation was the attachment of the berths to the sides of the car as permanent units, which effectively prevented the car from profitable daytime service as a vehicle for seated passengers. Drawing on the knowledge gained in his training as a carpenter, Pullman decided to create a more versatile arrangement, and during 1858 converted two obsolete sleeping cars of the Chicago & Alton Railroad in the manner his fertile mind had suggested. Neither this first pair of conversions, nor a modest number of improved models created shortly after the first pair, raised much enthusiasm among travellers,

but they did serve to provide Pullman with the opportunity to evolve his thinking. After a short visit to the gold-mining areas of Colorado, Pullman returned to Chicago with the determination to create the best possible car.

The new car emerged as the Pioneer, and marked a radical improvement in the type of comfort that passengers demanded. It was also much too large for service on the Chicago & Alton Railroad's system, however, so its fittings (valued at $20,000 rather than the standard $4,000 or so), such as carpeting, brocaded upholstery, polished wood, silvered oil lamps and gilded mirrors, served little practical purpose. However, in 1865 the body of President Lincoln arrived in Chicago on its way to Springfield for burial, and since the Pioneer was the obvious conveyance for the completion of the journey, the line was modified to allow the car's use. Later, the line between Detroit and Galena was similarly altered so that General Ulysses S. Grant could travel home in the car, which was later placed in regular service on the Chicago & Alton Railroad's system.

For the further exploitation of his concept, Pullman formed the Pullman Car Company in 1867, and his products soon became the very epitome of luxurious railroad travel. Although the new company's first cars were sleeper units, Pullman's range was soon expanded. The hotel car, combining sleeping accommodation with a kitchen and portable tables, was made for the Great Western Railway of Canada in 1867, and in 1888 the Pullman company made its first dining car for the Chicago & Alton Railroad. Beautifully

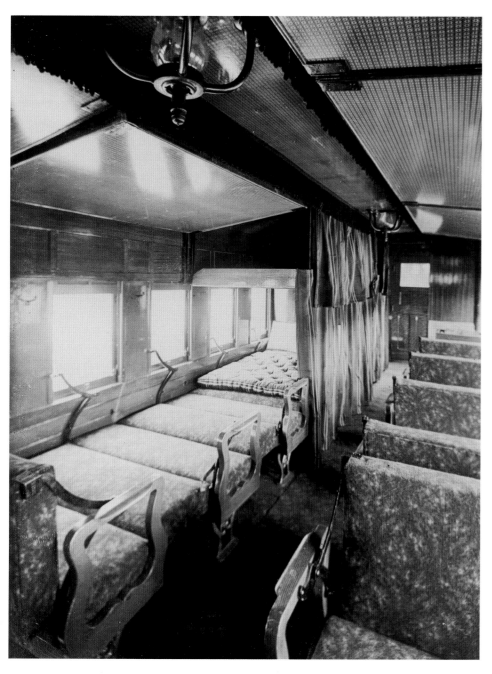

appointed day cars, known as Palace Cars, followed. Experience with these and other Pullman cars soon revealed that a connection between the individual cars would be advantageous, and in 1887 there appeared Pullman's vestibuled car, in which steel springs were employed to hold a steel-framed diaphragm over the platform at the end of one car against a similar arrangement on that of the next. This enabled passengers to cross in safety from one car to the other, and also made a major contribution to safety, by reducing the tendency of the cars's platforms to ride over each other. The introduction of the vestibuled car made it possible to create the so-called limited train with sleeping, dining, smoking, library, bathroom and even barbering facilities. This became very fashionable despite (or even because) of the higher charges that were levied for the use of such services.

Pullman did not only build the cars that carried his name, for each car also had its own Pullman attendant, carefully trained in the multitude of tasks associated with caring for the passengers. This concept lasted to 1947, when a case brought under American anti-trust legislation compelled the company to make a choice between building cars or operating them. The company opted for construction, passing responsibility for operations to a new consortium, until uncertainty about the future of American passenger travel led to the company to abandon this.

The success of the Pullman concept led inevitably to imitation. Many railroad operators manufactured their own cars, while other concerns, including the Woodruff and

RIGHT
Old and new: a coaling tower of the Chicago
& North Western Railroad and signals beside
the track at De Kalb, Illinois.

OPPOSITE
Train order semaphore signals at the
preserved Milwaukee Road station at Genoa,
Illinois.

Wagner companies, built and operated similar cars and specialized passenger services. The Pullman name retained it hold, however, and over time the company created new and improved cars to satisfy changing requirements. In 1907 there appeared the first all-steel Pullman; by this time, the standard accommodation of a Pullman car included curtained seating sections, which could be converted in the evening with berths, a gentlemen's smoking compartment at one end of the car, and a ladies's drawing room at the other. Air-conditioning was a feature that became increasingly standard from the late 1920s, while in the 1930s the so-called 'roomette' was introduced to replace the curtained alcoves with individual compartments that combined day seating, folding berths and toilet facilities. Each car was initially outfitted with 18 roomettes, but the staggering of the position of the floors and the arranging of one bed to slide beneath the higher floor and the bed in the next compartment to fold against the wall, allowed each car to be outfitted with 24 roomettes.

A large part of the discomfort typical of rail journeys in the early days of steam locomotion, over any except the very shortest of them, was their very length. The introduction of the Pullman and similar cars for the wealthier passengers, and of generally more comfortable accommodation in the standard cars for those of modest means, did much to improve the lot of the longer-distance traveller, but clearly a shorter travelling time would have also made a considerable difference. Thus the improvement in accommodation was paralleled by an increase

in average speed. Despite the fact that trains averaged about 40mph (64km/h) and inappropriately sported names such as 'Thunderbolt', those involved in long-distance travel still had to make frequent changes: even in highly industrialized and technically advanced New York, large numbers of train journeys began with a ferry trip across the Hudson, since only the New York Central

Railroad, with its Grand Central Station, had a terminus in the city, the only other railroad allowed to operate from this being the New York, New Haven & Hartford Railroad. This situation was improved only in 1910, when the Pennsylvania Railroad opened its own station on Manhattan Island. A consequence of this was to intensify competition on the route from New York to Chicago, which in the 1890s had

as many as 44 services every day.

The fact that the different operators operated over different routes, when connecting the same pairs of cities, inevitably meant that there were major differences in journey times, as a result of which, before World War I, the railroads operating services between New York and Chicago agreed on a 28-hour standard journey time. Since the distances involved ranged from the Pennsylvania Railroad's 903 miles (1453km) to the Erie's 996 miles (1603km), it was also decided that a dollar would be added to fares for each hour that any service subtracted from the standard time: faster travel might mean a greater fare. The leading lights on the New York–Chicago route were the Pennsylvania and the New York Central railroads, which operated their prestige trains, the Broadway Limited and the Twentieth Century Limited, in 18 hours (increased to 20 hours after World War I). Given the availability of Pullman cars on these two services, there was scope for a very large difference in price between the

On 16 November 1944, near Vinton, Virginia, a 15,000-ton coal train is hauled by the 2-6-6-4 A-class locomotive No. 1209, completed by the Roanoke shops of the Norfolk & Western in September 1937 at a cost of $120,394. The locomotive is shown here with an eastbound solid coal train on the way from the coalfields in West Virginia to Norfolk, Virginia. The white flags on each side of the smokebox denote an extra train, all coal trains being operated as extras. The locomotive was retired in August 1958 and sold for scrap.

slowest and least well-equipped services and their altogether faster and better-equipped counterparts.

In the affluent boom period of the 1920s, the railroads placed emphasis on service, but during this decade the motor car steadily became a more important rival to the train. Speed thus came to be a more significant element in railroad thinking. This led to the introduction during the 1930s of the streamliners, which were high-speed trains that attracted very considerable publicity as a result of their spectacular looks and high performance. Streamliners were thus a major weapon in the railroads's struggle to retain traffic at a time when it was being degraded by economic depression and the growing popularity of private transport. The first streamliner was introduced by the Union Pacific Railroad, using Pullman-built aluminium cars and an early diesel locomotive. Clearly an impressive name was needed to catch the interest and even the enthusiasm of the public. One of the first railroads to operate streamliner services, the Chicago, Burlington & Quincy Railroad, began the trend in 1934 with its Zephyr services. The initial Zephyr was a three-car train built by Budd of Philadelphia and used an early Electromotive diesel engine. Not all the new streamliners were diesel-powered, however. In 1935, for example, the Milwaukee Road launched its Hiawatha service with steam locomotives fitted with moderately efficient and visually stunning streamlined 'overcoats'. The Hiawatha was initially operated on the very competitive route between Chicago and Minneapolis-St. Paul, as noted above, but was then extended to include runs north to the shore of Lake Superior and west to Omaha, Sioux Falls and across the continent by means of the Olympian Hiawatha to Spokane in Washington state. Other western long-distance streamliners included such famous trains as the Atchison, Topeka & Santa Fe's Super Chief, launched in 1937 with diesel locomotion and Pullman coaches on the vast route linking Chicago and Los Angeles, and the Union Pacific Railroad's City of Los Angeles, City of Portland and City of San Francisco, that served the cities for which they were named.

It should be noted that while prestige services have inevitably attracted the highest levels of attention, such services have always

Line-up of Erie commuter trains at Jersey City, New Jersey, in 1950. By this time many older main-line steam locomotives had been relegated to secondary tasks of this type as main-line services became the responsibility of diesel-engined locomotives.

been in the minority of the relevant railroads's passenger operations. During the later part of the 19th century, for example, the railroads operated large numbers of special immigrant trains for the movement of families newly arrived on the eastern seaboard to the new lands they were going to settle in the west. Indeed, several of the transcontinental lines, mainly those operating in or into the north-western parts of the U.S.A., used agents in Europe to advertise the attractions of the new

country and arrange passage for the resulting flow of immigrants. The conditions on many of the trains that met the new arrivals were poor: the sleeping cars had only wooden benches along their sides as berths, and the cars were kept as open as possible so that they could be hosed down easily after they had discharged their passengers. At the other end of the scale, in terms of price and the facilities offered, were the luxurious private saloon cars for wealthy travellers. Built to the individual's

particular specification and limited only by the dimensions and the owner's ability to pay, these cars represented the last word in luxury. Several companies undertook such work; in fact, the Pullman company manufactured some 450 coaches for private customers before the great crash of 1929 ended this type of extravagance: Pullman's prices ranged between $50,000 and $350,000.

The other facet of railroad use is the movement of freight, and this type of

RIGHT
A railroad baggage cart, essential equipment at every train station and here seen at the East Broad Top Railroad's station at Orbisonia, Pennsylvania.

OPPOSITE
The Lima-built 4-8-4 locomotive No. 614 of the Chesapeake & Ohio Railroad in 1948.

operation preceded not only the concept of passenger transport but also the locomotive itself in even its most primitive steam-powered form. In its very earliest days, the railroad facilitated the handling of heavy loads, initially in quarries and mines. In the U.S.A. it was the commercial attractions of collecting

the agricultural produce of the country's westward expansion that first encouraged railroad operators to extend their tracks from the eastern seaboard toward the great rivers of the interior. These first planned to run their railroads in much the same way as the operators of toll roads and canals: the operator

would provide the tracks, and payment of the requisite fee would allow anyone to haul their own vehicles over them. The concept almost immediately proved ineffective, leading the operators to take complete control of all elements of the movement. This included the provision of the locomotives; the right types of

RIGHT
Like most other aspects of American life in World War II, railroads were affected by the need to give priority to war-time considerations. Train schedules were inevitably affected, this emergency schedule having been issued by the New York Central Railroad in 1945.

OPPOSITE LEFT
A key element in improving train safety was the Janney automatic coupler.

OPPOSITE RIGHT
The cover of a schedule of the New York Central Railroad.

War Emergency Train Schedules

Effective August 1, 1945 — Form 1001

car; depots where goods could be delivered, loaded, unloaded and collected; and the administrative system that made the whole system workable. These are the basic elements that still characterize railroad freight operations.

The same type of locomotives were initially used for both passenger and freight services, but it soon became clear that each could best be handled by locomotives designed and built for the task. Passenger services required the use of locomotives optimized for high speed with light loads, while those for freight needed locomotives optimized for low speed with heavy loads. In practical terms this led to the development of the freight locomotive with driving wheels that were more numerous but of smaller diameter than those of the passenger locomotive. With speed a relatively insignificant factor in freight operations, except where perishable agricultural produce was involved, the primary requirement became the movement of the maximum possible quantity of freight in each train, consequently some notably enormous steam locomotives were created specifically to work vast freight trains. During the period of steam locomotion it was generally impossible to locate the locomotive anywhere but at the head or tail of the string of freight wagons, thus limiting the size of any freight train to the load that could be supported by the couplings.

An earlier breakthrough in the control of long trains was the introduction of the quick-acting air brake. At first, freight cars were individually braked, which required the brakeman to move along the roofs of the cars to reach the wheels by which the brakes were

controlled, a system that was slow, inefficient, and fraught with danger for the brakemen, many of whom were killed. What was needed was a system that allowed them to be controlled from a single point in the locomotive, making it feasible for the brakes in every car to be applied simultaneously. By the 1870s the Westinghouse type of air brake, offering this capability, was entering large-scale service in passenger trains, but its introduction in freight trains, especially those of greater length, was initially less successful, as the time required for the braking force to be transmitted along the full length of the train could lead to severe shocks in the rearmost cars. By the mid-1880s a version of the

Westinghouse air brake system with the capacity for quicker action had been developed, the use of which made it possible for long trains to be stopped without significant delay and resulting shocks in the rear cars.

The adoption of a braking system that was universal on American railroads was important for a number of reasons, of which the most important was probably the growth of through-traffic, as this led to the spread of wagons belonging to different railroad operators over the entire rail network. This tendency was also a direct reflection of the growth of freight operations's size and importance. It also required the railroads to create car-accounting departments whose sole task was to keep track of the location of every one of the railroads's wagons: railroads were charged on a daily basis for the use of other companies's wagons, so the car-accounting department was a vital tool in the operations of each railroad to ensure that the right rentals were charged for their own wagons, and that the empty wagons of each operator were returned as rapidly as possible.

Time saw an increasing level of specialization in the wagons used for freight transport. In the early days of freight by rail, the three most common types were the flatcar, the boxcar and the coal car. Other types of car that later assumed large-scale use included the refrigerated car for the movement of perishable farm produce, and an ever-enlarging number of role-specialized cars. Coal has long been carried in larger quantities than any other type of freight load by North American railroads. The whole process

OPPOSITE
The Daylight-type locomotive No. 4449 of the Southern Pacific Railroad passes along a raised section of track of the Yolo Bypass in California at Midon, east of Davis, on a service between Sacramento and San Jose.

LEFT
The fate of many old and obsolete locomotives: shunting duties at one of the operator's yards.

became automated to a high degree, especially by operators such as the Norfolk & Western Railroad, which delivered huge weights of coal from mining areas of Kentucky and West Virginia for industrial and domestic use in the cities mainly to the south of the Great Lakes, and for export sales via its port facilities at Lamberts Point on Chesapeake Bay.

It was the task of the railroad operator to make up trains with loads from different companies for delivery to different destinations along and sometimes off the route to be travelled. This need to make up trains became inevitable after railroad routes began to meet and thereby open the way for the transhipments of loads, often from the lines of one operator to those of another. This frequently led to delays in the completion of many loads, and in an effort to overcome this problem there appeared a number of fast freight lines in the course of the 19th century. Established by agreement between the group's railroads primarily involved or between separate operators, the fast freight lines contracted with shippers to undertake the through shipment of their loads between different railroads.

After World War I, the task of handling individual cars and making up trains was facilitated by the automation of the classification yards where these tasks were undertaken. One of the first yards of this more modern type was the Markham Yard of the Illinois Central Railroad, just south of Chicago. But what allowed the introduction of large-scale automation was the development of the remote-controlled retarder, used in concert with power-operated switches and a hump to

OPPOSITE
Now a museum, the oldest railroad station in the U.S.A. is that of what is now Ellicott City, Maryland, built in 1831 by the Baltimore & Ohio Railroad.

LEFT
Open-end observation car.

RIGHT
Manually-operated semaphore signals on a
tower at Brighton Park, Chicago, Illinois.

OPPOSITE
The 2-8-2 locomotive No. 497, a unit of the
K37-class operated by the Rio Grande
Railroad, hauls an excursion passenger train
though the Cumbres Pass, Colorado.

enable all the yard's activities to be controlled from a central tower, with good all-round fields of vision. In the first period of North American railroad operations, the movement of all the cars in a yard was undertaken by individual switching of the engines to move them into the siding where their train was being made up. This was a slow and laborious system that was greatly simplified in the 1880s by the introduction of humps or artificial mounds, over which all the cars could be pushed in turn and then coasted downhill, using the appropriate switch setting, to their allotted sidings. The system was further speeded by the introduction of power-operated switches, but reached its definitive form with the installation of retarders, which are track-side beams that can be operated to grip the wheels of passing cars and thereby slow them down to allow full control of all the yard's activities from a central location. The Markham Yard opened in 1926, at which time the northbound classification section had 121 retarders and 69 pairs of switches feeding 67 tracks, with five towers to supervise operations.

The effective use of the retarder is based necessarily on a nice calculation of a number of factors, including the car's type, whether or not it is loaded, the car's degree of freedom in running, the strength and direction of the wind, and the route to the individual siding. The integration of all these factors is necessary for assessment of the amount of pressure each pair of retarders exerts on the wheels, to make certain that the car neither ceases to move before reaching the steadily varying numbers of other cars already at a halt

in the siding, nor crashes into them.

It was the very number of the variable factors, and the need for human crews to keep the cars under observation right through the switching process, that demanded the use of several control towers in each major yard, until the advent of the computer made it feasible to automate virtually the whole of the process and thereby permit a reduction in the number of control towers to one. Such automation is expensive in capital terms to establish, but allows significant savings once it has entered service. Manpower can be reduced, and the swifter and more accurate classification of trains makes for much more efficient use of the railroad's assets. To a very high degree automation makes the best possible economic sense in an operation that is dedicated to a single high-volume task.

For two primary reasons there was always the need for continued control of any freight train's movement after it had left the yard: the arrival of the train at its destination at the right time, and the control of all the

OPPOSITE
Locomotive No. 734 hauls an excursion train of the Western Maryland Scenic Railroad over Helmstedders Curve in Maryland.

LEFT
The fact that the day of the steam locomotive for main-line services was drawing to a close was signalled by the advent of diesel locomotives, such as this unit of the Union Pacific Railroad, seen here on 18 July 1937 hauling the City of San Francisco express near Hermosa, Wyoming.

Diesel-engined locomotion made rapid inroads into main-line services, for despite the initially greater cost of diesel-electric locomotives, they were cleaner to operate, easier to maintain and, in the medium to longer term, would repay the cost of the new facilities they needed through reduced operating and maintenance costs.

movements in a given area to ensure that there are no collisions. The first effective way in which this task was accomplished in the 19th century, was by means of the newly created telegraph system, used to issue train orders. Linked by telegraph to station operators, the central dispatcher sent orders governing the movements of all the trains on the line, which were then written out and passed to the engineer and conductor of every applicable train. The system ensured that each engineer was given his instructions, told of all other traffic on the line, informed of the priority accorded to the various trains, and all other relevant details. The system was of particular importance when any train had to move along a long stretch of single-track line with passing sections that trains moving in opposite directions had to reach at the same time: thus the engineer might be instructed to move to a specified passing point, with a loop in the track allowing him to pull off the main line and wait until the other train had passed before continuing. The engineer of the other train would have been told to move off but also warned of the first train and told where to expect to find it waiting in its loop. If the sidelined train was not in its appointed place, the train with the right of way would stop and telegraph the

The Union Pacific Railroad's original diesel-engined City of Los Angeles service is caught by the camera at the time of its inaugural run in May 1936, operating between Los Angeles and Chicago. At first, this was an 11-car service, but it was soon expanded to 17 cars.

The Turquoise Room of the Super Chief service of the Atchison, Topeka & Santa Fe Railway was one of the first private dining-room arrangements to be introduced by any American railroad operator, in this instance during the later 1930s.

dispatcher by means of a portable telegraph machine that could be tapped into the line at the side of the track. So important was the telegraph to successful and safe operation of the railroads that it was one of the fundamental rules that no train should depart without a telegrapher.

With the passage of time, improvement led to the introduction of block signalling for sections of any line where there was heavy traffic. This allowed the control of all the trains on that section by means of semaphore or coloured light signals. These were operated from a central control point with the levers for setting the switches, and later enhanced by an interlock arrangement between signals and switches: mechanically connecting all the controls, the arrangement ensured that a signal could be set, unless the individual switches were in the appropriate position for the instruction given. Block signalling was impractical for many parts of a large railroad network, and here the more modern system was centralized train control. This was developed during the 1920s, and placed the whole section of line under the dispatcher's direct control, with points and signals set by electrically-actuated control.

The nature of railroad freight operations was almost inevitably somewhat cyclic in

Good food and personal service were two of the main attractions of the prestige services that were operated by many main-line railroad operators from the 1920s. Here Fred Harvey, a chef on one of the Atchison, Topeka & Santa Fe Railway's Super Chief services, moves along the dining car to serve one of the meals he has just prepared in the adjacent kitchen unit.

ABOVE
Interior of a Pullman car of the Atchison, Topeka & Santa Fe Railway during the 1930s.

RIGHT
A bedroom suite in one of the 12 all-bedroom cars operated on the Atchison, Topeka & Santa Fe Railway's Super Chief services. Each suite provides two upper and two lower berths, two toilets, a dual wash stand, and a push-button radio.

nature: a type of freight vitally necessary at one time might then fall out of demand for some reason, be replaced by a demand for another but later resume its former importance. Thus while some aspects of railroad freight increased in volume and financial importance, others declined to greater or lesser extents. One of the most significant of these was the movement of cattle, which was one of the primary reasons for the extension of the railroads into the region of Kansas, where cities such as Abilene and Dodge City provided the points at which cattle herded from Texas were gathered for railroad movement to the great stockyards of Kansas City and Chicago. Speed of movement was clearly important when transporting live

animals, and here the Chicago, Burlington & Quincy Railroad was among the leaders, with average speeds of nearly 50mph (80km/h). The same basic pattern also held true for the movement of mail. This was first carried by trains in 1838 on a regular basis, following the decision of Congress that all railroads should be post carriers, although some mail services had been operated before this. From 1838 the movement of mail by rail grew steadily in capability and volume. Whereas the first mail had been moved in locked compartments, from the 1860s more effective use was made

of the concept after the railroad had reached St. Joseph and the jumping-off point for the Pony Express service for mail deliveries to California. Following the suggestion of a member of the U.S. Postal Service in St. Joseph, it was decided that mail should be sorted on board the train to avoid delay before being loaded onto the train. It August 1864, therefore, mail-sorting facilities, as already used in Canada and therefore modelled on the British pattern, were pioneered by the Hannibal & St. Joseph Railroad. Post office cars then became standard on many of the

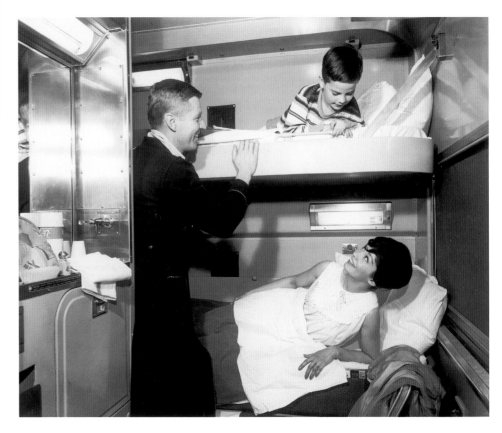

faster railroad services, with teams in these cars sorting the mail for the various points on the route. As the volume of mail increased, dedicated mail trains were operated. Like the cattle trains, however, mail trains have now become a thing of the past.

Almost as soon as the spread of the railroads had created the framework on which vast commercial and industrial expansion could flourish in American cities, this expansion began to add another, larger dimension to railroad operations. So while the development of the railroads spurred the growth of cities, the growth of cities now spurred the further development of the railroads. This expansion provided the means for the inhabitants of nearby towns to travel to and from work in newly established factories and businesses. These towns were gradually subsumed by the cities they supported to become suburbs, with the result that railroad services spread ever further. At an early point in this process of local growth, commuter traffic became a specialized form of railroad transport in its own right, characterized by its own types of rolling stock and, inevitably, its own operational problems.

In the decades following the end of the Civil War, railroads spawned the development of the suburbs. Industry and the railroads were

One of the most adventurous of any time, at least in its appearance, was this double-deck observation car used on the Hiawatha service of the Chicago, Milwaukee, St. Paul & Pacific Railroad (better known as the 'Milwaukee Road'), and seen here at Columbus, Wisconsin.

RIGHT
The 'beaver-tail' parlour car bringing up the rear of the Hiawatha express of the Milwaukee Road in 1935.

BELOW
The 4-6-4 F7-class locomotive No. 101 of the Milwaukee Road pulls out of Milwaukee, Wisconsin, on 30 August 1941 at the head of the 13-car Afternoon Hiawatha express service.

dependent on each other: industry could increase only on the basis of rail transport, and the growth of industry and the commerce it supported provided the traffic the railroads needed. The suburbs had a vital part to play in this process of mutual growth, providing both the workforce to operate industry and commerce and the market for their products. Large and regular traffic over the same routes seemed to be an ideal form of business to railroad planners. Even before the end of the 19th century, however, it had become clear that suburban services would be increasingly difficult, as commuter traffic required large amounts of rolling stock and locomotives, sophisticated organization and great efficiency, but would operate for only a few hours each day. Trains had to be run in both directions, but were filled only in one direction at a time, namely into the cities at the start of the working day and out to the suburbs at its end.

Maximization of passenger loads required the introduction of purpose-built coaches with minimal facilities, and these were of no use for other purposes. This was only the start of the railroads's problems, for the situation worsened with the passage of time. During the 1920s there began to develop serious competition from the private motor car, the 1930s saw a great economic depression, and World War II was followed by a further significant diminution of passenger traffic that coincided with the decline of steam locomotion in favour of electric and diesel propulsion.

Against a backdrop of sky and steam from a chocolate factory, these are ex-Chicago & North Western semaphore signals near the Clinton Street Tower in Chicago.

CHAPTER EIGHT

RAILROADS NORTH & SOUTH: CANADA & MEXICO

In 1876 this 4-4-0 unit was the first locomotive built at the Moncton shops of the Intercolonial Railway.

The large-scale development of railways in Canada was slow to get under way, largely as a result of low population density and the availability of alternatives such as water transport. Even so, the first Canadian railway was chartered in 1832. Established between the Richelieu river at St. John and La Prairie, across the St. Lawrence river from Montreal, the Champlain & St. Lawrence Railway was just over 14-miles (22.5-km) long but trimmed 90 miles (145km) from the river route, linking Lake Champlain and Montreal, that was currently the main line of communication between the New England states of the U.S.A. and the main city of Lower Canada. Services began on 21 July 1836, when a Stephenson Samson-type locomotive took an hour each way to haul two coaches on a round trip starting and ending at Laprairie. In its first years of operation, the Champlain & St. Lawrence halted its service when the rivers froze in winter, preventing the movement of the boats with whose operations the railway's services were linked, and started a schedule of services right through the year only in 1851, when an extension was completed to Rouses Point in New York state

to provide a connection with U.S. lines and so give passengers the ability to travel by rail right through to Boston and New England.

Other early Canadian railways were built

to bridge gaps in the river and lake transport systems that were still Canada's most useful natural lines of communication. As might be imagined from their nature, these linking

Locomotive No. 67 of the Canadian National Railway.

railways were generally short. The first was the Montreal & Lachine Railway that began operation in November 1848 between Montreal and the head of the Lachine rapids, the starting point of the river route to the west; in 1850 a railway was built to link the small town of Industrie (now Joliette) with the St. Lawrence river. The 12.5-mile (20-km) Carillon &

Grenville Railway was built around a stretch of rapids on the Ottawa river in 1854, while during the next year the Northern Railway was completed to provide a link between Toronto on Lake Ontario and Collingwood on the Georgian Bay of Lake Huron.

During the 19th century a fairly large number of other short railways was created,

providing a limited yet valuable service for the travelling public and the communities that the railways linked. There were also ambitious plans during the same period for longer railways, which all too often never got off the ground as a result of problems obtaining official permission from the different administrations of the separate colonies of

The opening, on 21 July 1836, of the first railroad in Canada, that linking La Prairie and St. John.

what was at the time British North America. Some of these schemes were realized, however, but only to the extent of small but nevertheless useful segments within the context of the larger routes that had been or indeed were still being planned. Typical of these was the railway linking Halifax and Truro in Nova Scotia, which was brought into service during 1853. By far the most significant of these routes, however, was that linking Longueuil, opposite Montreal on the St. Lawrence river, with Portland on the coast of the U.S. state of Maine: the Canadian section, more formally known as the St. Lawrence & Atlantic Railroad, combined with the Atlantic & St. Lawrence Railroad of the U.S.A. during 1853 to provide a rail service between Montreal and the sea, even when the Canadian city's natural access to the sea, the St. Lawrence river, was suffering from its usual winter freeze.

The creation of this year-round link with the sea is also of importance as the plans for its construction led to the 1849 Guarantee Act, under whose terms the government of Canada started to provide financial assistance for the construction of railways. A new line that gained an immediate benefit from the new law's provisions was the Great Western Railway, which was completed in 1856 and

provided a link between Niagara Falls, with its suspension bridge connection to Buffalo and both Toronto and Windsor, where another bridge linked the Canadian city with Detroit. Other funding for the construction of railways in Canada came from the mother country, where British companies saw profit in the improvement of intra-Canadian communications. During 1852 the Canadian government approved the plans for a British

company to build the Grand Trunk Railway, and by 1860 this great railway, with its celebrated Victoria Bridge at Montreal, providing a link with the St. Lawrence & Atlantic Railroad and a new line to Rivière-du-Loup, extended westward to Sarnia, via Toronto and Stratford on Canadian soil, and from Port Huron to Detroit on U.S. territory. A 999-year lease of the Atlantic & St. Lawrence allowed the further extension of the Grand

Trunk Railway to Portland in Maine. Unfortunately, the establishment of this important and impressive 800-mile (1287-km) unified route between the Great Lakes and the coast of the Atlantic Ocean had adverse longer-term implications.

In 1845 a royal commission on Canadian railways was established, one of the commission's tasks being the establishment of a standard gauge. This showed a considerable

Built by Timothy Hackworth in the U.K. during 1838, this 0-6-0 was delivered to a pioneering Canadian railway operator. The car is decidedly primitive, but at least provided accommodation enclosed against the worst of the elements and also the smoke and smuts emitted by the locomotive.

385

OPPOSITE
Another view of the early locomotive, optimistically named *Samson*, made by Timothy Hackworth for Canadian service.

LEFT
Celebrations of the arrival of the first train to reach Vancouver, British Columbia, on the occasion of the golden jubilee of Queen Victoria's reign on 23 May 1887.

56.5-in (1435-mm) standard gauge so that it could attract traffic from across the border from the standard-gauge American railroad systems via its interchange facilities at Detroit and Buffalo. The new Canadian national gauge remained standard for some 20 years.

The next major Canadian rail system was the Intercolonial Railway, which was the trunk line between Halifax and Quebec that had first been suggested as early as 1832. An early problem was the 1842 resolution of the border dispute with the U.S.A. over the eastern frontier line between the two countries, for this located part of the railway's planned route across the northern extension of the state of Maine, which delayed the creation of the Intercolonial Railway for some time. The advisability of uniting the separate British colonies in North America acquired a measure of urgency with the outbreak of the American Civil War in 1861, especially after the emergence of the possibility of the U.K. and

ABOVE
Spaced at the front, in the centre and at the rear, three locomotives of the Canadian Pacific Railway work a train of only eight wooden cars up the original 4 per cent grade of the Kicking Horse Pass.

RIGHT
A Canadian National 4-6-0 locomotive.

degree of foresight, especially when one thinks of the chaos that had developed in other countries as a result of their failure to fix on one gauge to cover the whole country. The commission fixed on an unfortunate figure, however, in the form of the 66-in (1676-mm) gauge currently used by the St. Lawrence & Atlantic Railway. All Canadian railways more than 75-miles (121-km) long were now compelled to adopt a gauge that had been created with provincial rather than national demands in mind. Among the Canadian railways that suffered most from this decision were the Grand Trunk and the Great Western railways: the latter had planned to use the

Canadian railway operators were faced with basically the same problems as their American counterparts south of the border: a few large cities and numbers of smaller urban centres scattered across a vast area containing broad prairies, high mountains, large rivers and, peculiar in North American practice to Canada and Alaska, frozen tundra. In Canada's case, though, the population was considerably smaller and the available financial resources considerably scantier in a country that nonetheless cried out for the benefits that would accrue from a long-distance transport capability. This scene was photographed at Hamilton, Ontario.

her colonies becoming involved. In October 1863 Sandford Fleming was appointed to build the railway and completed his survey early in 1865, recommending that the line of the Intercolonial Railway extend from the northern end of the Grand Trunk Railway at Rivière-du-Loup along the St. Lawrence river, before turning south-west through the Matapedia valley to the Bay Chaleur and

thence to Moncton, where a branch from St. John joined the main-line continuation to Truro and the existing railroad to Halifax. The provision of a railway connecting maritime provinces with Quebec and Ontario (as Upper and Lower Canada were now to be called) was built into the 1867 British North America Act, which created the Dominion of Canada as a confederation out of the previously

separate provinces. The chief engineer was Fleming, who succeeded in developing an excellent railway.

During 1873 Prince Edward Island, which had initially refused to join the federation, largely on the grounds of the Intercolonial Railway's cost, changed its mind after seeking unsuccessfully to create its own rail system; part of its incorporation into the Dominion of

A 4-4-0 locomotive of the Grand Trunk
Pacific Railway involved in the task of
constructing a line on Prince Rupert Island,
British Columbia, in 1910.

teams, and the construction parties that would follow in their wake, had to deal with three different types of country: the wooded terrain to the west of Lake Superior, the prairies in the centre of the dominion, and the deeply forested mountain ranges in the west. By 1878 Fleming had planned the route as a line following the northern shore of Lake Superior, heading across the prairies by way of Edmonton to the Yellowhead Pass, and finally reaching Vancouver on Burrard Inlet by means of the Thompson and Fraser river valleys.

In the time that the surveys were

LEFT
The Canadian Pacific Railway's locomotive No. 5935, a 2-10-4 unit of the Selkirk type for passenger and freight services, is seen soon after completion.

BELOW
In a scene of apparent chaos but in fact the result of careful organization, steam locomotives await their turn at the Turcott roundhouse at Montreal in 1943.

Canada had its railways taken over by the government and connected into the mainland system by train ferry. The Intercolonial Railway was completed on 1 July 1876, but by this time a far more ambitious programme had been launched. The spurs for this larger effort were the 1869 handing over by the Hudson Bay Company of a huge area to the west of Canada proper, and the 1871 incorporation of the colony of British Columbia into the federation as the vast westernmost component of the dominion, which now extended right the way across the continent from the Atlantic to the Pacific Oceans.

The condition that British Columbia fixed on its accession to the dominion was the creation of a rail link connecting the new western province with the existing eastern provinces, with work to begin within two years and be completed within ten. In July 1872 Fleming set off to begin the general planning of the route, and in the following year there began the detailed survey. This took almost eight years to complete, and at times involved 2,000 men or more. The survey

proceeding, a decision had to be made as to who should undertake the construction project. In 1872 it was decided that the task would be contracted to private enterprise, and the two companies which received the necessary charters were the Interoceanic and the Canada Pacific. In 1873 the government of Canada resigned as a result of the political scandal stemming from efforts to secure a merger of the two companies.

The completion of a line from Emerson, on the American border, to Winnipeg gave this central city an indirect means of railway communication with the eastern part of Canada by means of American track to Chicago and thence back north into Canada, but the rest of the decade saw little progress on the transcontinental line. In 1880 a sense of urgency was added to the question, for there was American agitation for the annexation of Canada's central prairie region. At this stage, therefore, George Stephen was persuaded to supervise the creation of a syndicate to take over the construction of the trans-Canada railway. In February 1991 the Canadian Pacific Railway Company was incorporated with Stephen as its president and James J. Hill, later the father of the Great Northern Railway in the U.S.A., as a member of the board. Hill made a fairly early departure when he disagreed with the decision to follow the route north of Lake Superior rather than proceed via Sault Ste.-Marie and across the northern part of the U.S.A. Even so, the contribution of Hill to the Canadian Pacific Railway before his resignation was very considerable, not least in his pressure to secure the services of William Van Horne as the general manager.

Horne had worked for the Illinois Central and the Chicago Milwaukee & St. Paul railroads before leaving the latter at the beginning of 1882 to join the Canadian Pacific Railway. With Stephen, who had earlier been the president of the Bank of Montreal, looking after the company's financial affairs, and Van Horne overseeing the more practical aspects of the company's operations, construction of the new railway finally began in earnest during 1882. A government grant of $25 million and

25 million acres (10000000 hectares) of land, as well as the short sections of track that were already in existence, constituted prime starting points. Progress presented enormous physical difficulties, especially in the crossing of the Rocky Mountains and, perhaps even worse, the traverse across the north of Lake Superior through a horrendous mix of swamp and rock. Even so, the line progressed and the track reached Calgary by August 1883.

One of the main reasons that the survey

Sir William Cornelius Van Horne was the first chairman and second president of the Canadian Pacific Railway, and a key figure in the development of the Canadian railway system.

of the potential routes for the Canadian Pacific Railway had opted for a more southerly route had been the fear that U.S. railroads, then extending rapidly over the north-western parts of the U.S.A., might draw off Canadian traffic if the route was fixed along a more northerly line. This meant that the line had to cross the Rocky Mountains between Calgary and Vancouver by means of the Kicking Horse Pass, as a result of which the track was faced with grades as steep as 4.4 per cent. Continued problems along the Lake Superior and mountain sections then coincided with a shortage of adequate funding to delay work until, in 1885, the government of Canada agreed to lend the Canadian Pacific Railway the required resources; this occurred after the importance of the operation had been confirmed when completed sections of track were used to ferry troops for the suppression of a rebellion in the area of Winnipeg. These new resources allowed the completion of the Canadian Pacific Railway on 8 November 1885, and by June 1886 the first scheduled through trains were operating between Montreal and Port Moody. The latter was just a short distance from Vancouver, the last section of which was completed in 1887.

The creation of this first Canadian railway across the continent to the Pacific Ocean spurred a rush of further development in the Canadian railway system, with the Canadian Pacific Railway itself in the forefront. One area that was to profit from this process was at the eastern end of the Canadian Pacific Railway's route where, because of rivalry between Montreal and

As in other parts of the world, steam locomotion continues to exert a strong fascination long after the disappearance of the steam locomotive as a genuine working engine. This is the 4-6-4 locomotive No. 2860, a Royal Hudson-type unit of the British Columbia Railway, hauling an excursion service from North Vancouver to Squamish late in 1970.

DECEMBER 5, 1943

GRAND TRUNK RAILWAY SYSTEM

IN CONNECTION WITH
CANADIAN NATIONAL RAILWAYS

CANADIAN NATIONAL RAILWAYS

IN CONNECTION WITH
GRAND TRUNK RAILWAY SYSTEM

A COMPLETE
TRANSPORT SYSTEM
Passenger-Freight-Express
Telegraphs-Hotels
Steamships - Air Lines

TO EVERYWHERE IN CANADA

within the context of traffic agreements the Canadian Pacific Railway had reached with the Minneapolis & St. Paul and the Duluth, South Shore & Atlantic railroads as protection against the increasing commercial threat represented by the growing northern railroad system being created in the U.S.A. by James Hill. In the region to the east of the St. Lawrence river, the Canadian Pacific Railway's system was pushed forward in 1889 to St. John in the province of New Brunswick by means of the direct route across the U.S. state of Maine. This route was created from an extension of the South Eastern Railway to Mattawamkeag, and a junction with the Maine Central Railroad. In the following year the Canadian Pacific Railway completed its transcontinental route by leasing the New Brunswick Railway system as the last link in its service to St. John.

William McKenzie and Donald Mann, who had earlier worked for the Canadian Pacific Railway, began in the 1890s to develop their own railway system. In 1896 the two men began to build the Lake Manitoba Railway up the western side of the lake for which the railway was named, before extending it to Winnipegosis with the help of federal land grants and financial assistance from the provincial government. In 1899 the railway's name was changed to the Canadian Northern Railway, and grew steadily as a result of a programme of takeover and construction supervised by McKenzie and Mann: the system developed links to Winnipeg, the border between Canada and the U.S.A., and Port Arthur on the shore of Lake Superior. As their financial resources

OPPOSITE
The Canadian National Railway's locomotive No. 6218, a 4-8-4 unit, is caught by the camera at Brampton, Ontario, in 1965.

LEFT
The cover of the Canadian National timetable of 1943, in the middle of World War II and therefore a time in which the most effective use of the Canadian railway system was of great importance to the Allied cause.

Toronto, the government of Canada had fixed a 'non-aligned' eastern terminus at the eastern end of Lake Nipissing. The Canadian Pacific Railway was already the owner of the existing line along the Ottawa valley to provide a link

with Montreal, and soon bought a miscellany of small railways to allow it to spread its schedule to Toronto and Quebec and create a branch to Sault Ste.-Marie in 1888. This programme of line extensions was undertaken

A 4-8-4 Confederation-type locomotive of the Canadian National Railway.

Railway was expanded westward toward the Pacific Ocean along the line established by Fleming through the Yellowhead Pass to Vancouver, and eastward in a long curve well clear of the northern side of Lake Superior to reach Sudbury and Toronto. By 1916, consequently, the Canadian Northern Railway was able to start scheduled services linking Quebec and Vancouver, while the inauguration of an electrified system through a tunnel under Mount Royal permitted services to a new terminus in Montreal and thence to an eastward extension of the system into Nova Scotia.

Over this period the Grand Trunk Railway had concentrated its efforts on developing its own network in Canada, while at the same time enhancing its connections with the railroads operating in the north-eastern part of the U.S.A. The 1897 opening of a new bridge at Niagara Falls and the addition of a new steel superstructure to the Victoria Bridge allowed the carriage of traffic, boosted by the Grand Trunk Railway's acquisition of the Central Vermont Railway, through to the city of New London on the coast of the state of Connecticut. However, the fiscal prudence with which the Grand Trunk Railway expanded did not match that of the Great Northern Railway and, finding itself somewhat over-extended financially, the Grand Trunk Railway called on Charles Hayes, lately of the Wabash Railroad. Hayes's new financial broom made a clean sweep and his linking of the Great Trunk Railway's services with those of the Wabash Railroad soon restored the Grand Trunk Railway's fortunes.

permitted, the two men enlarged the Canadian Northern Railway system through cost-effective construction where required and purchase where there was existing track; by 1905 the Canadian Northern Railway system extended from Edmonton in the western province of Alberta to Lake Superior in the east, with other small sections around Montreal and Quebec.

By the first decade of the 20th century Mackenzie and Mann wanted to develop their own transcontinental railway to rival that of the Canadian Pacific. Over a period of some seven years, therefore, the Canadian Northern

By the first part of the 20th century, Canada was receiving a swelling number of immigrants and its national economy was growing comparatively quickly, leading Hayes to think that the creation of a third transcontinental railway was financially feasible. This new operator was the Grand Trunk Pacific, created specifically for the task. During 1903 the Grand Trunk Pacific secured an agreement with the government of Canada for the establishment of a National Transcontinental Railway, based on the construction, by the government, of a line stretching from Moncton in the province of New Brunswick right across the provinces of Quebec and Ontario to Winnipeg, capital of the province of Manitoba. Once complete, this line was to be leased to the Grand Trunk Pacific, which was to undertake the construction of a line from Winnipeg to the Pacific coast in British Columbia. The government's eastern portion of the new route was planned to very exacting standards, with an eye to the shallowest possible grades, its course fixed through regions that were largely unsurveyed and only vestigially populated. The Grand Trunk Pacific's western portion, on the other hand, was in general a more-or-less parallel partner to the existing lines of the Canadian Pacific and Canadian Northern railways's western sections.

A primary financial anticipation of the planning of the new railway was the hope of drawing the grain traffic from Canada's water and lake routes on its way to the ports of the Atlantic seaboard for shipment to Europe. For this reason, the first part of the new railway was constructed from Port Arthur, at the head

LEFT
Installation of the engine in locomotive No. 9000 of the Canadian National Railway at the Kingston Locomotive Works in the course of 1928.

PAGE 400
Looking tired with the world and decidedly grubby, this is locomotive No. 3759 of the Canadian Pacific Railway at Montreal in 1959.

PAGE 401
Locomotive No. 972.

Off to the front: construction forces of the St. Paul, Minneapolis & Manitoba Railway (forerunner of the Great Northern Railway) are pictured moving up to the railhead, accompanied by soldiers for protection from hostile Native Americans. This 1887 photograph was made in what today is western North Dakota but was then the Dakota Territory. The railway was being extended in that year from Minot to Great Falls and Helena, in the Montana Territory, and four world records were established in the process. Construction began just west of Minot on 2 April and reached Helena, 642-miles (1033-km) distant, on 19 November.

of Lake Superior, grain-delivery services to the port beginning during 1910. At the other end of the new transcontinental line, the Grand Trunk Pacific ignored the well-established port and railway centres around Puget Sound and fixed its western end instead at Prince Rupert, a new port that was to be created on the mouth of the Skeena river near Port Simpson, some 550 miles (885 km) north of Vancouver.

One notable advantage offered by the new railway was the fact that it avoided both the Kicking Horse Pass route and the muskeg (a region of mixed water/partially dead vegetation bog, often covered by a layer of sphagnum or other mosses) around Lake Superior, both of which had been major obstacles for the Canadian Pacific Railway. Using a workforce of 25,000 men and large quantities of equipment and supplies brought into Prince Rupert by ship, the western section of the Grand Trunk Pacific was completed by April 1914, and in the following year the new National Transcontinental Railway line to the east was completed.

The Grand Trunk Railway, whose contract to operate the government-built eastern end of the National Transcontinental demanded an annual rental of 3 per cent of the construction cost, feared for its financial survival as the cost had been $150 million, three times the budgeted figure. Moreover, the fact that World War I was being fought bitterly in Europe had stemmed the flow to Canada of investment and immigrants. The

The Continental Limited, a Canadian National Railway service, crosses the Fraser river at Cisco, British Columbia, the Canadian Pacific Railway's main line being in the right foreground. At Cisco the CNR and the CPR, which follow the right and left banks respectively of the Thompson and Fraser rivers, change over to the opposite banks for the remaining 150 miles (241km) to Vancouver, British Columbia.

OPPOSITE
The Royal Hudson-type locomotive No. 2860 is seen above the Strait of Georgia during a British Columbia Railway excursion from North Vancouver to Squamish in the late 1970s.

LEFT
Richmond Station, Quebec, in 1930.

The Canadian Pacific Railway's Trans-Canada Limited passenger service, headed by the Pacific-type 4-6-2 locomotive No. 2327, leaves Windsor Station, Montreal.

Grand Trunk Railway now decided that successful operation of the complete National Transcontinental Railway, over both its own western and government-built eastern sections, was financially impossible. At much the same time and for the same general reasons, the Canadian Northern Railway discovered that it

could not return a profit on the operation of its own transcontinental railway. A royal commission, established in 1916, recommended that the best way to resolve the problems was the nationalization of the Grand Trunk, Grand Trunk Pacific, and Canadian Northern railways. It took some time to sort

out the three operators's financial situations, but by 1918 it had become feasible to create the Canadian National Railway Company to take over the three semi-moribund private railways. The Canadian National Railway Company initially took over the existing publicly-owned railways and also the Canadian Northern Railway, added the Grand Trunk Pacific in 1920, and absorbed the parent company in 1923.

The new board of directors was led by the American-born Sir Henry Thornton, who had started his railroad career on the Pennsylvania Railroad, become general superintendent of the Long Island Railroad and, just before his Canadian appointment, was the general manager of a classic British railway, the Great Eastern, a position he had held in World War I in parallel with two other posts, namely chief engineer of the Great Eastern Railway and director of railway transport in France. The highly experienced Thornton was well suited to the tricky task of creating a single effective system out of the disparate elements of the Canadian National Railway Company, and rationalizing the constituent elements's financial affairs and contractual obligations. In this monumental task Thornton was fortunate to have been given a free hand by the government of Canada, whose sole demand was that all outstanding commitments be honoured.

Thornton soon discovered that a large number of the lines that he now controlled needed major improvements, but in the following 10 years achieved wonders. Thornton turned the Canadian National Railway Company into a financially sound

The Canadian Pacific Railway's Trans-Canada Limited passenger service, headed by the D9c-class 4-6-0 locomotive No. 579, built in 1903, is seen near Lake Louise, Alberta.

A fast passenger service between Montreal and Ottawa leaves Westmount station in about 1900.

A construction crew works on the main line of the Grand Trunk Pacific Railway at Tête Jaune, British Columbia, in 1912.

Now replaced by a more modern structure, the Victoria Bridge was built in Montreal in 1859 to carry a single-track rail line over the St. Lawrence river.

RIGHT
Toronto was the 'stronghold' of the Canadian
Pacific Railway, one of whose 4-6-4
locomotives is seen here.

OPPOSITE
This 0-6-0 locomotive of the Canadian
National is now operated by the Conway
Scenic Railway.

The front and back covers of the pocket time card issued by the Western Division of the Canadian Pacific Railway for the services coming into effect on the division's lines on 3 July 1886.

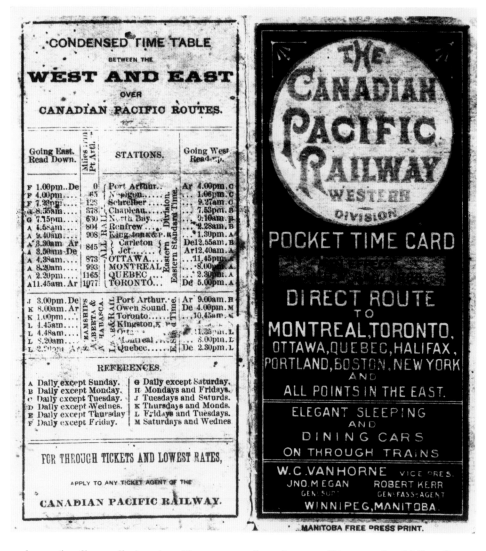

suffering financial difficulties in the 1890s, but then started to fare better as immigration to Canada accelerated in the early years of the 20th century. In 1899 the Canadian Pacific Railway created a new line through the Crow's Nest Pass, the southern crossing over the Selkirk mountains that had originally been rejected as a site for the original route to Vancouver, as it lay close to the Canadian border with the U.S.A, and this provided good access to major coal deposits in the area, which boomed and in the process boosted the profitability of the railway.

In this period of Canadian railway history, one of the most significant achievements, in construction and technical terms, was the creation of the famous spiral tunnels completed in 1909 to reduce the severity of the grades through the Kicking Horse Pass. Another major success of the same year was the Lethbridge viaduct over the Belly river on the Crow's Nest Pass line: more than 5,000-ft (1525-m) long, the viaduct is 314-ft (96-m) above the water and is the highest railway bridge in Canada. Other achievements included the 5-mile (8-km) Connaught Tunnel under Mount MacDonald, the opening of which removed a 450-ft (137-m) ascent to the top of the Rogers Pass.

At much the same time as it was accomplishing these and other technical achievements, the Canadian Pacific Railway was also building up its network of branch lines in the prairies. In the prosperous years of the 1920s, the Canadian National Railway Company pursued the same course, in spite of a vigorous level of competition. The economic depression of the 1930s, following the 'crash'

and operationally excellent system. He rationalized and also improved the network he inherited from its predecessors, and also launched the expansion of the system with the construction of lines into the Peace river area of northern Alberta and the addition of the

Long Lac cut-off between the old Canadian Northern and Grand Trunk lines, in the process trimming the distance between North Bay and Winnipeg by just over 100 miles (161km).

The Canadian Pacific Railway had been

A train service of the Canadian Pacific Railway climbs eastward in the Kicking Horse Pass above the Upper Spiral Tunnel, double-headed by the S2a-class locomotive No. 5813 and the T1b-class locomotive No. 5929.

RIGHT & OPPOSITE
Sister locomotives Nos 2822 and 2820 of the
Canadian Pacific Railway as seen in Montreal
on 24 March 1960.

In 1938, the Canadian Pacific Hudson-type 4-6-4 locomotive No. 2842 departs the snowy station at Windsor, Montreal at the head of its train.

An engine change at Moncton, New Brunswick, in 1943: the Canadian National 4-8-4 locomotive No. 6171 is backing onto a train travelling from Halifax, Nova Scotia, to Montreal. Moncton was a division point where all trains changed locomotives and hence a fascinating place for any visiting enthusiast. Contrary to much stricter conditions in the U.S.A., the Canadians were quite relaxed about railway photography at the time, despite the fact that World War II was still raging.

PAGE 418
The Canadian Pacific Railway's 4-6-2 locomotive No. 2471 leaves the station at Windsor, Montreal, at the head of an evening commuter train in April 1952.

PAGE 419
The Canadian National's 4-6-4 locomotive No. 5700 at Toronto in April 1952.

of 1929, ended this process and so reduced the demand for railway transport that passengers levels fell to little more than 50 per cent of their figure for 1928. So bad did the position become, moreover, that consideration was given to the merger and radical consolidation of the two major Canadian railway systems. For a number of political as well as financial and operational reasons, though, nothing came

of the concept and the two systems maintained their independence.

Clearly something had to be done to redress the situation, and a royal commission established in 1931 suggested a number of ways in which the co-operation and avoidance of duplication between the two operators could be improved. In the event, little was done, apart from the sharing of passenger

trains over the two systems's busiest sections between Montreal and Toronto. Then the worst of the depression were over toward the end of the 1930s and traffic began to increase once more. Next World War II demanded unprecedented levels of freight traffic, and the large scale of Canadian war production taxed Canada's railways to their limits, especially in the eastern part of the country as men,

RIGHT
The Canadian National Railway's locomotive
No. 4005 is seen at Winnipeg on 27
September 1957.

equipment, food and other items were
transported to the ports of the Atlantic
seaboard for shipment to the U.K. from
Halifax and St. John. Halifax was fed from
Moncton by only a single line, and this
exerted enormous pressure on the limited
capabilities of the line, which were maximized
from 1941 by the introduction of a system of
centralized train control.

The boom in Canadian railway transport
during World War II was followed from 1945
by a steep decline in demand as the
requirement for huge shipments to Europe
effectively ceased, and the combination of
improved road and air transport also took their

RIGHT
The Canadian Pacific Railway's locomotive
No. 5258 is caught by the camera on   1
October 1967.

OPPOSITE
The Canadian Pacific Railway's 4-6-4
locomotive No. 2860.

The Canadian Pacific Railway's transcontinental express in the period shortly before the outbreak of World War I in 1914.

RIGHT
The Canadian Pacific Railway's 2-8-0 locomotive No. 3607 is seen in service as a switching unit after being retired from main-line service.

toll of railway traffic. To ensure survival, the Canadian railways undertook a major effort to improve operational efficiency, a first step in the right direction being dieselization. The Canadian railways had undertaken a number of experiments with diesel haulage in the 1930s, and after a pause during the years of World War II, these were resumed once more. During the 1950s, therefore, both of Canada's major railway systems began the process of wholesale abandonment of coal-fired steam locomotion in favour of diesel-engined traction.

Another move prompted by the need to rationalize and streamline Canadian railway operations, and thereby achieve major improvements in cost-efficiency, was the 1961 amalgamation of the Canadian Pacific Railway's U.S. subsidiaries (the Minneapolis, St.-Paul & Sault Ste.-Marie, the Duluth, South Shore & Atlantic, and the Wisconsin Central railroads) into the single Soo Line Railroad with 4,500 miles (7240km) of track throughout the north-western part of the U.S.A. between the Great Lakes and the state of Montana.

The Canadian National Railway Company also expanded by acquisition of an overseas

The Canadian National Railway's locomotive No. 6218 departs from a station at the head of an express service.

RIGHT
A freight train of the Canadian National Railway near Canora, Saskatchewan, on 28 September 1959.

OPPOSITE
The 4-6-2 locomotive No. 2469 of the Canadian Pacific Railway at Toronto.

the construction of the new line was feasible only through the construction of several airstrips, so that supplies could be delivered by air, but good progress was made and by 1954 ore-laden trains were up and running.

Although the primary disposition of Canada's railway lines is along the east/west axis between the Atlantic and Pacific coasts or points between them, there are a number aligned along north/south axes. Typical of these are the iron-ore lines mentioned above, but others of note with this disposition include the Hudson Bay Railway, which is basically an extension of the original Canadian Northern Railway and reached Churchill on Hudson's Bay in the course of 1929, and the Ontario Northland Railway to James Bay, the southern subsidiary of

OPPOSITE
A 4-6-4 locomotive of the Canadian National Railway heads a cross-border passenger train service from London, Ontario, to Detroit, Michigan.

LEFT
A transcontinental train of the Canadian Pacific Railway in the early days of the service, perhaps 1893, at Glacier House.

BELOW
The camera catches a 4-8-4 locomotive of the Canadian National Railway at Moncton, New Brunswick, as it heads a train bound for Halifax, Nova Scotia.

system in 1949, though this was not altogether removed from Canada as it was that of the island of Newfoundland, which finally became part of the Dominion of Canada. The island's railway system had been launched in the later part of the 19th century, with Sandford Fleming as its chief engineer. For reasons of cost and the island's geographical isolation, the Newfoundland Railway system was based on a gauge of 42in (1025mm). Work on it started in 1881, but the line linking Port aux Basques with St. John was finished only in 1898. After the Canadian National Railway Company's takeover of the Newfoundland Railway in 1949, some of the island's track was converted to standard gauge.

Although, in overall terms, there was a slackening in demand for railway transport in

Canada in the period following World War II, there were some regions in which the demand for railway transport increased as discoveries of exploitable raw materials were made, creating the demand for equipment to be brought in and product to be taken out. Typical of such regions is the area some 350 miles (563km) north of the estuary of the St. Lawrence river around Knob Lake, in a virtually uninhabited area of eastern Quebec and Labrador. Here, it was estimated in the later part of the 1940s, vast deposits or iron ore, possibly about 10 million tons each year, were waiting to be extracted if the required transport could be provided. During 1950 this estimate paved the way for the start of work on the Quebec North Shore & Labrador Railway from Sept-Îles, on the estuary of the St. Lawrence river, to Schefferville. Work on

Hudson Bay proper. This railway was chartered by the province of Ontario during 1902 as the Temiskaming & Northern Ontario Railway, and attained James Bay in 1932.

The day of ambitious railway building in Canada was not completed by these routes in the eastern half of the country. In the west a classic example is the British Columbia Railway. The Pacific Great Eastern Railway was chartered in 1912 to build a route from Squamish through the Fraser river valley's timber country to link with the Grand Trunk Railway at Prince George. Little progress with the new line was achieved until the provincial government took control at the end of World War I, when work restarted. By 1921 344 miles (554km) had been constructed to Quesnel, but this was still some way short of the planned junction at Prince George. Work was again halted at this point, and did not resume until 1949, when construction of the extension to Prince George was started for completion in 1953.

Another with a north/south axis is the most northerly of all Canada's railways, a long-established private concern dating from the time of the Klondyke gold rush of the late 1890s. The 36-in (0.914-m) gauge White Pass and Yukon Route is 110-miles (177-km) long and was built between 1898 and 1900 from Skagway, where the prospectors landed after their sea journey to the Yukon, to Whitehorse, the capital of the Yukon Territory. The White Pass and Yukon Route lasted beyond the end of the gold boom, supported the U.S. Army in World War II,

and became very useful once more with the opening of lead and zinc mines in the Yukon Territory.

The development of the Mexican railroad system resulted largely from foreign capital and enterprise, attracted by national franchises or 'concessions', and was later encouraged by the payment of subsidies. This latter policy was adopted by President Porfirio Díaz in 1880 after the failure of an attempt to promote the construction of railroads by Mexican nationals working under a system of state concessions. Such a concession was not a corporate charter, as it was under legislation derived ultimately from English practice, or a grant of funds and/or other aid, but rather what was in practice a lease for a definite number of years to build a line on the basis of private finance. The state later gained ownership over the whole of the fixed property (the rack and other infrastructure) and an option over the movable property (the rolling stock).

The trials that confirmed the utility and practicality of the steam locomotive were undertaken in England in 1829, two years after the chartering of the first major railroad operation in the U.S.A. (the Baltimore & Ohio Railroad), and in was 1833 when the first consideration was given to the construction of a Mexican railroad, in this instance a line to connect Veracruz on the coast of the Gulf of Mexico with Mexico City. In August 1837 a concession was granted to Francisco Arillage for the construction and operation of such a line, with a branch to Puebla. A preliminary survey was made, but nothing further was

done and Arillage forfeited the concession as a result. There followed surveys for a number of other railroads, often undertaken by the U.S. Army's engineer corps. These resulted from the grant of other concessions, such as that of March 1842 received by José Garay for a line to cross the Isthmus of Tehuantepec.

In the middle part of the 19th century and through the regime of Díaz between 1877 and 1911, Mexican railroads were developed to open the way for the transport of raw materials to the Mexican border with the U.S.A. and to ports on both Mexican coasts, thereby facilitating the export trade, while other railroads were created to simplify the delivery of imported goods to Mexico City. Most of the Mexican railroad system was therefore surveyed, mapped and built between 1880 and 1910. Beginning in 1908, the consolidation of many of these railroads led to the Ferrocarriles Nacionales de México (National Railroads of Mexico), which thus controlled some 70 per cent of all Mexican railroad lines by purchase and, from 1937, nationalization.

By the middle of the 20th century, when diesel traction started to make serious inroads into the hitherto unassailed strength of steam locomotion, the railroads of Mexico amounted to some 12,500 miles (20116km), of which about 11,400 miles (18346km) were of standard gauge and almost all of the other 1,100 miles (1770km) of 36-in gauge. The Ferrocarriles Nacionales de México comprised a well-integrated system from Matamoros (opposite Brownsville in the U.S. state of Texas) and Ciudad Juarez (opposite

El Paso in Texas) to Suchiate on the Mexican frontier with Guatemala. Most of this system lay in the eastern half of the country, the principal exceptions being lines to Manzanillo, on the Pacific coast, and the east/west line of the Tehuantepec National across the waist of the country from Puerto Mexico on the Gulf of México to Salina Cruz on the Pacific Ocean. The 36-in lines of the Ferrocarriles Nacionales de México extended to the east and south-east of Mexico City toward Puebla and Oaxaca.

As well as the Ferrocarriles Nacionales, the Mexican government owned other lines such as the Kansas City, Mexico & Orient Railway, whose line extended south-westward from Ojinaga opposite Presidio in Texas, through Chihuahua to a projected connection with the port of Topolobampo on the Gulf of California, but with a gap of 199 miles (320km) between a point 78-miles (125-km) north-east of Topolobampo and a point about 190-miles (306-km) south-west of Chihuahua. Other government-owned lines not incorporated into the national system included the Mexican Railway Company linking the capital and Veracruz; the South-Eastern Railway extending south-eastward from Veracruz; and the Sonora-Baja California Railway with a 325-mile (523-km) line linking the head of the Gulf of California and San Diego in the U.S. state of California to the north-west and with the main Mexican railroad system to the south-east via Benjamin Hill in the state of Sonora.

In the western region of Mexico are the Southern Pacific Railroad of Mexico, the Mexico North-Western Railroad and a number of smaller lines that remained in private hands. The territory of Quintana Roo and the state of Yucatán also owned railroad lines within their respective areas. Until 1949 the Yucatán Railroad was completely isolated from any other, but the state-owned South-Eastern Railroad then extended its line from Veracruz to establish a connection. The main trunk lines effectively linked the most heavily populated parts of Mexico with a spreading fan of lines from Mexico City, and eight crossing points (between Mexicali-Calexico and Nogales in the west and Matamoros in the east) linked the Mexican railroad system with that of the U.S.A. Other lines linked Mexico City with Suchiate on the Mexican frontier with Guatemala, with the port cities on each of the Mexican coast lines, and with the most productive industrial, commercial, mining and agricultural regions of the country. There was considerable inter-connection between the various lines.

In overall terms, the Mexican railroad system used concepts, rolling stock and other facilities patterned on those of the U.S.A., even when not purchased directly from American manufacturers. During World War II a U.S. mission operated in Mexico to assist in rehabilitating about 1,900 miles (3060km) of key line to improve the transport of Mexican materials important to the Allied war effort. It is worth noting, though, that the weight of rail, maximum grades and curve radius, locomotive and other rolling stock types, and operating characteristics typical of Mexican railroad operations were generally less advanced than those prevalent in the U.S.A. at much the same time.

309, 314, 316, 330, 344, 345, 346
Mann, Donald 397, 398
McKenzie, William 397, 398
Mastodon 213
Mastodon-type locomotive 202, 208
Matt H. Shay 276
Mazeppa 193
McKim 193
Metropolis bridge, Paducah 177
Mexico North-Western Railroad 429
Mikado-type freight locomotive 267
Mikado-type locomotive 161, 200, 249, 258, 262, 264, 268
Milwaukee Road (Chicago, Milwaukee St. Paul & Pacific) 91, 93, 161, 259, 260, 316, 320, 326, 360, 379, 380
Minneapolis & St. Paul Rilroad 397
Minneapolis, St.-Paul & Sault Ste.-Marie 422

Mississippi & Missouri Railroad 40, 64, 67
Missouri Compromise, 1820 45
Missouri Pacific Railroad 40, 86, 118, 233
Moffat Tunnel 161, 164
Mogul-type locomotive 31, 206, 207, 266, 316
Mohawk & Hudson River Railroad 22, 27, 33, 36, 183, 186, 187, 190, 348
Mohawk-type freight engine 259
Monocacy 198
Monroe Railroad 28
Montreal & Lachine Railway 383
Montressor, Captain John 19
Morgan, J. Pierpont 101, 102, 103, 104, 106
Mount Clare 195
Mountain-type locomotive 280
Mud-diggers 193, 195

N
National Grange 100, 104
National Road 11

National Transcontinental Railway 399, 402, 406
National Transportation Committee 114
New Brunswick Railway 397
Newfoundland Railway 427
New Haven Railroad 216
New York & Erie Railroad 39
New York & Harlem Railroad 34
New York Central Railroad 35, 38, 39, 76, 101, 102, 109, 186, 208, 213, 228, 240, 242, 259, 266, 267, 274, 302, 304, 357, 358, 364, 365
New York Central & Hudson River Railroad 216, 218
New York New Haven & Hartford Railroad 35,104, 357
New York, Chicago & St. Louis Railroad 102, 291
New York, Ontario & Western Railway 164
Niagara suspension bridge 122, 171, 177, 385, 398
Niagara-type locomotive 259, 266, 304

437

ACKNOWLEDGEMENTS

*Association of American Railroads, USA: Pages 15 right, 20, 22 both, 23, 181, 190 below

*AT & SF Railway: Pages 351, 378 left

*Baltimore & Ohio Railroad Museum: Pages 12, 13, 14, 25, 32, 107, 159, 184, 255

*British Columbia Railways: Pages 395, 404

*Burlington Northern Railroad: Pages 122 below, 124, 146, 402

*Canadian National: Pages 144, 382, 398, 399, 403

*Canadian Pacific: Pages 217, 249, 393, 394, 406, 407 both, 413, 416

*Chicago & North Western Railway: Page 349 left

*Chicago, Burlington & Quincy: Page 136

*Delaware & Hudson Railroad: Page 195

*Denver & Rio Grande Railroad: Page 142

*Great Northern Railway: Pages 74, 99, 133, 147

*Gulf Oil Company: Page 190 above

* Harry A. Frye, New Hampshire: Page 250

*Illinois Central Railroad: Page 36 right, 39

Library of Congress, Washington DC, USA: Pages 9, 10 top, 21, 34, 35, 51, 52, 53, 63, 73, 77, 84, 87, 96-7, 121, 132

*Library of Congress, Washington DC, USA: Page 122 above

Milepost 92½, Leicestershire, England: Pages 5, 28, 106, 115, 116, 118, 132, 154, 156, 290, 310, 347, 396, 401

Milepost 92½, Leicestershire, England/Arthur J. Huneke: Pages 3, 7, 98, 108, 111, 112 both, 119 left, 125, 135, 141, 148, 149, 152, 158, 160, 164, 169, 174, 198, 220, 221, 223, 232, 240, 241, 247, 274, 276, 301, 332, 344, 367

Milepost 92½, Leicestershire, England/Brian Solomon: Pages 4, 6, 16, 17, 40, 76, 78, 79, 80, 81, 85, 89, 92, 93, 94, 95 both, 100 both, 102, 110, 113, 117, 119 right, 126, 129, 153, 155, 161, 162, 163, 165, 166, 167, 172, 173, 175, 176, 186 left, 178, 179, 182, 183, 186 left, 187, 191, 192 left, 192-3, 194, 199, 200, 201, 202, 203, 204, 209, 210, 211, 212, 213 top, 216, 219, 235 left, 238 above, 246, 256, 257, 258, 261, 262, 264, 265, 268, 270, 275, 277, 279, 281, 291, 292, 294, 295, 296, 297, 298, 300, 303, 304, 306, 315, 318, 319, 320 above, 322, 323, 324, 327, 336 right, 350, 352, 353, 358, 359, 362, 363, 364, 365 both, 366, 368, 369, 370, 371, 372, 397, 410, 411, 430, 431, 432, 433

Milepost 92½, Leicestershire, England/Frank Zahn: Pages 237 left, 400, 414, 415, 420 both, 424

Milepost 92½, Leicestershire, England/F.R. Dirkes: Pages 197, 242

Milepost 92½, Leicestershire, England/Howard Ande: Pages 354, 356, 357, 381

Milepost 92½, Leicestershire, England/John P. Hanket Collection: Pages 188, 385, 386

Milepost 92½, Leicestershire, England/Ron Ziel: Pages 143, 168, 177, 215, 224, 225, 226, 229, 234, 235 right, 237 right, 238 below, 239, 244, 245, 254, 269, 284, 325, 326, 328, 336 left, 339, 343, 361

Military Archive & Research Services, Lincolnshire, England: Pages 8 both, 10 below left, 11, 24 all, 29, 30, 36 left, 37, 42, 43, 47, 48, 49, 56, 57, 58, 60, 64, 103, 134, 137, 138, 139 both, 151, 180, 181, 185, 190 both, 195, 208 above, 213 below, 227 above right and below, 243, 251, 252, 331, 340, 348, 384, 387, 408, 412

Millbrook House Limited, Oldbury, W. Midlands, England: Pages 15 left, 18, 19 both, 31 both, 41, 46, 66, 69, 70, 75 above, 123, 150, 164 above, 170, 186 right, 189, 196, 205, 206, 207 both, 208 below right, 214, 218, 227 above left, 236, 271, 285, 286, 293, 299, 208, 320 below, 329 above, 337, 346, 383, 388 both, 389, 390, 391 both, 393, 405, 409, 417, 418, 418, 421, 422 both, 423, 425, 426, 427 both

*Milwaukee Road Photo: Pages 379, 380 both

*Missouri Pacific Railroad: Page 86

*National Archives, Division of Photographic Archive and Research: Page 61

New York Central: Page 341

Norfolk & Western Railway Company, Virginia: Pages 306, 338

Norfolk Southern Corporation: Pages 307, 360

Northern Pacific: Pages 38, 127

Personality Picture Library, London: Page 75 below

The Pullman Company: Page 355

Santa Fe Railway, Illinois, USA: Pages 128, 157, 311, 312, 313 both, 314 both, 321, 376, 377, 378 right

Southern Pacific Company: Pages 72, 329 below

Thomas Golcrease Institute: Page 62

Union Pacific Railroad Museum, Nebraska, USA: Pages 59, 65, 71, 90, 120, 130, 316, 349 right, 373, 374, 375

US Signal Corps: Page 50

York County Historical Society: Page 10 below right

*Prints/transparencies through Military Archive & Research Services, Lincolnshire, England.